Ristretto Rain

J. Michael Jones

Mount Erie Press Anacortes, Washington

This edition was first published in paperback in the United States in 2020 by
Mount Erie Press
Anacortes, Washington
ristrettorain@gmail.com
Copyright ©2020 Mount Erie Press
Identifier: ISBN: 978-0-9977591-6-7

To my wife Denise, who journeyed with me through the Valley of the Shadow of Death,
To my girlfriend, Greta, who taught me the art of living in the moment as only a Saint Bernard can.

CONTENTS

CHAPTER ONE

Rock Harbor

A dot on the horizon caught the young woman's eye, a speck no more than a single mustard seed cast upon the denim sea. She did not know that it was coming to find her and upheave her quiet life in this faraway place.

Halem stood flat-footed with one hand on the portafilter of the cherry-red and nickel-plated Lira espresso machine. The art deco apparatus, pumping and steaming, diverted her attention away from that dot and back into the space of the small coffee shop and her customer standing at the counter. The savory aroma of fine coffee soon infused the air around her, the familiarity of which comforted her, temporarily displacing the feeling of apprehension that clung to her like a shadow. The uneasiness stemmed from the events she was running from, and the fear they would eventually catch up with her.

Her opinion about Rock Harbor and her little shop, The Rock Harbor Coffee Roasters, was still not fully formed. She had left a life of friends and routine, moving to a place where she knew no one and no one knew about her. Was that a good thing? Was escaping the bad in Seattle, the things she wanted to forget worth this risk?

Halem had moved from Seattle's Capitol Hill to this remote village in the San Juan Islands ten months earlier. It was a hasty decision and such rash steps had not worked out so well for her in the past. At age twenty-three, it was the first time she'd lived outside of Washington's Emerald City, and she felt like she was still a little girl trying to find her way through, what seemed like to her at times, a cruel world.

She was a tall, thin woman. In her view, too tall and too thin for her own liking. By the time she was in high school she had the nickname "Beanpole," but as she thought about it, she had given herself that name and she was the only one who used it. As she had walked past the coffee shop that morning, coming to open it for business, the sun was just peaking over the North Cascades and onto their large front windows. There, she saw her reflection on those windows as if looking at a full-length mirror. She didn't like what she saw, and it was as if she had forgotten how tall and thin, she really was.

The stare of her tired hazel eyes moved gently from looking out at the peculiar dot far out on the sea, to the coffee cups stacked upside down right in front of her. Her gaze continued to slide from the cups down the front of the espresso machine to the two clear shot glasses, poised to receive the sweet ristretto. The freshly ground arabica beans sent out a nutty fragrance that penetrated deep into each corner of the twenty-by-thirty-foot shop. She loved that smell and wore the redolent of coffee in her hair and clothes with honor.

That aroma often provoked childhood memories of her uncle's pipe smoke. She thought it smelled delicious, sort of like smoked cocoa. So delicious in fact that when she was only six she swiped the smoldering pipe from her uncle's ashtray, took a puff out of sight behind the kitchen door, after which she promptly vomited on her new glossy, double-strap Mary Janes.

She considered the art of being a reputable barista, as trying to convert that wonderful bouquet of flavors into a liquid bath for the palate. She touched the glasses with her bright neon-nailed fingertip, positioning them precisely into their proper place. She grasped the black lacquered handle with her right hand and pulled hard, her elbow in lead, locking the sieve in place. As her eyes ascended back up the mirrored metal toward the function buttons, they paused to consider her own reflection. Her new haircut looked ridiculous. Her hair had been short-cropped, bleached, and left with long corkscrewed curls on each side, dangling down, across her ears. The curls ended in mint tips as if the ends of them had been dipped in green ink wells by a bratty schoolboy. It was her cosmetologist's idea. The woman didn't know much. She spent her days cutting the dirty bait matts out of fishermen's hair or trying to make old ladies look younger, thinner, and hip. Out of touch with chic, never would have made it in Seattle.

More than one coffee shop customer, typically a man in his fifties, asked Halem if she was a Hasidic Jew. Not funny.

She heard Kane, who was standing quietly at the counter, clear his throat. He was a big man in his early sixties, stocky framed of six-two or three in height. Sporting a balding scalp, bordered on the sides with rather long brown hair. He looked like a monk. He *was* a man of the cloth, a pastor... just not sack cloth.

She redirected her attention to the function buttons. Wasn't sure if Kane's throat clearing was meant for her, or just one of his plethora of nervous tics—throat clearing, scratching his head, tapping his index finger on the table, rubbing his face, or sniffing. All of which drove some of her customers batty.

Halem flashed Kane a comforting smile. She assumed he was watching to make sure she pushed the right button and pulled the glasses away before the weak, watery end of the shot went in, keeping the honey-colored crema in perfect proportions and only the purest decoction from the beans. Not only did he require a fine grind but a meticulous thirteen second extraction to make his cup perfect. Simply turning the pump off at the thirteen-second mark was not an option for Kane's ristretto. He wanted the perfect flavor of the purest part of the coffee bean, so he wanted Halem to pull the cup away at the precise time; according to him, there was a delay between stopping the pump and the cessation of the seeping of the coffee, so just pushing buttons was not acceptable. Since he wanted a double ristretto, she would have to repeat the entire process twice, but she had done it so many times, she could do it in her sleep... that is if she could ever sleep.

Kane also wanted his ristretto made into a cappuccino by adding precisely groomed micro-foamed milk. The normal customer was satisfied with straight espresso shots in their cappuccinos, including the watery ends of the pull. But Kane was fastidious. A real coffee snob. He would have been the biggest coffee snob even in Seattle, a city full of them.

Then there was Seattle's Rob.

Rob was different. Petite in frame but big with mental troubles. Each morning he wore the exact same button-up shirt, chartreuse Washington State Ferry raincoat, with built-in reflective stripes, and green dress pants. Every button of his brown shirt was buttoned, to the point he looked like he was choking. He even had to have the same ceramic cup for his coffee. He would wait for another customer to finish with it and the barista wash it out, rather than getting a different cup. They thought it was just his imagination as all their 200 cups were from the same commercial set. This was until one morning, when he pointed out that *his cup* had a hairline crack on the bottom, in the shape of a J. His last name was Johnston. Once they figured that out, they kept the cup out of service until Rob showed up... precisely at 8:33 a.m., or 9:10 a.m. on Saturdays and Sundays. Then he didn't show up at all. Three days later the baristas learned that Rob had been killed by a trolley car. He had his routine timed to the second. That morning Seattle had added another trolley car to their First Hill line. He stepped right in front of it. To Rob the world was static

Halem dreamt of a static world, where a mother remained the same—not where, going to bed, waking up, and going to bed again, would eventually lead to a mother getting older and dying from breast cancer, leaving her little girl with an inadequate father. She dreamt of a stagnant world where boyfriends, who had come to save you, would stay kind, handsome, mysterious... and sober, not turning out to have a temper... a bad temper.

"Ahem... Halem?"

Kane's throat clearing startled her. She realized that she had rested her finger on the button but had not pushed it yet.

"Sorry," she said as she pressed, and the pumps hummed.

"You seem to be especially distracted this morning [with the word *especially* indicating that he thought she was usually preoccupied, but more now]. Are you okay?"

"Yeah. I'm fine... just had my head in the clouds. Didn't sleep so well last night."

She returned her focus to the small glasses, pulling them away from the espresso flow at the precise time of thirteen seconds, maybe off by one because of Kane's question. She flashed the man another smile, as to show him never to question her reliability. She was the best.

After pouring the shots into a celadon glazed cup, she dribbled in steamed micro-foamed milk from a small, stainless frothing pitcher, creating a perfect fern design, down to the individual leaves, as if she had painted it with an artist's brush. Kane took the cup in his left hand and held his debit card in the air with his right. He waited until a small green light on the little square box lit up then slid his card in. Halem rotated the small tablet so that the screen was in his direction so he could "sign" his name with his finger. Then he cleaned his finger with a handkerchief. Never left a tip. It would seem unkind of him, especially being a pastor, to intentionally not give a tip. But at the same time, being a pastor of a small Presbyterian congregation in Eastsound left him with little spending money, even for handcrafted coffee. Halem forgave him, of course.

Halem questioned the frugalness of Kane making the thirty-mile, round trip, drive across the mountain and down the perilous dirt road in his old Land Rover. He gave her a lift to Eastsound once, for an emergency trip to get milk for the coffee shop. Riding in the old car with right-hand drive, made her feel like she was in the driver's seat without a steering wheel, and it scared the shit out of her. During the whole four-hour journey, they exchanged only a handful of words and most of those were her thanking him for his kindness. It was awkward.

But she knew that the trip over the mountain each morning was more than just a quest for the perfect cup of coffee for Kane. While she found that thought flattering, she knew there had to be more. She had heard of some pastors having secret places for sexual mischief, or alcohol inebriation. For Kane, she knew it was neither of those. But he was up to something, something he didn't want his congregation in Eastsound knowing about, but she just couldn't put her finger on it. Kane had a secret.

The pastor methodically made his way across the room, so the foam would not spill over the edge of the small cup. He took his seat at a white-washed wooden table pushed against the front window. In the center was a clay pot, with a cluster of rosehips and leaves. No roses, just the hips. It looked rather cheery, adding color to an otherwise drab writing space. It was his favorite spot, which the other regulars had learned not to occupy, particularly this time of morning. New boat arrivals or the vagrant tourists were the exception.

The table was one of the best perches, looking straight down the bluff onto the quaint harbor. Yet, there wasn't a bad table in the place. All of them looked down on the waterfront and out on the perfect bay. On warm days, the glass windowed walls could be fan-folded back, creating an outside space that seamlessly joined the inside, making it a glorious place to drink excellent coffee. The Rock Harbor Coffee Roasters was on the fourth level up the hillside and from that vantage point, customers could see beyond the natural harbor, through the rift in the rock and out to Puget Sound. On a clear day, the big volcano, Mount Baker, was visible, seeming to rise right out of the sea like a snow cone treat. Kane sat down his cup, opened his black briefcase, and pulled out a couple of magazines and an iPad. He was usually there at opening time to beat any of those ignorant tourists from occupying his favorite seat.

Halem flipped over the frothing pitcher and pushed it down on the glass rinser and followed with the two shot glasses. She grabbed a wet rag to wipe off the steaming wand. Wiped it down with intent, like a milk maiden cleaning the teats of her cow. She looked again in the shiny nickel plating to see her image and those curls. She hated her hair. She couldn't wait to get home to snip off those stupid hairy pendants. She took the coffee-stained wet rag and wiped the curls behind her ears. She stuffed the dirty rag in a clean utensil drawer and took out a new one from the towel drawer. She looked up, above the cups stacked on the Lira and out to the bay. Was the sun out? Had the morning fog finally lifted? Was the strange dot still on the water? Or was it just a smear on the window? The beauty of the bay sometimes pulled the breath right out of her, even after waking up to the same view for 340 consecutive mornings.

When Sandra, the fifty-year-old owner of the coffee shop, first recruited Halem from Capitol Hill to come to Rock Harbor as her barista, the two women were virtually strangers. Sandra had been a customer in her Capitol Hill shop on occasion but had never engaged in conversation with her until the evening that the woman asked her, on a whim, to come away with her to the San Juan Islands.

As Sandra drove them across the double-decker freeway bridge that evening ten months earlier, which started them on their journey north out of Seattle, she broke the silence by asking her, "What do you know about where we're going?"

"Nothing but it's in the islands."

Sandra had a look of surprise as she glanced at Halem and back at the highway.

Halem could see it in the lines on Sandra's face that she had concern and needed to speak. She leaned toward the woman, straining to hear her above the whine of the road and the wind rushing up and over the windshield, and into the open cockpit of the BMW convertible.

"Wow, I don't know where to begin. I'm just a bit taken back that you jumped at the chance to come with me, but you really don't know where we're going?"

"Does it matter?"

"Maybe not. But I thought you would at least need a few weeks to think about it. I was hoping by the next time I was in Seattle you would have decided. But you seemed so eager, that I just assumed that you knew all about the San Juans, their delights and, well, the downside of living in the bush."

"The bush?"

"Well, that's what we say, but it is certainly not the bush as compared to Africa or Australia's outback. It is rather lovely. Oh, I would say more than that. The village is Rock Harbor, on Orcas Island. It's stunning."

Halem continued in her listening poise and said nothing.

Sandra looked over at Halem and began describing Rock Harbor as, "One of those unique geological freaks of nature, like Devil's Tower, the Danakil Depression in Ethiopia, or Brazil's Mount Roraima."

Halem didn't respond, so Sandra added, "Sorry, but I used to be a park ranger years ago, before I married well and focused on art. Don't even get me started on the geology of Olympic National Park, I would talk for hours."

Halem gave her a blank stare as if asking her about Olympic National Park was the last thing on her mind.

"Well, Rock Harbor is a perfect circle, as if a giant sea monster had bitten out a half-mile diameter hole on the northeast flank of Orcas Island's Mount Constitution, and then filled it with crystal-clear water, seeping in from Puget Sound. The bay is deep, up to sixty feet at the center of the depression. It's separated from the sound by a fifty-yard-thick wall of bedrock, on which a few old cedars perilously rest, grasping the rock with their tentacled roots like beached octopuses. Cutting through this massive, natural break-wall, is a perfectly straight channel, only about thirty-feet wide, reaching out to Puget Sound. We locals prefer to call the sound by its old and more encompassing name, the 'Salish Sea.' We also refer to this channel, which connects the bay to the sea as simply 'the rift.' You'll get used to those terms. The passage is so narrow that it requires larger craft, such as fishing trawlers and yachts, to enter or exit one at a time. You'll love it there!"

Halem maintained her silence, tucked into her heated leather seat beneath the cool highway head wind. Sandra looked over as to make sure the girl was still listening, and Halem's squinting eyes indicated that she was.

"As I was saying," continued Sandra, "The harbor is beautiful. The village above it is built upon five manmade levels carved right into the rock of the mountainside. The only way in by car is by an old unmaintained logging road that comes down from Mount Constitution."

Halem's interest was starting to wane, not because she didn't want to know about Rock Harbor, but because her bladder was about to burst. She felt embarrassed to ask Sandra to stop as they had barely gotten out of Seattle. She was afraid that Sandra would think something was wrong with her that she couldn't hold her pee for more than forty-five minutes. But Halem did not want to get into the details of her personal life at this point, of how she had to sneak into her apartment and grab her things because of her sleeping, intoxicated, and often abusive boyfriend Finn, and that she didn't have the chance to pee. Nor did she want to get into the reason why she jumped at the chance to go to such a remote place on a whim. It too was because of Finn.

Sandra looked over at Halem and smiled. Abruptly, and with a sudden change of topic, Halem said to her, "I've gotta pee."

"Really?" asked Sandra with a perplexed look. "Uh, can you hold it until we exit in Mount Vernon, or do I need to stop now?"

"Now," said Halem in her manner of few words.

Sandra eased from the express lane to the right, across three lanes into the next exit ramp. She pulled into a gas station beneath a very tall and bright "Shell" sign. She sat in her idling car while Halem went inside. As Halem entered the bathroom, (which smelled like a mixture of Lysol and urine), she ran to a stall, dropped her pants, and sat down. Thoughts started to ramble through Halem's mind of how she must look to this nice, professional lady. Did she think Halem was crazy? Was she sitting in her BMW right then thinking, like in the movies, that Halem was raising the double hung window and escaping through the weeds behind the station? Was Sandra thinking she was sitting there with her jeans still buttoned and her sleeve rolled up and a heroin needle in her arm?

However, soon Halem was back in the car and they were on the road.

After an awkward fifteen-minute pause, Sandra spoke again, "Did you want to hear more about Rock Harbor?"

"Sure," came Halem's soft reply. "It sounds fascinating."

Sandra picked up where she had left off, "There's a small beach at the northern edge of the bay, called Crescent Beach, which is only twenty feet wide at high tide, making it too small and damp to build houses on. You'll enjoy swimming there on our few hot days... if you can bare the frigid waters. But the bay warms up more than the rest of the sound."

Sandra focused on driving for couple of minutes and then added, "Did I mention that we have our own waterfall?" Before Halem could answer, she continued, "Osprey Creek is a small creek that drops about twenty feet into the southern side of the bay. The falls creates a soothing sound throughout the village both day and night, keeping the inhabitants in a state of Zen." Sandra giggled.

Ten months had passed since that first ride to Rock Harbor and that state of Zen had alluded her. On this morning, between the dark basalt walls that framed in the rift, Halem could see the cerulean waters of Puget Sound. The sun was indeed out, with its rays dancing across the row of craggy snow caps of the rugged North Cascade mountains and glistening over the small rollers of the sound. While immersed in the ambience of the moment, what caught her eye again was that single dark spot on the blue canvas of the sea, something moving in her direction across the waves, bobbing on the surface. It was too small to be a fishing trawler or a sailboat, unless... perhaps... a day sailor. She looked down at her Lira and used her new, clean rag to wipe down the cherry-red steel ends and the nickel front. She hated streaks and had noticed several when she was observing her own reflection while making Kane's coffee. She wiped in counterclockwise swirls to shine it to perfection. Cleaning was her least favorite part about being a barista.

Halem glanced over the tops of the cups again to study the dot. Was it a kayaker? They do have those who are attempting to circumnavigate Orcas Island stop by for coffee. Their bay was the only put-out on the northeast side of the big island. If you follow the coastline, it takes three days even for a good paddler to finish the whole course. Sometimes they would set up their tents on Crescent

Beach for the night.

Halem looked across the café, checking out her customers. Her regulars were seated and "tucked-in" with their espressos, cappuccinos, macchiatos, and Ms. Van Dijk with her hot cocoa and baby marshmallows. On their tables were paperbacks, tablets, laptops and, in the case of Hank, a steampunk gaming computer.

The loudest people in her shop this morning, was a group of tourists. *Typical.* Three couples were sitting at the big table guffawing, talking way too loudly for the sensitive ears of the harbor villagers, who were used to being lulled to sleep at night by the soft white noise of Osprey Falls. Who the tourists were, who they knew, what they had, and where they were going were made clear to everyone in the shop, even without the intention of eavesdropping. They were sailors, as most outsiders are. They were traveling in a flotilla from San Diego en route to Anchorage. Apparently, Diane, the fifty-something busty woman with teased-out, long blond hair, (*obviously extensions*), was talking about managing the Seabreeze Hotel on Ocean Boulevard in that fair city. Apparently, young twenty-something men, per her own account, were always hitting on her. She described them as semipro athletes, body builders, entertainers, and millionaires. From the looks of her quiet husband beside her, he seemed to be hoping one of those suiters would eventually take her away. Halem chuckled with the thought.

While Diane seemed to see herself as incredibly beautiful, Halem never held that kind of body image. She hated her height, all six feet of it. While that may be ideal for a super model, it reduced her pool of men by seventy-five percent. A few short men would date a taller girl, but not so many. Her height made her feel unappealing. She wore flats that almost looked like ballerina shoes, even though it caused her feet to ache incredibly by noon. She also tended to stand with hunched shoulders.

Halem wasn't looking for a man right now anyway. Yet, she couldn't break those bad habits that insidiously became part of her, after her growth spurt when she was fourteen. If she really wanted men to stop flirting with her, she would have worn heels to look six-foot-four and keep her ridiculous curls. Maybe she did like the flirting after all, even if she didn't like men... at least at this point in her life. But flirting made her feel good. Gee-whiz. Her emotions were too messed up even for her to figure out, and she was too frightened to try and understand them any better.

Once again, Halem gazed out to the sea. The black dot had sprouted into a blot. She could see a rhythm in the object, and it was more than the waves bobbing dead wood up and down. What was it?

Disinhibition

The approach of the object in the sea was methodical and now seemed deliberate, coming in toward the rift. The progression slowed as it approached the narrow places. Halem walked back to the storeroom and returned carrying a burlap sack of roasted coffee beans toward the front of the kitchenette. The sack was only a quarter full—when she untied the white cotton string that held it shut, a few beans spilled out, which she kicked under the cabinet. The fact that the bag was almost empty, meant to her that it would soon be time to start the roaster. She loved bringing the green beans to a point of perfection. Her specialty was creating a true dark Italian roast, with minimal acidity but avoiding a bitter burnt taste.

Sandra bought her the best arabica beans money could buy. Most of them came as a direct trade purchase from Yemen, which was hard to get since a civil war had broken out in 2015 between the government and Houthi rebels. Sandra knew that she could not make a profit on such an expensive bean, but she wanted to support the Yemenis farmer, so they would not go extinct during this period of war-imposed destitution. These farmers were the ones who brought coffee to the world, at least in their opinion... but the Ethiopians have a different point of view, claiming to have discovered coffee.

She poured the last of the sack into a plastic hopper, which sat on a shelf just beneath the grinder. She took the limp sack back to the storage room and laid it in front of the big round cooling pan of the steel Probat Burns P 2 roaster. The roaster was satin black with a wide stainless-steel band around its middle. Sandra picked it out based on its color scheme because she wanted uniformity in the décor of the shop. The black case matched the Lira's black handles while the stainless complemented the stainless part of the espresso machine. Sandra wanted the roaster to be in full view of the customers for the atmosphere. Picking a roaster based on color made no sense to Halem, but it was installed long before she came to run the shop. However, it was a good machine, a grade higher although smaller than the one in her Capitol Hill café. The roaster had a double-walled roasting drum, which would greatly reduce the risk of scorching the beans. With that, Halem was satisfied. Sandra got lucky with her choice, knowing almost nothing about the premier coffee bean roasting process.

Halem walked back to the kitchenette area and closed the storage hopper under-the-bar. Took another look out to the sea. With the sun higher in the sky, the water was now a deep blue beneath an azure sky, and the light haze gave the scene a Monet, impressionistic feel. The strange object was still there and slightly closer and fuller.

Her father had taught her how to make a finger telescope, that she could make a pinhole with the tips of her index and thumbs of each hand. When you bring the four pinched fingers together, to create a tiny hole between them, it will magnify and focus the distant object like a pinhole camera.

After looking around the shop to make sure no one was noticing her, Halem raised her hands in front of her right eye, creating the tiny hole, framed in by the tips of the four fingers. It seemed to work as the object was becoming clearer to her. She could make out the rhythmic movement of each side of what appeared to be long oars. *A rowboat!* It wouldn't be the first to stop by, but it was unusual. The rowing club from Anacortes had come once, in three such boats, just as a day trip and a picnic on their Crescent Beach, followed by coffee in her shop.

The presence of a person, standing to her right at the counter and catching her peripheral vision, startled Halem. She dropped her hands and looked at the young man. "You scared me," she said.

Standing at the counter was a heavy young man wearing glasses. Blue and white flannel shirt, with a long tail hanging halfway to his knees. Unshaven. His hair a mess. A big, kind grin came to his face, and he chuckled in a most obnoxious laugh. Then he spoke in a bois-terous and deliberate voice, "I scared you? That's funny. I just walked in and you were looking at your fingers. I wasn't trying to scare you, Halem. Is something wrong with your fingers?"

"My fingers are fine. Jamie, you're late today. I wasn't expecting you."

"That's okay." He pushed his glasses up on his nose. "My mother made tacos last night."

Halem grabbed a cup to prepare his usual, a mocha with sweet-ened chocolate syrup. She was waiting for his further explanation, but when it didn't come, she asked, "So, how did her making tacos make you late this morning?" As soon as the words were out of her mouth, she had regrets for asking.

"Oh, when I eat a lot of onions," his voice disturbing the typically subdued customers. "It makes my bowels move. I went to the bath-room in mom's house to have a mega-shit this morning."

The big blond tourist elbowed her partner. The man turned to stare at Jamie. Halem was going to let it drop, but then Jamie kept going: "Once I was in the bathroom so long, I saw mom's Victoria Se-cret catalogs in the garbage can. So, I got excited looking at it and masturbated. That's why I'm so late."

Halem blushed, even though she had heard Jamie's unwonted replies at least a hundred times. Since he was mentally slow, she al-ways showed him extra grace with such comments. Nothing he said should have surprised her by now. But each time, she seemed more shocked. She made the decision to avoid further conversation and she refocused on his coffee, except to whisper, just above her breath, "I hope you washed your hands."

She quickly turned on the bean grinder to drown out any further comments from the young man. Once the beans were ground and weighed, and as she was hand-packing the portafilter, she heard the tourists again. They were giggling so hard in fact that Ms. Blondie, the one they called Diane, looked like she was about to wet herself. "I think we've sailed into Hicksville." They all laughed out loud.

There is something about Rock Harbor, maybe it is the isolation of the cohesive community, which makes the residents feel defensive toward outsiders, especially rude ones. She glanced over at Jamie, who had turned, squaring up his shoulders to the table of snickering tourists and was directly looking at them. *Poor thing.* He can't help what he says, yet he's so sensitive when people seem to disrespect him in return. The two characteristics didn't seem to be well suited.

Then she looked around the room as she locked in the portafilter and pressed on the pumps. *Hicksville? Really?* There sat Kane, with his PhD in comparative religions or theology... she couldn't remember for sure... but it was an Ivy-league school. *Princeton?* He'd written several books on ancient languages. At the table next to him was Henry Bohjanen, who they called "Hank," deeply into his game and oblivious to the world. Hard to believe that he was the first drummer for Nirvana. He left the band at their height, not because he wasn't good enough, but because of his intractable case of stage fright. Kurt Cobain had said in one of his last interviews that "Hank Bojo was the best damn drummer the band ever had, maybe the best the world has ever known." Halem, thanks to her mom and dad's involvement with Seattle's grunge band movement, knew exactly who Hank was the first day he walked into the coffee shop, although he was a man of few words. He never offered small talk, just a "thank you," when she served his drink.

Next to Hank's table, sat Alaskan fishermen Roger and Daniel. Roger spent two tours in Iraq and one in Afghanistan. Got a Purple Heart and returned home to take over the family fishing business when his dad got sick with lung cancer. *Hicksville? Really?*

Then there was Ms. Van Dijk, with her own high-end design label, with boutiques in New York, San Francisco, and Milan. Sandra told Halem all about the woman. She maintains her home here, to avoid the limelight, so she can think and design. *Hicksville? Give me a break.*

About that time the loud word, "Halem!" pierced the air beside her. "Wake up Halem and finish my mocha."

She smiled at Jamie and quickly poured the waiting shots into his cup. "I wasn't sleeping… just thinking."

"I hope you were thinking about fixing your hair. Those curls look goofy."

"Yes, Jamie, I *know*. I'll cut them off as soon as I get home tonight."

"I liked your ponytail the best. Why'd you cut it off?"

She didn't answer.

"Doesn't matter, you're still gorgeous. I would still love to have sex with you, even with the goofy curls. I'm still a virgin, you know."

Halem paused, turned robotically, and looked at him in the eyes, as if to say, "Naughty boy, shame on you." She went back to making his coffee.

"I bet Judy talked you into it. Cutting off your beautiful hair. My mom says she's a quack. She's not licensed you know. She started out cutting Bob's hair and then the other fishermen's like my dad. I guess she's the only hair cutter in town. She's okay for men. She cuts my hair. Most of the women go over to Anacortes to get their hair done."

She handed Jamie his eight-ounce mocha. He gave her his usual five-dollar bill allowing her to keep the extra twenty-five cents as a tip.

Then Jamie walked directly to the tourists, who were at the tail end of their long giggle session. He strolled up behind the loud blonde and just stood there. He sipped his mocha with a loud slurping sound, leaving a white whipped foam mustache, making him look like a little boy. The tourists were all quiet but still snickering under their breaths, which Halem could tell from their quivering heads. They were pretending Jamie wasn't there and made no attempts to engage him in conversation. He sipped his drink again. "So… where're you folks from?"

With her back turned the blonde said, "San Diego. Ever heard of it?"

Jamie took another loud sip, "I like the Gulls."

The man, to the right of the blonde, looked at him with an astonished glare, "Really, you know who the Gulls are?"

"I like the Swiss goalie, Berra."

The blonde finally turned around, "So, you have ESPN here? I can't believe it! I didn't think a satellite signal could beam this far from nowhere."

"I've been to three games in San Diego. My granddad is James, James the first. I'm the third. Granddad is retired from the Navy and lives in San Diego. He has season tickets." Jamie sipped his mocha again, "Where're you heading, in your boats?"

The man, to the right of Diane, said, trying to be serious, "Alaska... I guess you've been there too."

Halem took a deep breath. She had to get there before things started to get ugly, which usually happened with Jamie and tourists. Jamie had almost drowned in Alaska and to ask if he had ever been there could set him off.

"Yeah, Dad commercially fishes there all the time and I sometimes go with him." He licked whipped cream from his upper lip. "Dad says that he has to save California yuppy sailors on almost every trip. So, maybe you need me to go with you... you know, to show you the way."

The group looked at each other, smiling, just about to break into belly laughs.

"Do you know about the Seymour Narrows? Sailors run into trouble there all the time, especially in bad weather," added Jamie.

Halem, fretfully took a cinnamon roll out of the display case and stuck it into the microwave.

A man, across the table from the blonde, trying to muster a serious tone, answered, "Yes. I'm the navigator for the group. I've studied the route and have the best electronic equipment. I'm familiar with Seymour Narrows and the other tight spots along the way."

"So, you've been through them before?" asked Jamie.

"Uh, no. But I've studied them on maps."

Jamie, after taking yet another sip added, "Do you know how to use a sextant? You can always lose power for your navigation equipment."

The group sat in silence until the blonde woman said, "Oh, you do know that a *sex-tant* isn't a device that you use to masturbate with, don't you?" Immediately, the whole group burst out in loud laughter.

The man beside her, trying to refrain his laughter long enough to speak was finally able to spit out, "Yeah, I'm sure his *semen*-ship would be a great asset for us!" The whole group howled until one of the men literally fell out of his chair.

Jamie just stared at the blonde, who was then laughing the hardest, clearing his throat, he mumbled, "You aren't as pretty as you think you are. It's obvious that you have fake hair... and fake tits."

The microwave dinged. Halem grabbed the roll and carried it over to the table next to Kane. "Jamie, I've a hot cinnamon roll for you. It's on the house. Hurry, before it gets cold."

Jamie walked in slow precise steps in the direction of the table, which held the cinnamon roll. He knew he was being conned but didn't mind. He looked back at the table of tourists and said defiantly, "That's okay, I wouldn't want to go with you anyway. My dad can bail you out if you get into trouble." He took a seat at the table, facing through the window, out onto the bay. Halem laid her hand on his shoulder and whispered, "Ignore them. They're assholes. They'll be gone soon."

As she turned away from the table, she looked out the window, only to catch the sight of the dot, a rowboat in full bloom, entering the outer rift. A small white boat, with one person aboard, pulling the paddles against the sea and pulling the Rock Harbor world toward him with his powerful strokes. Certainly, it was a "him" at the oars.

With a clean towel in hand, she walked toward the tourists' table. Smiled. Collected their empty cups. Wiped up the crumbs, which she dropped in a flowerpot. It appeared that Jamie was watching the white boat as well. Watching and carefully sipping his mocha. "Jamie's special to us," she whispered. "He's had a brain injury..."

"You think?" said the blonde.

Halem gave her an annoyed look and continued. "He almost drowned when he was nine. He fell off his father's fishing boat in Bristol Bay." She walked to the other side of the table, closer to the woman, and said in a low tone, "He was in a coma, I think his mother said, for about three months. If the water had not been so cold, he would've died. But he did have a brain injury. He's not as bright as he could've been. He had to drop out of school. They call it *disinhibition*. No ability to filter what he wants to say, so he says exactly whatever he thinks. He means no harm. It's a brain injury."

The blonde gave a big, fake, crocodilian smile. "Maybe he'd been better off if the water had been warmer."

Halem wasn't sure what she meant. Was she saying that Jamie would have been better off dead? She had just told the woman that the cold water was what had saved his life. Was that what she was trying to imply? Then, Halem felt rage fill her chest and face. Hear her pulse in her ears. Her own emotional inhibition was in full effect, so she gathered up the dishes and headed back to the kitchenette, ignoring the comment, saying nothing.

She put the empties and dishes into the dish washer then paused to gaze at the bay. The rower was now in plain view, inside the rift and nearing the harbor, rowing what looked like an old wooden skiff, white hull, red gunwales. In the middle was a bare, wooden mast around which a sail was wrapped and tied out of the way. He used the long oars with great skill. Clearly a man, although, with his back toward the shore and with his rather long, curly hair, could have been mistaken for a woman. His muscles were masculine. He was dark, so dark, it was hard to tell his race. A well-tanned Caucasian, Hispanic, or lighter-skinned Black.

The rower pulled hard with each stroke, rotating the blades, seamlessly to being parallel with the water, from the finish of the stroke back to the catch. He moved like a skilled dancer with the sea as his partner. With the revolution of the paddle blades, she could see his shoulder blades, likewise, rotating beneath the back of his shirt.

Halem gathered a few more cups from the plastic bin on the other side of the bar. Stacked the remaining dishes into the dishwasher. Almost full. Time to turn it on and then focus on the roasting. Then she heard Jamie. *Now what?*

"Halem, this mocha tastes like crap. That's not like you."

She felt another blush sweep across her face. She was an expert, one of the best in making good espresso, which was the linchpin of a good mocha. Was Jamie playing some type of game with her?

Halem grabbed the glass out of his hand and sipped it herself. Something *wasn't* right. The *milk* was bad. She had forgotten to taste the milk!

Keeping fresh milk in her shop was always a problem. They brought in several gallons at a time, and if they did not use them up fast enough, they would start to sour. The village had no store, and all their groceries came in by boat or over the treacherous mountain road. Sandra wanted to put the extra milk in her chest freezer at her house, but Halem was afraid freezing would cause it to separate and become watery. She was a perfectionist, and this morning she felt like a coffee monkey.

Halem looked across the room. At least four of the tourists had a coffee product with milk in it. Kane had his ristretto-based cappuccino and Hank had a regular cappuccino, so they both had the bad milk. Even Ms. Van Dijk had milk in her hand-made hot cocoa. *Why hadn't anyone said anything?* Jamie was the canary in the coalmine, always the first to speak. He would let her know when it's too hot, too cold, or... when she has a bad hair style.

She pulled the gallon jug out of the refrigerator and sniffed it. Yeah, it was bad with a smell of buttermilk. Why had even Jamie waited so long to tell her? His mocha was half drunk. Apparently, the San Diego tourists had distracted him. She threw the gallon in the garbage with such force that some of it splashed out and onto the floor. She quickly wiped up the mess and stuffed the soiled towel, out of sight, into another drawer.

"Excuse me everyone. I just found out that our milk was sour. I'm so sorry. So, either I'll make you a new cup on the house, or you can get your money back."

Kane smiled, "I noticed something wasn't right with the milk, but the coffee was perfect."

She looked at Hank, head set on and unmindful of what was happening around him. Ms. Van Dijk smiled, "I'm fine. But you should check the milk each morning before you start using it." Halem never understood why some people state the obvious. Was it just to be discourteous?

The tourists of course were doubled over in laughter. She stared at them, waiting for a response. Then Jamie, still standing beside her, said, in an ill-humored voice, "Don't laugh at her! She's the greatest barista in the Pacific Northwest. It was just bad milk." They said nothing, just allowed their hilarity to slowly waffle away into the awkward air of the room, and they resumed their previous conversation.

The morning passed, and the coffee enthusiasts had filed out one by one, with few new customers wondering in. By the afternoon, Halem was eagerly waiting for things to slow down so she could start her roasting process. She wished she could roast while the shop was open, but she wasn't about to take a chance on someone interrupting her at a key moment in the process. Thirty seconds late on dumping the roasted beans into the cooling tray could ruin them. Yemenis beans were too expensive to waste. Men risked their lives to get the beans out of the country. It would be a shame to ruin them with a bad roast. When the roaster was running, she constantly watched the beans through the brass port window. When getting close to finishing, she sampled the beans through the coffee tryer.

The tryer is a small scoop, with a wooden handle, which slips through a hole in the cast iron drum into the roasting chamber. As the drum turns, it spills the beans into the scoop producing a reliable sample. While most roasters would examine the beans' color and even sniff them, Halem liked to pick a bean out and toss it into her mouth. Play with it on her tongue for texture. Slowly crush it with her molars for hardness. Then lay the crushed bean remains on the different taste buds across her tongue. This tasting would take a couple of seconds yet provide Halem with precise information about the roasting process. Interruptions during this forty-five-minute process could lead to a disaster.

When the tourists left, just before noon, they filed by the counter. Since they said nothing when she made the announcement about the milk, she had assumed they were happy with their drinks—but then they wanted their coffee re-credited onto their debit cards. She couldn't make eye contact with them because she felt so angry. Those people disrupted the other customers, were rude to Jamie, and now they were leaving and paying for nothing. It was these things that stood as a constant reminder to Halem that life is not fair. The most awful people come out on top, while the rest, like her, struggle to find one tiny piece of happiness.

Kane, as usual, was the last one out as Halem closed the shop at five. He gathered up his books and journals, stuffed them back into his briefcase. His first drink of the day was always his ristretto-based cappuccino, but he had order a cortado—with the new milk—and a rosemary roll in the afternoon. As he handed Halem his empty cups at the counter, she asked when he was coming back. He usually visited two or three times each week. He looked into the air as if to think and said, "I think I'll be back on Friday."

"Be careful crossing the mountain," she said as she closed the door and locked it behind him. Finally, the shop was empty, and she could start roasting! It was the best part of her paltry life with no future to look forward to, no past to remember, no friends to share the present. Just making coffee.

Chapter Three

The Barista

Sandra had rescued Halem from her life in Seattle's Capitol Hill ten months previously. The stout naturally salt-and-pepper haired woman came into the Emerald City Beans one day and noticed the barista hard at work, making coffee, waiting on customers, and prepping the roaster.

The shop in Capitol Hill was much larger than the shop on Orcas Island. The Seattle shop was spacious, with the ambience of a coffee roasting factory. The large roasting area there was framed-in on three sides by rustic thirty-foot fir tables. The roasting apparatuses were all clad in hammered copper with brass accents, giving them the appearance of a fine collection of industrial art sculptures. Additionally, there were more than twenty smaller tables scattered throughout the huge room. The ceilings were dark, but open, exposing the old beams from the late-nineteenth century, when it was built as a city stable. While it once housed horses that pulled buggies through the dirt and brick streets of frontier Seattle, it became the premier place in the city for high-end coffee, serving several hundred demanding patrons per day. In that posh shop, most considered Halem the best among the best.

Halem had noticed Sandra as a repeat customer and—a remarkably attractive woman. She was rather striking, especially considering her middle age, shoulder-length hair, with no attempts to cover the emerging gray, and stocky frame. She carried herself with great confidence, a trait that Halem coveted.

One afternoon, when Halem came to clear Sandra's coffee cup from her table, Sandra grabbed her wrist and asked, "You wouldn't be interested in working in a new coffee shop in a gorgeous, but isolated place, in the San Juan Islands? Would you?"

The word that stood out to Halem that morning wasn't *gorgeous* but *isolated*. It was about that time she was realizing the precarious-ness of her relationship with her boyfriend, Finn. She immediately said, "Sure." While Sandra had been the originator of the question, she appeared to be a bit taken back by Halem's swift and confident response.

Sandra, with raised eyebrows asked, "Really?"

Halem was concerned that her quick response might give her away. Would this nice woman figure out that she was running from something? Or maybe her swift actions would communicate that she was flippant, not taking the offer seriously. She was serious. She had been looking for the chance to escape from Finn and Sandra's offer seemed to her as a sign.

Finn had swept into Halem's life like a hell-bent knight on a mis-sion. He was dark, witty, wacky, and kind. He was about the exact same height as Halem but referred to himself as six-foot-two, while she was five-eleven. He met her on the light rail when he was stand-ing beside her, holding on to an overhead strap. He looked down at her, seated beside his right leg, her elbow tapping his thigh with each bump of the train as it crossed asphalt streets. She was reading a book, but he couldn't see the title. "What's that you're reading?" he asked.

She smiled at him and showed the stranger the front of her book, John Updike's *Rabbit Redux*. Finn began to laugh uncontrollably, leaving her to think she was reading something that was unaccepta-ble to him or even silly. She blushed and pulled away, wrapping herself—cocoon-like—back in the pages, not to read, but to escape from the threatening world of strangers inside the train. She always had this feeling that strangers were judging her, how she looked, her clothes, and in this case, what she was reading.

Once he contained his giggle, Finn reached into his oily leather bag, which hung by a shoulder strap over his left hip, and pulled out a well-worn copy of Updike's *Rabbit, Run*.

Ensuing small talk led to a date, well, sort of. Finn picked her up at the coffee shop when her shift ended that evening. They walked down Broadway. He darted into a Walgreens at the corner of East Mercer and bought a bottle of Rebel Yell, Ginger. There was a local grunge band playing a concert in the Bobby Morris ball field a few blocks away. His idea was to go, taking Halem with him. Finn, unabashedly, grabbed a quilt he saw behind a dumpster on Harrison Street... obviously a homeless person's vacant bed. He had a wild sense of humor and thought it was funny.

"Finn!" said Halem with a nervous laugh. "What's he going to sleep on? Ew... that's nasty."

Finn shook it hard and then put it over his back like a cape as he skipped down the sidewalk, dodging bystanders, getting several steps ahead of Halem. He stopped and spun around to look directly at her, walking backwards and said, "Don't worry, we'll give it back on our way home. He won't miss it." Then he turned and pretended to run down the sidewalk, swerving left and right between pedestrians with his left arm outstretched, his right still clutching the dirty blanket tight around his neck, pretending to fly like Superman.

They arrived at the park packed with people, all standing or laying on the field, freshly wettened by a late afternoon drizzle. Finn laid the blanket down over the damp grass and patted on it to motion for Halem to join him. She grimaced and slowly sat on the edge of the stained quilt. They eventually laid on it, on the muddy ground, and sipped Rebel Yell straight from the bottle for the rest of the evening.

Halem was not a hard liquor drinker. Things became a blur for her as Finn kept passing her the bottle and lifting the bottom as she sipped, making sure she had a good gulp. She and Finn made love right there in the park, rolled up in the grimy blanket, on the wet-dirty ground, in front of everybody, save the darkness, and with a man she hardly knew. No one really seemed to notice, anyway, as a fog of cannabis hung over the crowd.

Finn invited her to come home with him, to live. She agreed on a subdued impulse, restrained under his overwhelming confidence and the Rebel Yell sifting through her veins that it was the right thing to do. Her reckless decision to go with Sandra was like this previous agreement to go with this man that she didn't know. Maybe accepting Sandra's offer so quickly was Halem's later attempt to remedy the previous bad choice to go with Finn.

Finn helped her walk to the light rail that night and then to her home in the Belltown district. It was a roundabout way to get home, requiring a long walk north. But Halem liked the modern, quiet train. Her home was a small humble apartment on the third floor of a yellow-brick building built in the 1920s. After her mother died, her father had become withdrawn. More like a walking corpse. Got up in the morning, before Halem. Left for his job at the Seattle Public Library by nine-thirty. Halem would lay in her bed until he was gone, avoiding him. She couldn't face him, and the hopeless sorrow written on his dusty, sullen face. When he came home at night, Halem would be at work. When she returned from her job at the coffee shop, he would be asleep in his easy chair, empty beer cans in the floor, one on the arm of the Lazy Boy. She'd pick up the cans and cover him with a blanket. She never knew if he spent the entire night there or got up and went to bed later. This was the crux of their relationship for the six years following her mother's passing.

Her mother was full of life... before it was pilfered from her. She filled their house with flowers, songs, and the smell of baking cardamom and cinnamon bread. Halem felt guilt that the pair of breasts, which had sustained herself when she came into this world, took her mother away. It was a primal feeling of responsibility that she knew didn't make any sense. Her mother would still have breasts if Halem had not been born, and she still would have succumbed to breast cancer, although Halem read once that lactation and breast feeding could be a risk factor for cancer.

Her memory had become opaque by the passage of time. But she remembered her father in better days. She could still see him playing the mandolin and singing silly songs with her mother. He had written many of them himself. She recalled him bringing home old computers and books from work and things of the world for them to explore. They had a huge library of their own, made up of books the

Seattle Public Library was discarding. Amazing how much he could strap on to a bicycle and within its basket.

Halem's father had always said that the price of true love was loss. Halem didn't know what that meant at the time. But he died with the love of his life. His loss was immeasurable, as was his love. The apartment was nothing more than a mausoleum, save the polished marble. Cold, dark, and damp, even in the dry, sunny days of Seattle's summer. The yellow bricks of the building's façade seemed to be in mourning, as they had turned brown with greenish, algae-stained mortar lines, especially near the ground. On the outside, the building smelled like wet mold. The apartment reeked of staleness, with the scent of her mother's lovely flowers long faded away.

Halem went away with Finn without resistance. It wasn't just the paralyzing influence of the alcohol. It was the metaphorical knotted bedsheets dropped from the window, down which the damsel could escape the dreaded tower. If she didn't grab the chance, it may never come again—or so she thought. She couldn't afford to live in Seattle on her own salary. She knew it wasn't fair to her father to leave like that. He deserved better. She'd left out of a deep place of despair.

She took all her important things—clothes, phone, toothbrush, brown teddy bear. Stuffed them in a garbage bag. Slung it over her shoulder as she prepared to walk back to the train. Never left a note or said goodbye to her father. He was already gone, gone from this earth. She saw his silhouette in his chair. His barreled chest slowly rising and sinking, leaving the stink of beer. His thinning frontal hair laid precariously across his brow, and his redden cheeks fluttering with each snore. Apparently, on this night at least, he wasn't going to his bed. She looked around the living room for the familiar blanket but didn't see it. "I need to cover him," she said.

Finn threw the dirty quilt, the one they had taken from the homeless guy's nest, the same one they had made love on, over him and laughed. Halem felt the disrespect in the gesture but kept silent, which she later regretted.

Her father really did deserve better, but he would never know the story woven deeply into the blanket's soiled fabric. It was just like the dirt the priest had thrown on her mother's casket as they lowered her into the ground on that windy day in Lake View Cemetery. It was just dirt, but as a young girl she didn't understand; she felt it was an act of disrespect from the padre. You wouldn't throw dirt on a living person. Her mom deserved better too. But she would never know. When Halem stepped back from his chair, a tear tumbled from her face. Finn wiped it off with his grimy finger. But that is where the empathy ended. "Really?" his question intruded into the poignant moment.

Finn had a rather bare studio apartment on the edge of Capitol Hill, only a couple of blocks from the coffee shop. It was simple. A beige futon on the floor, purple sleeping bag on the futon. In the bathroom was his comb, soap, and towel. Beside the futon was an old steamer trunk full of his poorly organized clothes. On the back of the door were two rows of wooden pegs, each, except one, with a hat hanging from it. The hats were an assortment of styles including a fedora, a couple of newsboys, a Panama, at least two baseball, and one stovepipe. All dirty and well-worn. Finn probably commandeered them too, from dumpsters or the street-sleeping homeless. He also had rows of empty whiskey bottles across the windowsills, all four of them. This was Halem's first feeling of concern about his drinking. The concern came from a passing place of clairvoyance, quickly brushed aside like a single gnat in her hair. But that feeling never left her. It floated peripherally, not in view, but not out of sight, either.

As she got to know Finn, and it took almost a year to do so, she encountered his demons. He was an alcoholic. The spirits bewitched his demeanor, fueling a vent of anger that Halem found terrifying. He was also kind, handsome, and exciting... when restrained. He was also a liar and manipulator.

Finn was not an avid reader. He had never opened Updike. He had seen her on the light rail several times the days leading up to their first conversation. He thought she was pretty. Very pretty, so he said... although she didn't believe him. He had written down the name, Rabbit Redux, when he saw it on the cover of her book a few days before he spoke to her, and then visited the Mercer Street Books to look for a copy. He wanted to find the same title but only found Rabbit, Run, in the used section—worn, tea-stained, and dog-eared—and purchased it as a simple prop. *A setup.*

Halem lived in denial... until he slapped her. Slapped her face. He apologized. She accepted. Then it happened again. Soon there was no daylight of soberness into which he could inject the slimmest apology. It was time to leave. Oddly, although he hated her when he was wasted, he was also madly in love with her and would not give her up easy... when he was sober. But she had terrifying glimpses into the dark places of his soul, into the hollow nooks and crannies where his insecurities resided. It was time to leave.

Escaping to a remote place was what she needed. Sandra's invitation required no thought. At the end of her shift, she packed all her belongings into two garbage bags. Slightly bigger bags than the bag she carried in from her dad's apartment. She had to do it in haste while Finn was unconscious from drink.

As they drove from the coffee shop to her apartment, Sandra explained that she had been observing her and knew that she was a hard worker and, "A damn good barista because I had tasted your coffee several times. One of the other baristas told me you were the best." Asking Halem to come with her was no accident.

Sandra turned out was quite a talker and, unlike Halem, didn't hesitate to share her personal life. As they drove through Seattle, heading to the freeway, she explained that she was previously married to a lawyer in Queen Anne. Her ex, Bret, was a good guy, but liked women... other women. He liked them lightly, not deeply, and he seemed to think that was ducky. One woman wasn't enough for him. Sandra had put up with it for years, focusing on her art. But one day she had simply had enough. It was never just the other women, but to accommodate those relationships, he resorted to habitual lying. It was the lying that she finally couldn't take, so she left him. The settlement left her with seven figures. He was a lawyer and should have known better, however, his narcissism never allowed him to imagine she would leave him, so a prenup had never presented itself to him. This is where she made the connection between her personal life and Halem. Now she had a good income from investments, the coffee shop had no pressure to make a profit. She explained that creating a world-class coffee shop in this isolated village was a project for her, like a hobby. She looked over at Halem and smiled, "This will be a great job for you. No pressure. Just having fun, doing what you love."

On that first day, ten months earlier, when Sandra and Halem rode north out of the city in Sandra's convertible, they were complete strangers. Now they found themselves in an employer–employee as well as a landlord–renter relationship.

Halem seemed to have left her voice in Seattle that night. She just leaned against the side window and let the cool wind blow through her hair, causing her bleached-golden ponytail to whip to the left and the right, as if behind a galloping colt. She was listening to Sandra's conversation and her detailed history about Rock Harbor but without engaging. The exception was when she had to ask her to stop to allow her to pee. She was both scared and feeling safe. Finn would never find her in the San Juan Islands, but what else waited for her there? Was it worth the exchange?

After Sandra finished narrating her introduction to Rock Harbor, and the history thereof, she allowed several miles of quiet asphalt to move beneath them before speaking again. Then, she moved the conversation into a more personal space.

"Are you from Seattle… I mean were you born there?"

"Yep."

"Oh… do you have a family?"

"Yep."

"Do you live with them? I mean that apartment that I picked you up at, is that your parent's place or do you live on your own?"

She pictured Finn passed out on his shabby futon as she stuffed her belongings into the garbage bags.

"My own."

"Well, that was progress: a two-word answer."

Sandra suddenly shifted into a quieter mood. Focused on the road. Halem felt like her evasive answers was giving Sandra doubts about her. Was this idea of employing Halem a mistake? Worse than that, maybe Sandra was worried that she was one of these kinds of quiet strangers, a young, mixed-up woman that you see on *Dateline* or *48 Hours*—the kind who seems sweet but poisons their landlords or chops off their fingers with a rusty hedge pruner while they sleep.

After a few minutes, Sandra picked up where she had left off, almost like she had been in a trance. "The Rock Harbor Roasters isn't a large shop, not like the one on Capitol Hill. It is quaint with six tables, one being a refectory table that would seat eight. There's a bar around the espresso machine and the ordering counter right inside the door. Maybe it would accommodate twenty customers at most. The roaster is in the back. Everything is brand new."

A few more miles of quiet roadway passed. The sun was going down over the Olympic Mountains, and the air was getting cooler. "Do you want me to put the top up?"

"I'm fine."

Sandra turned up the heat and the heated seats to compensate for the cooler, evening air. She told Halem how she loved riding in a convertible, especially when it was barely warm enough to have the top down. The air seemed so refreshing, like it had a higher concentration of oxygen than regular air. When other convertibles would pass her with their tops up, she felt that they were looking at her and thinking that she was a wild and crazy woman. A real bad ass. That was her ambition at least.

"So, what's with the name? It's pretty, but I haven't heard it before."

Halem sat up. "Well, my mom and dad were rockers. They were like groupies or something like that in the 1970s. They followed several bands across the country. They named me after Van Halen."

Sandra thought for a moment and then said, "But your name, at least on your nametag, is spelled H-A-L-E-M, isn't it?"

Halem snickered. "Yep. My mom misspelled it on my birth certifi-cate. She had seen the name 'New Halem' in the paper that night, you know the town in the Cascades. I think a rockslide had closed the access to New Halem, and they were flying in food or something like that. Then she accidently spelled my name that way... or, at least that's how she described the story to me." She paused. "She wasn't very smart. Mom wasn't. But she was very funny and full of life, just not well-read."

"Was?" asked Sandra.

Halem, for reasons she was not sure, decided to lie. "Oh, I mean *is*. She isn't very smart but she's funny. I think I said wasn't, thinking of my childhood... but she still is. I mean she's still funny and full of life."

"And your father?"

"Uh, he works at the Seattle public library."

"He's a librarian?"

"Not really. He's the one who stacks books, restacks books, moves bookcases, and more manual work."

"Is he nice?"

"Nice? Uh, I don't know."

"How could you not know if your father was nice or not?"

"I guess he was." She wrapped her ponytail in her hand to keep the wind from flapping against her face. "I mean... uh, well, he's very quiet."

"Was he always a quiet man?" asked Sandra.

"No... not really."

A few minutes of silence passed, as Sandra focused on the road. Halem closed her eyes, as if she were about to go to sleep.

"Why did he," said Sandra, "I mean your father, why did he be-come so introverted?"

Halem remained silent. It wasn't so much that she didn't want Sandra to know the real reason her dad was so quiet, which was in response to her mother dying, but that she didn't want Sandra to know that she had lied to her when she spoke of her mother in the present tense.

The evening sky grew dark, the blue progressing to purple, indigo, and violet as the sun drifted further out into the Pacific Ocean, en route to bringing Asia its dawn. The top of Mount Baker to the east was set aglow in contrast to the darkness seeping into the lowlands like poured molasses. The wind over the glass windshield was growing colder and denser. The airstream was the only sound that filled their ears.

Sandra asked louder than before, "Why did your dad become so quiet?"

Halem responded with force. "I don't know!"

Sandra didn't pursue the thought. They traveled to Mount Vernon and exited onto a state highway heading directly west, toward Puget Sound.

"What's your ambitions in life? Do you always want to be a barista? I mean you could be. You're good at it."

"Being a barista isn't so bad. I wouldn't mind doing it for a few years at least," said Halem.

"So, it isn't your dream job?"

"Hmm. No, being a writer would be my dream job."

"Really? What kind of writer, I mean, what genre?"

Halem sighed, "Sci-fi. I love reading it, and I dabble in writing it now."

"That's a little unusual for a girl, isn't it? I was guessing it would be romance. Have you published anything?"

Halem chuckled, "No."

"What are you working on now?"

Halem turned her head to look out the side window. "It's about the internet. You see, the number of connections of the internet, worldwide, rivals the number of neurons in the human brain, which is eighty or ninety billion. So, in my story, the internet starts to take on consciousness and becomes like a person, but a very benevolent person, who wants to fix the broken world. Then some people start to see the internet as a god."

"... I know it sounds corny," Halem quickly added.

"No, it doesn't. I was just trying to get my head around the concept. It sounds fascinating, maybe even a little provocative."

"I have a friend who's a literary agent. She helps writers get published with some of the big publishers. Uh… well, she's my ex's sister-in-law, she's married to Bret's brother, but we are closer than that. We are good friends even if Bret wasn't in the picture. Maybe I can set you up with her… I mean, once you have something good written. Uh, not that anything you write wouldn't be good, even the internet becoming a god story, is good."

A few minutes passed and a few more miles of rolled asphalt unrolled beneath them.

Sandra pulled over to the shoulder. Halem looked at her, curious. "I'm putting the top up… you know, so that you can hear me better." She pushed the button and a high-pitched whine followed. The black top came forward and latched onto the windshield. Sandra locked it in place by turning a latch. Then she pulled back out onto the highway.

"There's only one road into Rock Harbor and it follows a tortuous course of switchbacks and hairpin turns with no guardrails. There's deep ruts, especially in winter, making it impassable except for maybe a jeep."

Halem gave her a raised eyebrow. "Do you have a jeep? Can we drive it in the dark?"

Sandra chuckled as she came to an intersection where the Farm to Market Road met State Highway 20. As they were waiting for the light to change, she continued. "We'll get there like everyone else… by boat. We'll park at the marina in Anacortes, where I keep my car, and load my stuff onto my powerboat. It's about an hour and half trip."

"In the dark?"

"Sure. I've done it many times. I'm experienced at the helm of a boat. My ex—you know, Bret—had several boats both power and sail. He taught me a lot. We even sailed to Hong Kong and once to Mexico. After I had proved my seamanship to him, he left the boat in my hands for long segments of the Asian trip while he went back to Seattle for business. I sailed alone from Hawaii to Taiwan." She looked at Halem and added, "Your first lesson about boats, the front is the bow, the rear is the stern, facing the front, the right side is the starboard side and the left is the portside. You will need to remember those. I'll add more terms later."

The light changed to green, and Sandra pulled out onto the highway. "During that trip, you know, the one to Asia, I *thought* that Bret was back in Seattle taking care of business. Instead, I later found out that he was shacked up with some bimbo he met on the beach in Honolulu. A woman with giant boobs like she had escaped from a circus' freak show." She laughed.

"Really?"

"Yeah, really. But turns out that wasn't his first or his last. Our entire twenty-year marriage was him going from woman to woman behind my back, like a disorientated hummingbird going from flower to flower looking for the sweetest nectar. Eventually I figured it out. But he made my life comfortable. I had an art studio right on the water in South Lake Union. I could focus on my art and live like a queen, even if I sold only a painting every six months. Bret had millions."

Sandra paused for a minute.

"Then one day I decided, for self-respect, that I couldn't go on living like that. It was the lies more than the women. To me, having a woman on the side is disrespectful, but lying to me, is audacious. Like him saying he was working back in Seattle when he was really living in a beat-up Winnebago with this bimbo—I don't even think he knew the bitch's name—on the beach in Lanikai. So, I left. I thought about moving to France. I had a settlement in the millions and could do that. But oddly I chose Rock Harbor as my new home. I went there just to air out my brain for a few days and fell in love with the place. It's a strange but lovely spot. I like the isolation, yet proximity to Seattle. It's full of eclectic, but wonderful people. This includes the few year-round residents and the constant flow of outsiders."

"Men are jerks!" said Halem.

"Oh, I've met some nice men. I just made a mistake when I married Bret. I don't know, maybe it wasn't a mistake. You measure an experience by how it turns out in the end. This end to that relationship isn't so bad. Even Bret isn't so bad if you can look past his womanizing and lies. If I could just open the back of his head and tinker around inside a bit. If I could cut those womanizing wires, he would have been a fabulous husband. Now that would make a great science fiction story. But who knows, maybe it was my destiny because now I have the freedom to do my art in a quiet place and to give a gift of a high-end coffee shop to a small village. I would have done it all over again if I had the chance, but with less naivety."

A few more miles passed, and Sandra spoke again, "Rock Harbor's so small, maybe fifty year-round residents, but lots of tourists, that it couldn't support anything more than a little café with a big, Bun coffee maker. But I want to bring in the best of the best in the craft of making good coffee. That's why I'm inviting you."

"I hope I don't disappoint you."

"Besides the year-rounders, we have the transients. We have the regular transients, which are usually fishermen. They fish in Alaska or Puget Sound and keep their boats in Rock Harbor as a safe and convenient place to berth them. If there's a short off season, say between Chinook and Dungeness crabs or Coho, they live on their boats for a month, until they're ready to go again. But our biggest transients are the tourists. They come by sailboat, kayak, or power boats. Their stay is brief… taking a lot of photos, asking a lot of really stupid questions like, 'is Rock Harbor real?' leaving a lot of trash, which we must take back to the mainland by barge, and then they disappear. To them, Rock Harbor is an intriguing place, like a Disney exhibit, but the small footprint bores them quickly and the turnover rate is quite high, with dozens coming and going every day, at least in the summer."

Sandra then drove across a big bridge. It looked like a work of art in concrete, like a giant vibraphone, sweeping up slowly, starting a half a mile away from its midpoint. It rose above the saltwater to a height that would accommodate even the tallest masted ships. At the top, the northern winds tugged the car to the right and left in little jerks. They drove down the other side of the bridge, up and over a big hill, and then through the well-lit island town of Anacortes. They left the settlement on the west end, heading toward the water.

They passed rows of beautiful homes on a steep hillside, with big glass-paneled-framed decks, all looking out over the water. They turned down toward the harbor. It was dark and quiet along the road, with silhouettes of dry-docked boats, up on stands or sitting on trailers, parked in graveled lots. They pulled into one of those large parking lots, which held an assortment of cars and boats. As they drove slowly between the rows of cars, the stones beneath the rubber tires popped like popcorn. A cold, damp draft came in from the quiet water and poured in through Halem's window, bringing with it whiffs of seagrass. They parked in a spot in front of a large worn number "252" stenciled in yellow paint on a horizonal telephone pole, which sat, delicately, on concrete blocks. Sandra grabbed her pocketbook and opened her door. Halem stepped out onto the gravel and watched Sandra walk into the shadows.

"I'll be right back!"

Halem must have been standing in the frigid emanation of Puget Sound as it was getting much colder. Colder than even riding on the freeway with the top down. She couldn't see into the dark but could hear the lapping of small waves on stones, tinkling like crystals. She could not tell where the land ended, and the water began. Two feet away? Ten? Fifty?

A loud rumbling sound interrupted the soft tones of water on stones, the new sound coming from across the dark street. Then she could see Sandra pulling a large metal cart beneath a streetlight. She pulled it across the road, onto the gravel parking lot, and behind her BMW. She caught her breath and looked up at Halem, who had wrapped herself in her own arms, rocking back and forth, trying to ward off the encroaching chill.

"Don't you have a coat, sweetie?"

"Isn't it still summer?"

"You can throw your stuff in the cart. We'll get warm soon."

Sandra pulled out her nice leather-trimmed canvas duffle and sat it in the cart. Halem sat her two garbage bags on top of Sandra's stylish duffle. They emptied the tightly packed trunk and back seat, including several large grocery bags, boxes of wine bottles, jugs of milk, and a hundred-pound burlap bag with "Product of Yemen" stenciled across the side. It took both to lift it. They stacked them in the cart, precariously so it wouldn't tip over.

Sandra and Halem pulled the cart back across the graveled lot. They picked up speed when they hit the blacktop and then had to resist the pull of gravity as they went down the aluminum ramp to the dock. The end of the ramp was connected to two rubber casters, which rolled back and forth as the floating dock rose and fell with passing waves. Each turn of the wheels made a high-pitched squeak, compounding the chill moving down Halem's spine.

They walked to the end of the dock. There, tied up to the horn cleats, was an aluminum boat with an enclosed white cabin, sweeping forward like a maritime spaceship. It took up the front half the boat with an open deck in the back. Smoke-tinted windows surrounded the cabin in the front. Braced on the stern was two large, black Yamaha outboard engines.

Sandra stepped into the rear cockpit area and the boat rocked. She looked back at Halem, standing with her fingers still on the cart handle. "Okay, hand me those things."

Halem, still on the dock, started to hand Sandra the contents of their over-packed cart. Sandra stacked the supplies neatly in the back of the boat. Halem started to step in but Sandra spoke quickly, "Wait sweetie. Take the cart back to the top of the ramp and leave it. By the time you get back, I'll have the engines running and we will be ready to cast off."

While Halem was walking down the dock and up the ramp, she heard the soft rumble from behind her. Bubble-bump… bubble-bump… bubble, bubble, bubble-bump… bubble, bubble, bubble, bubble.

On the way back Halem walked through a bluish cloud of gasoline smoke, drifting from the boat, which made her cough. The cabin was lit up inside, with lights in the bow and stern. Sandra came out the door of the cabin, leaving the outboard motor idling, *tat tat tat tat*. She walked around the right (starboard) side of the cabin to the bow and motioned for Halem to follow her from the dock side. She said, while pointing, "Untie that rope and throw it to me."

Halem struggled to release the rope and threw it in Sandra's direction. She caught it and coiled it up on the foredeck of the boat.

Halem was catching on as she followed Sandra to the stern. Sandra shouted above the noise of the engine. "Untie it and then jump in. Watch yourself as you step across our stuff and come up to the cabin. I'll pull out as soon as you are onboard and settled."

Inside, there was a high-backed captain's seat in front of the controls on the forward right side. Behind the captain's seat was a small sink and a door to the head. On the left or portside, there was one forward-facing, padded low backed chair, which would seat one, and behind it a small table and behind that a bench seat that would seat two. Halem took a short-backed seat on the left, in front of the small built-in table. Sandra, sitting directly in front of her and to her right in the captain's chair, flipped a switch on her dashboard and the interior lights went out.

Halem studied the woman as she took command of the boat's controls. Sandra was her Moses, leading her across the Jordan. Would it be her Promised Land?

Chapter Four

Jordan's Crossing

Halem watched as Sandra navigated through the harbor. They passed boats and yachts of all shapes and sizes on both sides, threading the narrow channel just above idle speed. Each dock had a single dim streetlight overhead. Most of the boats were dark, reflecting only a faint surface glow from the nearest streetlight. A few boats had interior lights on, apparently with occupants inside.

As they pulled into more open water but still inside the break wall, Sandra pushed the throttle level forward and the speed picked up slightly. Once she cleared the jetty and was now in the sound, she sped the boat up, causing the bow to rise in the water. There was a silhouette of land rising out of the water on their portside. It went up high, blocking out a third of the western starlight. Sandra nodded and said, "Burrows Island, nice place for a picnic."

Once she was past the narrows between Fidalgo and Burrows islands, she pushed the throttle further, opening the boat up to almost forty knots. Halem felt the bow rise and bounce over the one-foot waves. Looking back at Fidalgo Island, she let her eyes follow the steep hill rising from the water's edge to a crown of dark evergreens. In clusters along the crest of the hillsides were homes, lit-up like miniature villages around which a toy train would run.

"What do you think?"

She paused, taking it in. "It's nice." She looked out the window. "I mean, I've never been in a boat before."

"Never?"

"Never, ever. Well, I've ridden the ferry out to Bainbridge, but I haven't even done that in a few years. I did have a one-day rowing and sailing class in high school, but that was on Lake Union and in a tiny boat."

They sped across the Guemes channel and out, passing on the south side of the tall and wooded Cypress Island. There were a few other boats, lights on, out on the dark water, so dark that it could have passed for ink. To the north they caught the glimpse of a larger ship with a row of rectangle windows set aglow by interior lights near the top. "Tanker... coming down from Alaska" said Sandra.

In the far distance were small clusters of lights, marking human settlements. To the starboard side, Sandra pointed out the lights, noting they were from the Bellingham area. She couldn't make out the individual sources to the lights, but the general tinsel reflected into the coastal mist.

Sandra reached up, turned on and then adjusted a spotlight to shine out in front of the boat. "When you're on the water in Puget Sound, you always have to be mindful of dead logs. Some people just call them *deads*. I'm not sure if it means a dead log or that *you* would be dead if you encountered one. If you hit a big one, while going fast, it could ruin your day."

As they circled around the southwest corner of Cypress Island, a dark silhouette appeared in the western sky before them. On that silhouette were sparkles of intermittent lights, coming from high-perched homes.

"That's our island!"

"That's Orcas Island?"

"Yeah! Precisely, that mountain is Mount Constitution. We'll be coming in view of Rock Harbor once we circle north."

Halem continued to look at anything she could see in this dark world of water. It reminded her of the stories that she had read about astronauts journeying into space. Leaving the lighted world they crossed a well-demarcated line into the blackness of space, where the curve of the blue earth is suddenly visible below, and the visible stars suddenly appear, kneaded deeply into the pitch of deep space above them. On one small island, she could see a couple of lights, presumably a small cabin or house, standing out like terrestrial stars. She looked back over her shoulder to see the lights of Anacortes; however, Cypress Island had now eclipsed them, hiding them from sight. Sandra turned toward the north through the Rosario Strait. After twenty minutes, they turned back to the northwest and around the northeast corner of Orcas Island.

The digital screen on the boat's dash flashed in brown, yellow, and blue.

"What's that?"

"It's my radar. I want to keep track of other boats out here." She paused, standing on her tiptoes to look directly in front of the bow, then dropped back down on her heels. "Sometimes these dumbass tourists drop anchor right in the middle of a damn boating waterway. Then they kill all their lighting to enjoy the ambience of being on the sea at night. Pure stupidity. I almost hit a small sailboat one night doing that. It was before I got my radar. I would have hit it if I had not seen the reflection of my spotlight on a port window just in time. I turned hard to the starboard and just missed them, but I was so close I could see the whites of their bugged eyes and could tell it was a merlot in their half-drunk glasses." I yelled at them, 'Dumbasses!'"

Halem was looking at the Bellingham glow on her right when Sandra added, while pointing out the front window, "Hey girl, look over there… there's home."

It seemed surreal, but right in the flank of the tall dark mountain, down near the sea, was a perfectly shaped and lighted circle. It was more like a stack of lighted circles, reminding Halem of a scene in one of her favorite old movies, *Close Encounters of the Third Kind*, where the aliens had a base at the foot of Devil's Tower. From the water it looked like a spaceship, with the rings of concentric lights, climbing above the murky water, surrounded by the complete darkness of the forested mountain side.

Sandra turned the boat sharply to the portside as they moved toward the harbor. As they approached the outer basalt bastions, the walls seemed to grow in stature and to tower over them. The buoy-mounted navigation lights led the way to the rift and gave Halem the feeling of a spacecraft being directed into the landing bay of its mother ship. A red light on the right and green on the left showed them where to land. Sandra pointed at the buoy lights and said, "We're going between the lights. Your next boating lesson is in the saying that sailors use, 'red on the right on return.'"

They moved further into the rift, and, for the first time, Halem could see the actual village, at least a narrow slice of it. As they went farther into the bay, now with the outboard motor at a crawl, the field of vision slowly widened as they emerged from the inside opening of the rift. Sandra looked over at Halem, who was standing, leaning into a side window, and looking up at the top of the walls on each side of them as they passed between them. She looked up the terraces directly in front of them. *Gorgeous.*

When the boat fully exited the rift, into the harbor, Halem stepped outside the cabin door and spun around so she could take it all in. So incredibly beautiful in the still night air. The water was as still and shiny as black-lacquered glass, reflecting the layers of lights from the village above. In front of them were five semi-circles of illuminated buildings perched on perfect ledges, one above the other like the layers of a fancy cake with one big circular piece cut out. The lights ran almost completely around the harbor, except for the wall and rift, which was now behind them. To the left was the waterfall, dropping into the bay. Beyond the docks on the starboard side was the small falcate beach, which must have been Crescent Beach. It was wide on this night as the tide was low, looking like a quarter moon, coincidentally, being illuminated by the real moon's last quarter, which was just rising in the east.

"Who built all of this?"

"God."

"What does *that* mean?"

"It's natural... at least most of it is."

"How can this be natural? It looks perfect... and artificial."

Sandra turned down between two docks, one with a big "C" on the end and the next one with a big "D." She reduced the speed again until it was a slow and deliberate *tat... tat... tat.*

"Well, like I was telling you during the drive here, if you were listening, the harbor itself is natural. However, they had to carve out the places for homes up on the bluff."

Sandra stopped talking as she turned to pull into her slip. She suddenly grabbed her spotlight, tilting it downward toward the water directly in front of the boat. "Dammit!" She put the boat in neutral and then briefly in reverse then back to neutral. The jolt forced Halem to grab a handhold. "Idiots," said Sandra in a slightly softer voice.

Halem didn't note what Sandra was seeing—at first. Then she saw a lime-green tandem kayak, in the water and tied up to the dock.

"Idiot tourists. Who in the hell would tie up a kayak like that? You pull your kayak or canoe out of the damn water and put it on shore. Bill must have been drinking today."

"Bill?"

"Our so-called, part-time harbormaster. He takes impromptu days off to cuddle his bottles of cheap wine and today must have been one of those days. Otherwise, he's as sharp as a tack and would never let someone do this in a private slip."

They sat in the dark water idling. "The harbor's almost full tonight," said Sandra. "This is *my* slip. The only open ones are at the far end, and it would be a real effort to get all our stuff up to the house from there."

She looked at Halem and back at the kayak. "Okay, here's the plan. I'm going to pull up to the kayak; then I'll turn the helm of the boat over to you. I'll try to jump from the bow over the kayak to the dock. Then I'll untie the damn thing, push it away, and make space for my boat. Then you pull it in."

"I don't know how to drive a boat!"

"I've seen you around a complicated espresso machine and roaster. This'll be a piece of cake."

Halem gave her a wide-eyed look. "A piece of cake?"

Sandra pulled her toward the boat's controls. "You drive a car, don't you?"

"Yeah… but even that's been a while."

"Here's the throttle. It is intuitive. You push it forward to go forward and the further you push it, the faster it will go. Then when you pull it back, you will feel it click into the neutral position, where the boat sits and idles. Then pull it back and the props will reverse and back the boat up. The steering wheel is just like one in a car. You probably won't have to touch it."

A piece of cake?

"So, here's the plan," Sandra went on. "I'll put it in forward and let the idle push the bow forward, pinning the kayak to the dock. Then I'll walk up to the bow, throw the dock line over the kayak and onto the dock. Then I'll jump onto the dock myself. I'll signal for you to reverse the boat. You'll pull back the throttle, feel it click into neutral, then pull it gently further back into reverse for about three seconds. Then push it forward, back to neutral. I'll hold the dock line, so you don't float away. I'll untie the kayak and then push it out of the way, then I'll pull the boat to the dock and tie her up."

Seemed simple enough, and it went exactly as planned. The only awkward moment was when Sandra was standing on the bow in her skirt. She had a rather wide gap to jump, more than she realized until she was standing next to it. Landing on the kayak would mean that she would likely hurt herself and end up in the drink. So, she hiked up her dress around her waist and stood on the bow just in her pantyhose. Crouched down low, and then leaped as hard as she could, with the rope in her teeth. Cleared the kayak and caught the dock just by her tiptoes.

Walking away from the now safely berthed boat, the two women pulled a large, four-wheeled wagon filled with their stuff.

"Are you just leaving the kayak in the water?"

"Damn right," said Sandra. "It can't go far. It would be highly unlikely that it could float out and thread the rift out to the sound. Maybe the owners will have to take a swim, that's if it doesn't float over and hang up on another dock."

"Won't they find out it was you since your boat has taken its place?"

"No. We take care of our own here... and if they dare untie my boat in retaliation, Bill will throw them out of Rock Harbor... if he's sober."

They pulled the wagon up the steep ramp to the first shelf. *Shelf* was the term the locals used for the five major levels. Sandra's house was on the fourth level, the same as the coffee shop. They walked past the harbormaster's—now closed—office, past two wooden homes to the start of the stairs, which the locals called the "escalator," although it had no moving parts, being cut into the basalt. A crimson metal railing on both sides of the steps offered support for the climb. Each shelf had a forty-foot flat crossing or landing to reach the next part of the staircase. Constructed beside the stairs was a narrow-gauge rail track, built upon a steep wooden trestle, giving it the appearance of an old wooden roller coaster. Upon the tracks sat a large, walled stainless-steel tram car, which the locals called simply "the tub," attached to a cable. Sandra and Halem moved all their belongings into the tub. Sandra pushed the button marked *4* and the winch jolted on and began to spin. The tub slowly started to climb on its own.

Then they started up the staircase on foot. Halem looked around again, across the bay where the untethered kayak seemed to have come to rest against a big commercial fishing boat, trying to take it all in.

At that moment, they came to the first landing. A man was sitting in front of one of the nearby homes smoking a rolled cigarette. "Hi Jason," said Sandra. He waved back with the tarred fingers holding the cigarette. Sandra paused, like she was going to introduce Halem. But she didn't. She just whispered for Halem's hearing, "Fisherman."

They caught up to and then passed the shiny tub rolling up the elevated track. They paused to catch their breaths, then the tub passed them again and continued up to the next level with a grind of the cables and a squeak of the wheels.

As they reached the second shelf she paused again to suck in the cool marine air. "It's funny but we all make it a habit to race the tub up to the level we are going," she said. "You can beat it if you're not too tired or winded." The tub passed them again with its six squeaking metal wheels.

They arrived on the third shelf. Sandra paused to catch her breath once again and said to Halem, "Turn around."

She could see above the outer wall and over toward Bellingham with her bright lights, now seeing the individual lights from houses and buildings. "This place is crazy gorgeous."

They climbed to the fourth level without talking as if both had become breathless and could no longer keep up with the tub. A four-wheeled cart, just like the one they used at the harbor, sat at each landing, including the fourth.

"Sure is," said Sandra. "I mean it sure is beautiful. Let's drop off our supplies in front of my house, which is just ahead. We'll park the cart there and unload it after I show you the shop. But remember, always bring the cart back to the trolley as soon as you empty it, because others might need it. I don't have the key of the coffee shop on me, but we can look through the windows."

They walked about two hundred feet along the shelf, passing several homes. Sandra's house was a cute framed house with shutters, like a small Cape Cod, with a row of Adirondack chairs along the front. Then there was two houses and a chalet-looking structure with an outside patio. The entire front of the place was clear glass above which was a sign, in big letters, *The Rock Harbor Coffee Roasters*.

"I know, the name is simple," said Sandra. "But I like it, and that's what counts."

"It's a good name," said Halem as she put her hands above her eyes and against the glass looking through the window. Behind the counter sat the brand-new Lira.

"Your Lira is better than the one we had on Capitol Hill."

"My Lira?" asked Sandra. "That one is now yours... all yours." She gave Halem a hug. "Welcome to Rock Harbor, dear... your new world. I hope it just brings you good things."

Chapter Five

Closing Time

It was now ten months after that introduction to Rock Harbor, and Halem knew her way around the shop as if she'd been there for years.

On this evening, she immediately started to prep the roaster, making sure the drum and cooling tray were clean and the burners were igniting. She dragged a hundred-pound burlap sack across the floor and toward the roaster. It had *PRODUCT OF YEMEN* stenciled diagonally on the front. She cut the white cotton string, which had sewed the top of the sack together. The bag popped open, releasing just a hint of coffee from the unroasted beans. She ran her hand through the contents, allowing the green coffee beans to flow between her fingers. She loved the feel of the fluid beans sweeping around and through her hands. She could tell where the beans came from by touch alone. It was by their texture. The Yemenis beans were more irregular, rough, and chipped. Once the Yemenis dry them, with the cherry fruit still on, they pass between centuries-old grindstones turned by donkeys or camels until the bare bean remains. It was heartwarming to think that the last time humans touched them was when the Yemeni farmers themselves hand-picked out the remaining sticks and loose cherry husks before bagging them.

She preheated the roaster's drums and made sure they were turning properly. Since her beans were "high-grown arabica" beans, coming from farms at the 3500-foot elevation mark, she had to wait to load the roaster when the temperature reached 398 degrees. What they call "hard beans" are from an even higher elevation, in the highlands of Ethiopia. Those denser beans require an even higher starting temperature because they are so compressed.

A sudden knock on the coffee shop's door startled her. *Shit!* "Who the hell could that be?" She used the touch screen on the side of the roasters to shut everything down. The knock came on the door again. "I'm COMING!" she shouted, with a bit of irritation in her voice. She wiped her hands on her apron, kicked a few loose coffee beans under the roaster, and headed toward the door.

Halem recognized the dark, tall man standing outside—*the rower!* Had the broad shoulders, muscular arms, the long curly black hair she'd observed from afar. It had to be him. He certainly wasn't from the village—nor was one of those annoying tourists.

She froze, one foot locked in front of the other in mid step. Was he safe? Sandra had warned her of shady fishermen who showed up in town now and then and could be dangerous. Rock Harbor even had fugitives drift into town, thinking that, since they had no police, it would be a good place to hide. But, as her eyes studied the man's soft smile and felt the warmth of his deep brown eyes, seeing the playfulness of him having his nose pressed against the glass like a stooge, all these things told her he was kind.

Halem finished her step, added another, and then another until she was next to the door. The muscles of his arms were well-shaped, completely filling inside the sleeve of his white cotton T-shirt as he held his arms up, hands shielding his eyes so he could see through the door and into the lighted shop. He sported a short stubby beard. Solid black. She blushed. Her fear shifted from him being dangerous to her feeling intimidated by his good looks.

"WE'RE CLOSED!" she shouted through the glass door with a nervous and muffled voice.

He began speaking. Halem could see his lips moving, but with the exhaust fan running behind her, she could not make out a single word. She rotated the deadbolt until it clicked, and the door relaxed within its frame. She turned the brass knob slowly, opening the door about an inch, and said, "Excuse me? I couldn't hear you."

In a pleasant and soft voice, seasoned with a slight British accent, he repeated, "Is there any way a new stranger in town could get a cup of coffee? I've been at sea for two days and have a terrible caffeine headache."

Halem dithered. She wanted so much to get the roaster going. She also felt pity for the rower and his need for caffeine. But the deciding factor was his mystique. There was something that drew her to him. Yeah, he was dark and tall, to meet the proverbial requirements for handsome. He was also muscular, apparently from rowing. But he had such a sweet smile and kind voice that drew her to him the most. Beyond that, there was something odd, in a positive way, which made her want to know more about him. This could be their only contact, as many people drift in for hours or a single night and are just silhouettes cast across the next morning's sunrise, as they float away to who knows where.

Halem shifted her perplexed look into her big crooked smile. That was another feature that she didn't like about herself; when she smiled the right side of her mouth was always higher than the left. She noticed it in pictures of herself and then started to avoid smiling when photos were taken. But this evening, the smile was spontaneous and completely crooked. "Sure, I can make you coffee."

She let him walk in and closed the door behind him, locking it.

"Were you cleaning up?" He asked.

"Oh, I just finished. I was starting the roaster for my weekly coffee roast. It's a very delicate process and needs my full attention."

"Oh, I'm sorry to intrude. I saw your hours sign, that you close at 5 p.m. and I knew that I just missed you. But if you're busy, I can try to make do until morning... but I was just hoping that maybe I could get one cup of brew."

"I don't mind. What do you want?"

"A simple doppio espresso would be wonderful."

Halem checked the roaster's touch screen controls again to make sure she had shut everything down properly. Roasting would have to wait. She walked back to the Lira. She put a scoop of beans into the grinder and paused before flipping it on. She turned back to the stranger and asked, "Would you be interested in ristretto shots? That's my favorite when I'm hungry for coffee."

He cocked his head, "Hmm, honestly, I've heard the term but don't know exactly what that means?"

Halem explained, "Ristretto is an Italian term that means 're-stricted.' It's a way of making an expresso that captures only the purest or best possible taste of the coffee bean, by restricting the amount of water and giving the bean the full exposure to the exaction. You can increase that exposure by grinding the beans more finely, almost like a Turkish coffee grind, and keeping the volume of water low. But you can't grind it too fine or grains will go through the filter screen and into the cup, making it truly a Turkish coffee. Some baristas believe that the fine grind itself will restrict the amount of water that goes into the cup because the tamping is denser. However, others, including myself, believe that you also must watch the time of the extraction and not let it exceed fifteen seconds."

"Wow, I thought I knew a lot about coffee, but you learn something new every day. Sure, I'll take a restricted… uh, how did you say it?"

"Ris-treh-toh."

Halem set the grinder to a finer setting and flipped it on. She sifted the grounds onto a scale until it reached fifteen grams, and then put it into the portafilter. She tamped it down with a measured part of her body weight. It used to be a quarter of her weight but now that she was thinner, she had to bear down with about a third. She locked the portafilter into the machine and placed a small, clear Lungo cup under both spouts. She looked back up at the man, who sat at the bar right in front of her. She pressed the pump button and watch carefully as the water temperature and pressure rose.

It was a bit surreal, as earlier in the day, she was looking above the cups on top of the machine to see a small dot out at sea. Now, when she looked above the same cups, she was looking directly into the dark brown eyes and sun-kissed cheeks of the same rower. At this moment, a single freckle on the tip of his nose was bigger to her, than his entire boat was a few hours earlier. She glanced at the cup under the spout. As the honey-brown coffee dripped out, she looked back up at the man and smiled.

"You apparently know what you're doing," he said.

"I should hope so. I've been doing this for five years. Since I graduated from high school."

"I've drank espresso from seaports around the planet, and I can already tell, by your touch, the way your handle yourself around the machine, and the smell of the beans that this will be a world-class coffee."

As she handed him his cup, he sat it down and then reached across the bar with his right hand, "Hi, I'm Winston… like the cigarette." His hands were rough and calloused.

"I'm Halem."

"Hay-lem? How do you spell that?"

"H-A-L-E-M, like in the town, New Halem."

"I'm not familiar with it, but Halem's pretty… I mean, the name's pretty… The girl Halem is of course pretty as well, with lovely curls and the delicate neck of Cleopatra."

She blushed. She had forgotten about the stupid curls. She was too speechless to say, "thank you." She regained her composure and added, "New Halem's a local mountain town."

"Were you born there?"

"No, I was born in Seattle… but that's a long story.

She started wiping down the machine. "Where're *you* from?"

She disconnected the portafilter, turned it over, and hit it on the previously cleaned knock box. She wiped off the countertop around the area. She then opened the clean utensil drawer and stuffed the dirty towel in it, pressing down on the towels already crammed in there to make room.

"Nowhere." Winston sipped his coffee, sat it down, and looked inside the brim of his cup. He started rubbing his cup between his hands, as if it were a genie's bottle.

"I saw you rowing in this morning. When you were still far out at sea, I saw you. You were a dot, then a blot on the blue water, and then a man in a rowboat. Now you're here in my coffee shop drinking my coffee. So, if you are from nowhere, where did you sleep last night?"

"Nowhere... actually, I was rowing all night."

"From somewhere."

He sipped the coffee again and let it glide across his tongue like a real connoisseur. "That's really good." He said with a smile and a wink. She had never seen a warmer smile, one that incited a deep pair of supporting dimples.

Halem rolled her eyes. "You say that because you're so caffeine-deprived."

"Roche Harbor was my last stop... and this is not just replenishing my caffeine tank, it's the best coffee I've had in months... maybe years."

"Roche Harbor, that's a long way... and you rowed the whole distance?"

"Yep. I mean, I wanted some good wind to pull my sail, but I had none. The air was as still as poured glass, so I eventually put the sail away to reduce my drag. So, yeah, I rode here on oars... oars and sweat."

"Where were you before that? You're not from the San Juan Island, are you? I mean, I know that's where Roche Harbor is located on San Juan Island, but it isn't home, is it? I detect an accent, so I know you weren't born in the states. I just can't tell if it's British, Australian, or who knows, maybe from New Zealand?"

"Nope. I was in Canada, before Roche Harbor."

"And before that?"

"Uh, Port Townsend and then Port Angeles before that."

"But where are you from... *originally*?"

"I was born in Cleopatra Hospital in Cairo, Egypt. That's how I know you look like the queen, because they stamped her profile on my birth certificate. Forgive me, but I said that earlier, about you looking like her, not with a flirtatious intent, but I had the sense that you needed to hear that you resemble one of the most beautiful women the world has ever known. And I guessed that even if I said it, you wouldn't believe it."

Halem just stared at him with a squint. If felt a little creepy, like he was reading her mind... or soul. Was she really that easy to read?

Winston looked back into his cup, "But I was only there, in Egypt, for six months before we started moving. We were in India, Tibet, Jerusalem, Pakistan, Paris, London, back to India, then central Africa, and it all became a blur."

"Was your father in the military or something?"

"Nope. He was in the British Foreign Service. He had something to do with regulations of international banking. In other words, he wasn't James Bond." He smirked, "He was like an accountant. My mom... she's Egyptian."

"Oh, I get it now! They named you after Winston Churchill. I mean... considering that your father was British."

He shook his head. "Well, that's what my mom used to say. But, to tell you the truth, I think it was the cigarette. My dad had a life-long affair with the slender white body of the smoke, behind my mother's back. He would say that he was 'going out.' I could watch him from my bedroom window in Lahore or Paris, or wherever. He would walk down the nearest alley and pull a cigarette out of his hat... literally. Then he would lean back, out of sight and light it up. I could see the smoke cloud around his head in the shadowy light. I could smell tobacco on his shirt and breath when he returned. I found the motherlode one day in his coat pocket. The brand was Winston. Only then, did I realize that my namesake was the cancer-stick and not the Prime Minister." Then he quietly laughed. "My little brother was Nigel."

"That must have been tough, I mean, finding out you were named after a cigarette brand must have been horrible."

"Oh no, just the opposite. My family didn't know Churchill at all. However, Dad had a profoundly personal and enduring relationship with the cigarette. So, oddly as it may sound, I was honored he named me after his greatest love in this world. My mother threat-ened to leave him if he ever took up smoking again. So, the smoke must have been more important than her because he took his chances. She smelled the tobacco on his shirt too, I'm quite sure, but didn't want to say anything because she knew her leaving him was just an empty threat."

Halem had no follow up questions but stood and stretched, like she was ready to move on. She still wanted to get the roaster going and needed it done that night to have enough beans for the following day. But she was also so intrigued with this stranger that she hated to have this moment escape her. She sat back down on her stool and decided to wait him out, to keep him engaged in conversation until he closed it off and left. Roasting into the wee hours of the night was not that unusual for her.

"You've got coffee beans to roast, don't you?"

She nodded.

"Would you mind if I stayed and watched? I have nothing else to do, and the coffee roasting process has always fascinated me."

"Yes, that would be fine."

She preferred to roast alone. She needed to focus. She was the main roaster when she worked at the much larger Emerald City Beans. That roasting machine took two people to operate, as they did five different roasts of 100 pounds each. Matt was her co-roaster there. They would not start until 11 p.m., when things were quieter. They tried, as she was doing this night, to roast right after closing time, which was 6 p.m. at the Capitol Hill shop. However, in Seattle, there was a constant flow of people knocking on their door at that time of day. Most commonly, just like with Winston, someone would knock on the glass door, looking above the big "CLOSED" sign to mumble, "Are you still open? I saw the lights on." At the end, it was her favorite night of the week because she didn't have to go home to Finn's intoxicated rage.

Matt and her grew to love those all-night roasting sessions. He became her best friend. Considering that he was not interested in women (he had a boyfriend of his own), she knew that she could get as close to him as she wanted, emotionally, and have no confusion of motives.

Matt was the only person on the planet that she told about the bad part of her relationship with Finn. She felt horrible leaving on a whim, without telling Matt where she was going. But she knew that Finn would come into the coffee shop demanding to know where she was. She wanted Matt to be able to look Finn in the eye and say, with integrity, that he had no clue but, "One day, Halem didn't come to work and no one knows what happened to her." Matt had enough intuition to figure out that she had taken off to escape Finn.

Winston's motives were not so clear. Did the rower want to stick around because he was really interested in the coffee roasting process? Or, could he have interest in her as a woman. He did make the comment that she was pretty, and he didn't have to. Maybe he was just being kind and was simply a coffee fanatic. And if he did have some romantic interest in her would she be just another nameless girl that he tries to sleep with in each port he visits?

She found him to be profoundly handsome and mysterious but different than Finn's mysteriousness. Finn's wackiness centered around himself. He was more of a mystery in the pure sense of the word, while Winston felt to her as more of a mystic. How did this Winston know that she didn't consider herself attractive? Was it because she *wasn't* attractive, and he was being kind to say she was? Finn, on the other hand, was never so observant as he was desperate for his own attention. Winston, on the other hand, was quiet, and more outwardly focused or at least it seemed that way. This hunch became more apparent as the night matured.

Halem pulled two bar stools toward the roasting area. She invited Winston to sit and asked if he wanted another espresso.

"Yeah, that would be fabulous."

She went back to the Lira to make another doppio espresso. For the third time that night, she thoroughly cleaned the area with a dishtowel and stuffed that dirty rag in an ever more jammed utensil drawer, so jammed that it was almost impossible to get it fully closed. Winston watched her with great curiosity.

She tested the turning of the roaster drum, which she could hear, and rechecked the temperature settings. She operated this machine from a touch screen. She watched it fire up and then cool down. Then she poured the beans out of the sack into a large bucket. Inspected them again, removing just a few cherry husks, chaff, and sticks.

"The Yemenis do a great job cleaning the beans before shipping."

She explained each step to Winston. Once the machine reached 398 degrees Fahrenheit, it was time to pour the beans in. She needed to devote her full attention to the process, so he obediently sat silently. He watched her move instinctively from the touch screen to the portal window to see inside, and then as it approached completion, she pulled out the wooden handle of the coffee tryer.

The long metal scoop came out full of smoking beans. She sniffed them. Picked up one with her fingers and placed it on her tongue. She held it in the open air, tongue stuck out, to cool before pulling it into her mouth. She reinserted the coffee tryer back into the brass-framed hole within the front of the roaster. Crushed the bean in her mouth with her molars. She closed her eyes to focus. She worked her tongue to let the pieces sit on each of her taste buds. She waited two more minutes and repeated the process. After the third time, as soon as the crushed bean was on her tongue, she immediately reached over and opened the discharge gate to allow the hot smoking beans to flow onto the cooling pan. A blade and brush started to turn to keep the beans in constant motion and to remove any roasted chaff that were still sticking to the beans.

Halem let out a soft sigh, which indicated to Winston that the tense moment had passed, and he could speak to her again. He watched her continuing to shut down the machine. Then he broke the silence, "Okay, we've been talking about me all night, so let's talk about you."

Halem turned off the cooling tray and the propane supply as the last step of finishing the process. She pulled her hands through the finished beans, allowing them to flow between her fingers. *That's how a warm surf on a Caribbean beach must feel.* Back and forth she waved her hand. She was thinking about the fact that she has never felt comfortable talking about herself. What could she tell the man that he would find interesting? She wasn't born in some exotic place. Only visited Portland and had never traveled outside the United States. Never even applied for a passport. After her mother died, she felt that the dark hand of fate had reached down and covered her life, so there was no reason to imagine, or to take the kind of risks that you would build dreams upon. Moving to Rock Harbor was the exception. Who would be interested in her boring life if they knew the truth?

"Hello, Halem... did you hear me?"

She shook her head as to wake herself up from her daydream. She pulled her fingers out of the tray. Then she smiled, picked up an empty burlap sack, and positioned it to catch the roasted beans. She opened the tray door and the brown beans began to pour into the bag. Winston helped her hold the bag open.

"This always reminds me of Willy Wonka's chocolate waterfall." She said as she picked a couple of the freshly roasted beans out of the flow, handing one to Winston and putting one in her mouth. She chewed on hers, and Winston followed her example.

"Yes, I heard you earlier, the part about talking about me. I guess I was just thinking about what would you wanna know? I mean, compared to you, I don't have much of a tale to tell."

"Well, my main mission now, the reason I'm still adrift at sea after four years, is because people fascinate me. When someone tells me they don't have an interesting life, that means I will be the fortunate first to hear. I love fresh coconut milk. Cutting off the end of the thick, tough husk and letting that sweet milk drip out from deep within. That's how the introverts' stories are to me."

"You think I'm an introvert?"

"You just said you didn't like sharing your stories... or that you didn't have stories good enough to share. Something like that. That's an introvert in my book."

Halem filled the hopper under the espresso bar with scoops of the still-warm beans from the sack.

"You're being a little melodramatic, aren't you? I mean, you really don't know me, and you've labeled me as introverted. I'm not sure that's fair. And the coconut thing. That sounds poetic but probably a line you've used before."

"I'm sorry. I spend months alone... just with fictional characters in books. Lately, a lot of those books have been poetry. Maybe that's why I came across that way. I meant no harm. I just have to get used to being with people again, each time I make port."

"That's alright."

Then she closed the bag, tied it tight, and dragged it back to the storage area. She looked back at Winston. Was she in some theatrical daydream? Was this really one of the most striking male specimens she had ever laid eyes on? She figured that tomorrow she would realize this evening would turn out to be some grand hallucination, maybe from a caffeine intoxication, and the man never existed in the material world. But if the man was real, where was this going? Should she let him into her private world?

It was seven-thirty. She had been talking to Winston for over two hours. She was feeling comfortable enough to criticize him for being melodramatic, yet she felt intimidated as he was completely out of her league.

"I have all night," he said, noting her looking at the clock.

"Where're you staying anyway?"

"So, you are redirecting this back to me?"

"No, I didn't mean to. But I was just thinking, if we were to talk much longer, I don't want you going out in the dark with no place to stay."

"That's thoughtful of you. But I do have a place. A rather nice place. When I came in, I asked the harbormaster about rooms. He took me to the *Savage Susan*. The owner rents out the captain's quarters when it's in port. Bill, the harbormaster, acts like the landlord. Smells a little like fish or crab... something fishy... oh, and a little like beer, otherwise it's nice."

"Bill, what do you think of him?"

"The same. Smells of fish and beer, but nice."

"Hey, I need to test my batch with a pour-over, you've probably had enough, right?"

"I would love to taste your new coffee."

"You have to keep in mind that beans need to rest overnight before they reach their full potential. So, don't judge this batch too harshly. You'll need to come back for the best taste tomorrow."

"I will."

Halem's face lit up.

She ground the beans in a hand-crank grinder. She set up two cups for a pour over. The smell of freshly brewed coffee filled the room, displacing the stale sea air.

Winston, as he watched her pour, asked, "Doesn't drinking coffee this late keep you awake?"

"Maybe. I never sleep well anyway, caffeine, or no caffeine."

She brought Winston his coffee. With her cup now in her hand she asked, "So, what do you wanna know?"

"Yum… that's delicious. Let's start with the basics. You said you were born in Seattle but where did you grow up?"

"Seattle… Seattle for both."

"Okay. Tell me about your parents?"

Over the next three hours, she told him about her wonderful years growing up. Her parents lived simple lives without much material wealth. They loved the arts, especially music. Song filled their lives, and it wasn't unusual to have musicians dropping by for jamming session in their kitchen. Even her parents occasionally performed, professionally. Her dad played a variety of stringed instruments and her mom kept the rhythm on the tambourine, claves, or maracas. Her mom also sang—she had a great voice that could have been even greater with training.

She told Winston about the morning that her mother found a big lump under her arm and went to the doctor. It was hard for a 10-year-old girl to understand the relevance of that. She remembered her mother saying she was worried about her breast and a growth. But she was thinking that her mom was worried about growing a new breast, under her arm. It was confusing. But then doctors' appointments became the center of their lives. Her mother had a mastectomy, bilateral. It wasn't until Halem saw her mom's new, flat, nipple-less chest did the shock sink in.

Winston listened with perfect attention, only taking his eyes off her to sip his coffee now and then.

But things went from the peculiar to the bad to the horrible (with the mastectomy) to a surreal chronicle, as if she were watching a movie about someone else's life. Her father's mood drifted from happy to somber. He grew anxious and more irritable as her mother became thinner and weaker. Then, one rainy morning, her father had her pack her school backpack and overnight suitcase and drove her to his mother's, her grandmother's house—to live. He said he was doing this for her good, so her grandmother could keep her in school and to avoid the "distractions" of her mother being sick. It was dreadful. She only visited her parents weekly and watched their lives from a distance. It was like watching a story that she needed to be part of, but she had been written out of the script.

Halem said, "It was as if he had picked me up and set me on a different track from the two of them, going smoothly into a fake, peaceful world; while the world I had been a part of, the one with my father and mother, took a sharp descent into bedlam. I can never forgive him for what he did to me."

Her mother eventually became too sick to sit up or participate in real conversations. Halem never doubted that she would recover, but what did she know? With her physical separation, Halem knew little about the treatments and was not present, or realized, the moment that hope was worn out. Her father started to drift into mourning weeks before the death. It was the last she had seen of her father, her old father. That was the end of dialog. She went through the emotions of the wake and the graveside, but she felt nothing. She was numb. She loved her mother profoundly, and the horrors of losing her, at age eleven (having just had a birthday unnoticed), she could only cope with it as a fictional story. But when something is fantasy, there's no place for closure… or a simple goodbye. She concluded, "The story just ends, you pick up your stuff, and you walk away."

Winston listened as if nothing else mattered. She felt embraced by his dark eyes, and he seemed to have dialed his ears into her voice. He was quiet, only expressing empathetic sighs and occasionally asking questions for clarification. That's how she knew he was really listening.

Halem picked up their cups and put them in the dishwasher. Then she finished the story about her parents. Her father picked her up a month after the wake. Had an uneventful life through middle school and high school. Felt like she could write down every word her father said to her during those years, on a single piece of paper or even a Post-it note. "Why was he punishing me?"

Then she talked about Finn. She was so in love with him—at first. She believed that he was the door back to normalcy—he wasn't. She felt bad for just walking out of his life. But when she told Winston about the heavy drinking, the physical abuse, and the emotional neglect, he simply said, "I'm really glad you left. Sandra was truly a godsend. People like Finn often suffocate those around them, even those they genuinely love, under the blanket of their own insecurities."

"Sandra certainly *was* a godsend."

But then Halem finished talking about Finn by stating, without thinking, that "I'm not interested in dating again… not for a long time."

As soon as those last words had slipped over her coffee-coated tongue, a part of her had remorse. There was a little girl inside of her, who was being swept away by this stranger and wanting to leave the door ajar for something more than a friendship. But he had a way of drawing her out, things that were part of her obscured heart.

It was now ten. The time had flown by. She felt exhausted but with a strange sense of relief. Winston had created a catharsis, but she didn't realize where this would eventually take them.

When she got to the part about Sandra coming into her life, she paused. Not that she didn't have more to say, but the exhaustion was winning. She looked out the front windows. The full moon was inching over the southside of ice-cladded Mount Baker, setting the high glaciers aglow once more, but now in white light as if they were heated to a thousand degrees. She walked to the front of the shop and folded her arms across her chest, leaning her head into the hard plate glass of the folding door. She heard a screeching on the floor and looked back to see Winston returning the two stools to the bar. He sat on one, facing her and the lemony moon beyond her. "You live in a beautiful place."

"Sure do."

"You know what nautili are, don't you?"

Halem thought for a moment then walked back to the bar. "Well, I know what a nautilus is. Sandra has some from Morocco, cut in half and cemented into her shower. She's into geology. She likes all kinds of rocks. She was a park ranger many years ago."

Winston smiled. "*Nautili* is just a plural form for *nautilus*."

Halem blushed.

"They have been around since the beginning of time and I'm sure that the ones in the shower are fossils from millions of years ago. But they still exist and swim in the sea. I've seen them. They add layers to their shell each year, going around and around. When they are old, they have ten or more completed circles. As they grow, they move out and occupy the new broader part of their shell and they wall off the smaller old narrower parts. Air fills the old empty shell, which gives them buoyancy, helping them to swim upright. But when they are threatened, they pull back inside and close off the outer entrance with a tough leather-like hood."

"And why are you telling me this? Do you just like nautili or are you going to make a point?"

"I'm making a point, of course." Winston's dimples re-appeared above his angled jaw.

"People are like nautili," he said as he drew an imaginary spiral on the bar top in coffee grounds with his finger.

"We live in the outer chamber of a complex shell. When we feel threatened, we pull in and close our hood. However, the human shell, rather than being walled off at the end of the chamber, can continue deeper and deeper into the spiral, terminating in a labyrinth of our most primeval self. Once you have moved back beyond a couple of turns, it is dark there, and difficult, if not impossible, to find your way out."

"What're you implying?"

"Halem, your father is lost deep inside. I bet he's still a decent man, but he doesn't know the way out. Once you're lost like that, beyond several dark turns, it is virtually impossible to find the way out on your own. You've nothing to illuminate the returning path."

"You're probably right. I think he's lost forever. But, you know, I'm not sure if I care. He did it to himself... and to us."

Winston sat quietly for a moment then said, in a soft, contemplative voice, "I didn't say *forever*. The operative words I said are, *on your own*."

"I hope you're not implying that I'm the one to save him. What I should do is march into his apartment and chew him out... telling him exactly how I feel and how much he's hurt me."

Winston sat up in his chair. "Someone needs to... I mean to save him, not to chew him out. I think you love him too much to be angry at him, because you do realize how much he has suffered too. But someone needs to be the mythic Lady with the Lantern, who searched the dark storm-battered Cornish coast for her lost child and lost sailors, to bring them safely home again."

"Why me?"

"Who else?"

"I guess you expect me to save Finn too?"

"Nope. You can't save Finn."

"Why is it that I can save my dad, but I can't save Finn? Isn't he locked up inside his own shell due to some fear too?"

He looked up at the clock. It was approaching midnight. He looked back at Halem and asked, "You wouldn't have anything here to eat, would you?"

"So, like that, you're going to change the subject?"

"Not at all. I want to dive deeper into your question, but I just happen to be hungry. I only had a bag of salted peanuts in the shell to eat since I left Roche Harbor. I spit a chain of shells into the water between San Juan Island and here. I thought I would find something to eat in town, but it's too late. So, all I meant is I'm famished."

Halem walked around the bar into the kitchenette. "We have some left-over rosemary and olive oil rolls."

"That sounds perfect."

"How many?"

"How many do you have?"

Halem looked into the refrigerator, "Looks like six."

"Okay,"

"Okay, what?"

"I will take all six rolls."

"Really?"

"Are they expensive?"

"No, that's not the point. They're on the house because they were made yesterday morning, and three-day-old rolls aren't good enough to be sold."

"I'm ravenous. I would eat them even if they were covered with mold... but they aren't... are they... covered with mold?"

"Of course not."

"Your relationship with your father was very different than your relationship with Finn," said Winston. "It has a much firmer foundation on which you can stand. You have your history of... how old are you anyway?"

The bell chimed. "I'm twenty-three." Halem turned and opened the microwave, taking out the plate of rolls.

"So, you and your dad have a twenty-three-year history together," he said.

"But I haven't seen my dad in ten months, not since I left Seattle."

Winston scratched his head. "Okay, let's say twenty-two years. But my point is that you have a long history with him. Secondly, you have a blood connection, which means a lot. Most fathers have an instinct to protect their children. Sure, there are some sociopathic fathers who don't care, but those are rare. I know that your father wasn't one of those." Then he stuffed the first roll into his mouth.

Halem pinched off one of the rolls still on the plate. "How do you know he wasn't? I mean, that he wasn't a sociopath?"

"Hmm, these are *dee-lish-ous*, even old… it's like they've aged like cheese. Think about it. Why would he take you to live with his mother when *your* mother was dying?"

"I guess I was in the way. He was being selfish."

Winston rubbed his eyes. Getting sleepy. "Of course not, Halem. He sent you away to protect you from the great, *dreadful,* which was coming. Maybe, he made the wrong choice, but I'm confident of the motive. In some, ill-conceived thought, he imagined that if you were in the normalcy of his mother's house, the pain could not find you there. He was willing to walk down that dark track alone, but—I admit mistakenly—wanted to spare you."

He put another roll into his mouth, this time the whole thing.

Swallowed and cleared his throat. "So, as I was saying, you have a solid foundation with your father. You can draw from that foundation, as you enter that dark place to bring him out. But, even with that strong footing, there's still some risk. However, with Finn, it's entirely different. You had little history, not a blood-link or any kind of substance. There's not a strong footing for you with him. If you attempt to save him, the nautilus will become a vertex, pulling you in. You said he hit you? So, there's no instinct of protection with him. He would consume you like a drowning person accidently pulling under and drowning their rescuer in an act of self-preservation. Finn is also salvageable like all humans are, but not by your hands. He only needs your prayers."

He took the last roll. It was now midnight.

"Halem, we can discuss this more later. Reflect on the things we've talked about tonight and we'll return to the topic in a day or two."

"That means you'll be back? I mean, we have so many visitors who are here for just one night."

"Sure. I want to get to know people in this town and I think the Rock Harbor Coffee Roasters would be the perfect place to meet them... while drinking great coffee too!"

"Then, maybe I'll see you tomorrow... or I mean later today?"

He walked to the door and left. Halem grabbed her backpack from the back of the shop. Walked over to the roaster to make sure the gas was off. Turned off the lights and stepped outside, locking the door behind her. She then came upon Winston who was leaning back, against the side of the shop, looking at the full moon. It had now traversed a quarter of the night sky and had turned from yellow to cream. She leaned against the wall beside him. Wasn't sure why she stood there, but some type of impulse pulled her to do so. He spoke, almost as if he had an afterthought suddenly entering his mind. Still gazing at the moon, he said, "Halem?"

"Yes?"

"Did you cry at your mother's funeral?"

"Uh... I don't think so. I was eleven. It was such a shock. I didn't understand what was happening. I don't remember crying. As I said, the whole thing was like a movie that I was watching. Someone else's horror flick."

"When did you?"

"When did I what?"

"Cry?"

Halem went quiet.

After waiting for a couple of minutes, Winston asked, "When are you?"

"When am I going to cry?"

"Yep."

"It's been over ten years for Pete's sake! The season for crying has come and passed."

He gazed at the moonlit sky. "When we first moved to Madras... Madras, India, I was about eight. I was frustrated because it was a hard place to ride bikes in our small village, which was about ten kilometers from Madras proper. The roads and hillsides had these crazy ditches everywhere. I didn't understand their purpose… until the monsoons hit. We arrived at the end of their dry season, and the ditches were empty. Then, when the deluge came for a month, it was difficult to fight the floods. Workers had to constantly clear the trenches of debris. Otherwise, the streets would flood, not to mention the fields and their livelihood." He paused to look at the moon again.

"Tears are like the monsoons," he went on. "They must go somewhere, or they'll destroy the entire village. If you dam them up, then someone will starve."

Halem sensed a romantic ambience. She just needed to wait for the moment to shift a little from the serious talk about crying. Maybe it was a spell cast by the moon. Maybe it was the quietness of the night accented by an occasional hoot from a great horned owl, somewhere, up on the dark forested side of Mount Constitution. No harbor in the world, not even Riomaggiore, could look more beautiful than theirs on this night. Or again, maybe it was the fact she was leaning against a wall beside one of the most handsome and fascinating men she had ever met, who really was totally interested in her. She would not have been surprised if he had tried to kiss her at that moment. If he had tried, she thought she would kiss him back. But… he didn't try.

Then, as if Winston could hear her thoughts, he said, "Halem, I'm glad you told me that you are not interested in men right now. You must know too, that I will be leaving again, in a matter of days… and there's no stopping that."

With no words left to speak, they both started to walk. They walked toward the escalator, which led to the lower levels. Halem passed Sandra's house and walked to where Winston turned to descent the stone steps. "Goodnight Winston," she said. "It was a pleasure meeting you."

He did a little bow, "And it was a pleasure meeting you, Miss Halem."

He was several steps down the stairs when she yelled, "You have a brother?"

"What?"

"Never mind, we'll talk about it tomorrow."

Then off he went, down the steps, almost skipping. His figure vanished into the lower shadows, but she could still hear the tapping of his shoes on the basalt and the rustling of seagulls, when he disrupted their perch along the railings. She felt a soft hurt, a hurt spun from what could never be, pass through her, and then scatter into the nocturnal draught, coming down from the dark mountainside. *Where was this going?*

Chapter Six

Jamie

Halem arrived at the coffee shop the next morning, all sleepy-eyed and dangling her keys against the metal deadbolt, as she tried to find the one for the lock. She had three brass keys that all looked the same, and it always seemed that the last one she tried was the one that worked.

The crystalline rays of a bright daybreak's sun were struggling to lift Halem's brain out of the muddled-ness of profound sleep. Going to bed after midnight wasn't the problem. That, she could manage. Sleeping only a few hours at night was her norm. But it was lying awake for almost the entire night, suspended within the glow of a post-Winston wonder. She had not fallen into the deep stages of sleep until just before her alarm went off. The piercing sound jolted her back into the cognizant world but with lingering cobwebs filling the empty spaces of her mind.

She was stunned. She wasn't sure what happened the previous night. Did the most interesting man she had ever met, come rowing in from the sea, like some aquatic knight, and engage with her in the most substantive conversation of her entire life? Is that what really happened? Or was it an amalgam of dream and reality?

Soon after finding the right key and opening the door, she heard the rhythm of squeaking, rolling wheels coming down the stone terrace. Sandra passed across the glass windows at the front of the shop, pulling a handcart loaded with three stacked boxes. She turned at the corner of the building and came through the side door, with a racket of clatter as the cart bumped over the threshold, hitting the door as it automatically closed behind her

"Good morning Sunshine!"

Halem responded with an ersatz smile, mumbled something

about good morning, and quickly refocused on setting up the software on the check-out tablet.

Sandra sat the boxes in a row on the counter. "I baked these this morning, so they should still be warm."

"Thanks," responded Halem, with a bit more sincerity.

"What's the matter darling. You're not hung-over, are you?"

"Didn't sleep so well."

"I heard you come in really late. Is everything okay?"

"Yeah, things are perfect. I roasted last night."

"Was there a problem? I mean you're usually done roasting by eight. It's none of my business, but I was worried."

"I had a guest. A tourist came in late and wanted coffee. He watched me roast and we spent the evening talking."

"Really?" Sandra smiled. "He?"

Halem didn't respond so Sandra added, "Do I have a sense that you are smitten?"

"NO! It wasn't like that. He's just quite interesting."

Sandra put the bakery goods into the showcase. Placed some in the freezer. Halem looked at the clock. Seven fifty. Ten minutes to opening.

"Is he a nice guy?" Sandra asked. "I mean, we get some pretty seedy characters around here—even people running from the law."

"Yes. You told me that already. This man, well, he's fine. He seems to be one of the smartest men I've ever met."

Halem started unpacking the dishwasher. Heard the door open— and there stood Winston. She lost her breath. She hadn't expected him to come in so early after she had kept him out so late. Sandra smirked. She knew it had to be the man.

Halem regained her composure. "Oh, hi... I'm surprised you're up already."

"Yeah, me too."

"Sandra, this is Winston... uh, and Winston, this is Sandra my boss. Uh, my boss and my landlord... oh, and friend."

They shook hands. "Well, I hope I'm more to her than just *a friend*. I am her best friend in Rock Harbor and, in ways, her surrogate mother... until she gets back to Seattle to her own."

Winston glanced at Halem but remained silent.

The three of them stood in stillness, not knowing what to say.

"Okay, gotta run," said Sandra. She grabbed the empty cart. "Oh Halem, I'm going to Seattle today, did you need anything? Of course, I'll get coffee beans, but besides that?"

Halem thought for a moment. "I'll text you with a shopping list." She didn't want to talk about tampons in front of the stranger.

"It was a pleasure meeting you Sandra," said Winston. "Have a safe trip to Seattle."

As he walked toward the bar, Sandra flashed Halem a big smile and a thumbs-up. Then she was out the door, the cart rattling behind her.

"Are you having coffee this morning."

"I can't wait to taste your beans now that they've rested from the roast."

"I just thought you might be coffeed-out."

"No, I even slept like a baby after three late-night cups. Two days of hard rowing can do that to you."

"I should try it, you know rowing. Might help me sleep better... Doppio?"

"What about a cortado?"

"Certainly."

Halem put a scoop of her newly roasted beans into the grinder and turned it on. Then she sifted out a precise amount on a scale and placed them into the portafilter, grooming them to perfection. She pressed down with the tamper and twisted a quarter of a turn, Winston watching her every move.

"You move like a danseuse." Before she had the chance to respond, he added, "Any more thoughts about our conversation?"

She frowned while continuing to work on the coffee. Then she paused and looked up at him, while wiping the dusting of ground coffee off her hands with a dishtowel. "If you're thinking about my need to help my dad, I don't think I can do it."

"You cut your curls off." He said.

"Yep."

"Why?"

"People thought they looked funny."

"What people? I thought they were cute. What matters is did you like them?"

"No, I didn't."

"Well, then, I guess that settles it," replied Winston.

She finished his coffee and poured in the foam, then a small bead of her mocha syrup, working it in a swirl from the center out to the edge. Then she used a toothpick to make ten lines across the swirl, creating a etch spiral design.

"It looks and smells perfect. I've never seen anyone make that design before." He tried to sip it, but it was still too hot. "So, Halem, you must do it, you know, helping your dad. If you don't do it, who will?"

"There's nobody else. He's pretty walled-off. He doesn't even have a pet... or a plant. He did have a King Charles Spaniel named Fred, but then he died from bloat, and he never got another dog."

"Then it's your mission, and you can do this." He attempted to drink his coffee again; this time he got one quick sip in. "That's fantastic... meaning the drink. The beans are great with just a hint of the cocoa." He cleared his throat and continued, "Halem, I was reflecting, you know, about last night. I've been thinking that we must take care of you first, then you will be ready to help your dad."

"Me? I need help?"

"We all do."

"What kind of help do you think *I* need?"

Winston took another drink of his coffee and swallowed and then cleared his throat again, "Well Halem, you need to forgive your dad, and yourself... and you need to grieve."

Halem continued to work, hastily, getting the last of the shop set up. Walked from behind the bar to the tables to straighten them up. Dusted crumbs off the tables into the floor. Her busy movements seemed to be venting some of the frustration. It dawned on her that she had forgotten to sweep the previous night, so she pulled out the straw broom and quickly swept it across the floor. Then, she lifted the large rubberized welcome mat, which was just inside the door, and swept the dirt under it, then she laid the mat back on top of the dirt, crumbs, and sand. Winston watched this with great curiosity and raised eyebrows.

As Halem was finishing out near the front of the shop, she noticed something on the terrace that caught her attention. She quickly ran back and put the broom away and started working to set up things at the bar.

She looked at Winston and whispered, "Here comes Jamie. He's a regular. He had a brain injury... uh, but he's nice."

Then she thought for a moment as Jamie turned the corner of the shop, walked up the side and was reaching for the door. He tried to open it, but it appeared to be stuck. Halem walked around the end of the bar. As she passed in front of Winston, still seated on a barstool, she added, "Don't be offended if he says outrageous things. He can't help it."

She reached the door and turned to look at Jamie through the glass. He was still struggling to turn the doorknob. "Wait a minute Jamie! It looks like it's locked." She turned the button in the middle of the stainless-steel knob and the door unlatched.

Jamie immediately pushed it open. "Halem, why do you have the door locked? It's a quarter after the hour, and you already have a customer." He indicated Winston sitting at the bar.

"Jamie, it must've been an accident. I unlocked it this morning, and then Sandra was here with a cart. I think she accidently locked it again as she left. It's easy to push that button in by accident when you turn the knob." *Maybe Sandra locked it on purpose to give Halem and Winston privacy.*

Jamie walked up to the counter. Halem followed but then went around the end of it, returning to the Lira. She pulled the bottle of mocha syrup back out of the refrigerator and started to work on Jamie's sweet drink.

Meanwhile the sea-spray-swept visitor reached out his hand and said, "Hi mate, I'm Winston."

"You smell like body odor,"

"I'm sorry but I was rowing hard for a couple of days and I haven't found a shower yet."

"Are you Halem's boyfriend?"

Winston chuckled. "No... I mean... uh, it would be an honor to be so, but I'm just a traveler who stopped by Rock Harbor."

"Well, then, why did Halem have the door locked, and you two were in here alone?" He looked Winston up and down. "Your hair is greasy."

Winston chuckled and remarked, "You're right, my head needs a good washing as do my armpits."

"Jamie!" said Halem, "I told you that it was an accident, you know, locking the door."

Jamie looked at Winston, "Is that your Whitehall tied up at the dock?"

Winston raised his brows. "Yes, as a matter of fact it is. But it's not really a Whitehall but a Norseboat. They're remarkably similar. I'm impressed that you know boats so well. I'm also impressed that you noticed my boat in a harbor full of them. You're a vigilant man."

"I should have known it was a Norseboat because of the red stripe of paint beneath the gunwale. It's my job each morning to look for new arrivals. I let Bill know because he wants to make sure they've paid their slip fee. Bill is either too drunk or too hung-over in the morning to do that himself. My mom says he's an alcoholic."

"I paid him when I docked."

Jamie looked out the front window with a cold, thoughtless stare. Then he looked back at Winston. "I do know boats. My dad's a fisherman. I sleep in my dad's boat now. It's my house... when dad's not borrowing it to fish. It's a 1990 Delta Seiner called, *Molly's Miracle*. It's fifty-eight feet and one of the biggest boats in the harbor. It's tied up in front of mom and dad's house."

"I noticed it when I came in. It's flying a Jolly Roger isn't it

"The flag's mine. Mom says I act immature because I'm mentally handicapped."

Winston seemed puzzled. "Well, old mean pirates flew Jolly Rogers, and I don't think anyone would call them childish, at least not to their faces. You're certainly smart about boats."

The two men stared at one another for a moment, as Jamie didn't take the social clue that it was his turn to talk. Winston asked, "And what's the story behind that name? You know, the name of your boat?"

"It's named after me... and my mom. They call Mom 'Molly.' She prayed that I would live after I had drowned. The doctors didn't think I would. So, when I woke up in the Anchorage hospital, they called my waking up Molly's Miracle because she was praying a lot when I was dead. Her real name is Mary, but everyone on the boat always called her Molly. My Dad's name is Dale. His real name is David, but, for some reason, they started calling him 'Dale' when he was a kid and it stuck. Well, Dad's real first name is James, James the second and that makes me the third. So, it's really James David... but they still call him 'Dale.'"

Halem served up Jamie's drink.

"You cut your curls off. Good for you!"

"Thanks."

"Halem, would you let me fuck you for charity?"

"WHAT ARE YOU TALKING ABOUT!"

"I'm brain-damaged. I'm turning twenty-one in a few months, and I'm still a virgin."

She pointed at his nose. "No, Jamie, and don't ever ask me something like that again." She went back to cleaning her Lira, embarrassed as hell.

The door opened and in walked the tourists from San Diego—and the timing could not have been worse. Five of them this morning, lacking one of the men from yesterday. *Shit.*

"You think I'm fat, don't you?" asked Jamie.

He then walked toward a table, mocha in hand.

"Hey, sit here with me mate," said Winston, patting the bar stool beside him.

Jamie looked perplexed. No one had asked him to sit with them before. Most people wanted him to sit as far away as he could.

"I don't think she likes me because I'm fat."

Winston looked under the bar at Jamie's midsection, "Oh, I hadn't noticed. You must not be too fat because your belly fits under the bar."

Halem was getting nervous. The San Diego tourists, lining up at the ordering area of the bar on her right, and there was Jamie sitting at the bar with Winston, on the other side of her espresso machine on her left. Her fear was that Jamie would say something serious that the tourists would think is hilarious.

Halem kept her eye on the San Diego group but her ears on Jamie and Winston. She had a sense that Winston was intentionally distracting the young man.

"Jamie," Winston said with a soft voice. "Why is it so important for you to lose your virginity?"

"I want to be a real man, like other men, and [as if Winston had not already heard] I'm turning twenty-one soon."

"So, Jamie, losing your virginity makes you a man?"

"Yeah, and I want to learn to drive a car too. I would be able to already, but I live in a place where there are no damn cars or roads. No highway except the logging road, and I would be crazy to try and learn to drive up there."

"I bet your dad lets you steer the *Molly's Miracle*."

"Of course. All the time."

"That's manlier than driving a car. I know a lot of men who drive cars but only a few who can captain a ship, and those are the most masculine men I know."

Jamie seemed to be soaking in those words when Winston spoke again. The tourists were congregating around the order area. Halem moved closer to her Lira, standing on her tiptoes, to hear Jamie and Winston on the other side. She was dying to hear the rest of the conversation.

"Jamie," said Winston. "The jungle is full of orangutans, hundreds of which lose their virginity every day. Do any of them become men?"

"We are ready to order," said the loud blonde over at the ordering area. Halem played around with the dials of her Lira to stall. "Just a minute, I'm calibrating my machine."

The blonde laughed and said, "I hope you've calibrated your milk." Then she burst out laughing in her high squealed voice that sounded to Halem like some exotic, New Guinean bird's mating call, a call that went along with her bobbing chest.

She heard Jamie respond that orangutans do not turned into men.

She looked through the cups stacked on top of the machine. She took down the top ones to give her more space to hear and to see. She needed them anyway for the large order from the tourists. She could see Winston's face, as he smiled large and his dimples arched backwards to support the grin on each side. He said, "Jamie, do you know what really makes a man out of a boy?"

Jamie looked back at him, baffled. "What?"

Winston motioned for him to come even closer.

"Empathy."

"What's that?"

The blonde said in an annoyed voice, "We're ready, are you going to take our orders or not?"

"Uh, I'm listening to my machine to make sure it's running right, just a minute."

"That girl would never make it in a big city. She's probably never been off this island..." then she giggled and added, "Maybe never been outside Rock Harbor."

"It's the almost magical ability to look into someone's eyes and to feel exactly what they're feeling at that moment," Winston went on telling Jamie. "That's really what makes a boy a man. It's like a supernatural power. Many boys never become men."

"But I'm brain-damaged. I don't think I could do that. Mom always tells people that I don't have the ability anymore, to be kind."

"Jamie, you can identify even the most obscure boats. Surely, you could learn to identify people's facial expressions or their tones of voices. Think of the expression that someone makes on their face, is like the shape of a boat hull and their tone of voice is the arrangement of the superstructure or masts. I understand that being under water injured part of your brain, but you can find other ways around that injury. I think you're very smart and have the potential of being as kind as you are smart."

Jamie seemed pleased with the statement.

Winston pointing to his own face. "Look at me and tell me what this face, which I'm about to make, means." Winston flashed as soft smile, where his dimples barely broke the surface. "So, what am I'm feeling if I make that expression?"

Jamie shrugged his shoulders. "I don't know."

"When my lips turn up on their ends, I'm smiling. When I'm smiling a little means I'm happy. Whatever I'm doing or whatever you are saying to me at that time, makes me pleased. If I have a big smile, with my mouth open, it means that I think something is funny. Let's test this, and you see if you can identify when I'm happy."

Winston made a series of faces, all with some form of frown or a look of shock, and then he gave him the weak smile again. Jamie's eyes lit up.

"That's it, that's the smile."

"So, that means I'm happy doesn't it."

"I guess so."

"See Jamie, you can do this easily. And do you know something, that big aluminum ship you sleep in isn't Molly's Miracle... you are. You beat death. That makes you a superhero. Very few people do that."

Halem wiped her hands on a dishtowel, smiled at the tourists, and asked, "So, what can I get for you." They began spouting out orders, "A cappuccino, no make that two cappuccinos, one small and one large, one with lots of foam, one quite wet, a black tea, a doppio with a touch of milk..."

"You mean a macchiato?"

They all looked stunned, and she just added a macchiato to her mental list, realizing they didn't know what it was.

Another member of the party added, while pointing to a slim red-haired lady beside him, "And we'll take a pour-over and she would like an iced mocha."

"Got it," said Halem. She punched several buttons on the tablet and looked up and asked, "Is this on one tab?"

One of the men announced as he pushed his way toward the front of the group, "I'll get this one."

"That will be twenty-three dollars and twenty-eight cents."

The blonde looked disturbed. "That doesn't sound right. Did you over-charge us? How many drinks do you have?"

"Five. Which averages out a little over four bucks each and tax."

The lady didn't look convinced and Halem added, as the man was inserting his credit card into the little white box, "Just go to your tables and I will bring your drinks to you."

The blonde smiled, "Well hon, did your coffee machine sound okay?"

"Sound okay?"

"Yes hon, when we were waiting you said you had to listen to your machine to make sure it was running okay... so, is it? That's all I'm asking, as I sure don't want our coffee coming out of a defective machine."

"Oh, it's running perfectly." Halem felt her anger rise.

As the tourists headed to the big table, the blonde, and a thin dark man, the one who had paid the tab, and the red-head lady, paused as they passed Jamie and Winston. The blonde looked at Jamie with a look of contempt and said, "You're here early. Apparently, your mom didn't make tacos last night, did she?"

Jamie said nothing.

"She must have burned her Victoria's Secret catalogs."

Jamie said, sternly, "Why are *you* still here? I thought you were going up the Inland Passage."

She chuckled. "No wind son. No wind. You may not know that

sailboats need wind."

"I'll vouch for that, that there's no wind," said Winston. "That's why I had to row here. However, Jamie's one of the smartest people I know regarding things nautical."

"And who might you be?" asked the blonde in a flirtatious voice.

Winston offered his hand. "I'm Winston... like the cigarette... and [looking at all three people still at the counter] you are?"

The blonde said her name was Diane, which Halem had forgotten from the previous day but preferred to think of her as "the blonde," or "the obnoxious blonde."

Jamie turned his back to study his mocha, as if in defiance.

Winston asked, "So, you're heading north, are you?"

"That's right," said the blonde. "As soon as the weather permits. We hope to stay in Vancouver a few days before we leave civilization—and you?"

"I'm heading that way too."

"Sailing alone?" the redhead asked.

"Probably, unless I bring Jamie here with me as my scout and navigator."

"Maybe you would want to join our flotilla," asked the Blonde. "What kind of sailboat do you have?"

"Oh, I have a sailing and rowing skiff."

"A skiff?" asked the blonde. "As your main boat? Are you serious?"

"Yes, yes, and... yes. But it's actually a seventeen-footer Norseboat."

The man in the triad spoke up, "So, you're trying to take a sailing skiff, Norseboat, or whatever, up the Inland Passage and you need this boy as your navigator? That sounds reckless. What do you have for navigation?"

"A sextant, compass, and pocket watch."

The blonde and redhead snickered. Winston didn't seem to get the joke. Jamie did as he turned around to face them, like he was thinking of something to say, probably something rude.

"That's it?" asked the man.

"Yep," answered Winston.

"Do you know how to use a sextant?" ask the sailor from San Diego.

Winston allowed the question to hang in the air for a moment. Finally, he answered, "I think I do. I mean, I left Singapore four years ago with my boat, a sextant, compass, my pocket watch, some dried fish, a bladder of water, going west, and it's gotten me this far."

The coffee bean grinder came on; then the Lira pumps hummed as Halem continued working on the drink orders.

"Holy shit!" said the man. "You've honestly rowed or sailed that thing all the way here, through the Panama Canal and the whole bit?"

"Nope."

"Well hell, I didn't think so."

"I'm sure you skipped the Atlantic," added the blonde.

"No, what I meant, after I had crossed the Atlantic, I sailed around the Caribbean for almost a year. Then I decided to go down the east coast of South America, around Tierra del Fuego and back up the Pacific coast. I didn't want to miss anyone, so no I didn't take the Panama Canal."

Halem passed behind them with a tray of drinks. "Drinks are ready."

The blonde asked, "So, you knew people along the way?"

"Yeah, I do now. I know a lot of them. People like my mate Jamie here, and Halem, whom I just met."

They started to walk toward their table and the man, asked, "So, if you have so much sailing experience, why do you need this boy to go with you?"

"It's a tricky passage, and Jamie's a local and experienced in that route. I think he's a brilliant seaman. I picked up a local guide in Oyster Bay, who sailed all the way with me to Cape Town. I picked up a passenger in Isla de los Estados, who helped me sail through Beagle Channel."

The group at the table broke into a collective chuckle when Winston had said the word *seaman*. He didn't get that joke either.

On her way back to the bar with her empty tray, Halem over-heard Winston talk about passengers. It crossed her mind that he might even ask her to go with him to Alaska, if she played her cards right. *Just maybe.* However, he had been referring to only Jamie go-ing with him, so she quickly dismissed the thought, as she brought nothing to the table, no sea experience, nothing except making cof-fee, and who needs their own private barista while at sea? Then, it crossed her mind that here was a boy who lost half his brain and still had more to contribute than she did.

The day passed in the usual sense with the same regulars coming and going, except for Kane. There was a new, three-man sailing group that came into town in the afternoon and came directly into the shop for some "good coffee."

Jamie and Winston had left together about 10 a.m., as they were going out the door, Winston mentioned something about Jamie showing him around the harbor and giving him a tour of *Molly's Mir-acle*.

It was near closing time, and Halem assumed she'd served the last customer of the day, when Winston reappeared at the door.

Winston.

Looking more handsome than the last time she had seen him. Shaven. Hair clean and shiny. Wearing a white button-up shirt and black jeans. A big smile gripped her face as she felt the breath drawn out of her lungs again.

"Looks like someone found a shower."

"Yep. Jamie let me use his on the *Molly's Miracle.* I was going to use the one on the boat where I'm staying, but it only had cold sea water coming out of the faucet."

"Really?"

Winston nodded. "Apparently, the potable water tank is empty, and Bill is going to look into filling it back up. Brackish water's okay for flushing toilets but not much else."

"Did you want another coffee?"

"That would be wonderful."

She put beans into the grinder. "You wanna a doppio?"

"I'll try something a little different. You can't make an authentic Turkish coffee, can you?"

"Of course. Grounds in?"

"Is there another way?"

"Some Americans want me to pour it through filter paper." She set the grinder for the finest powder. Then opened the cabinet beneath the bar, moved some things around, and came up with a copper ibrik (a Turkish coffee boiler with a long wooden handle).

"You're kidding me! You have an ibrik?"

She came up with two Turkish demitasses (small, white cups with gold trim).

"You're incredible!"

She gave him a crooked smile. "Of course, I have the proper supplies. How else would I make Turkish coffee the right way?"

"The last one I had was in Seaside, Oregon, and it was made in a mug... in a microwave."

"Sounds atrocious."

"It was. I thought about using it to varnish my boat, but I respect my boat too much for that." They both laughed.

Halem put two demitasse-filled cups of water into the ibrik, "How many lumps of sugar?"

"One."

She put two lumps of golden sugar into the ibrik, one for each cup.

"Are you making yourself one?"

"Yep, one of my favorite ways to drink coffee. I just don't put in the effort unless someone else wants one too."

She took the ibrik, by its long wooden handle, over to a small propane burner, which had, until then, gone un-noticed. Turned the dial on the burner, it sparked and lit, then she sat the metal pot directly on the flames.

They were both startled when Hank, leaving through the door with his computer gaming gear, said, "Good night Halem."

"Good night!"

Halem said to Winston, "I was going to introduce you to Hank. He's a little shy and keeps to himself. Maybe next time." As the water came to a boil, she used a small silver spoon, and poured in two heaping spoonsful of the fine coffee grounds and slowly stirred. "Can you lock the door before someone else comes in?"

And he did.

As the coffee came to a boil again, she spooned off the caramelized foam and dripped it into the bottoms of the two empty cups. Then she poured in the coffee.

They sat, drinking the thick dark coffee from their delicate, gold-rimmed cups. "Halem, as I was saying this morning, as a starter, you need to forgive your dad."

She sighed. She didn't like his intrusiveness. "It doesn't matter now. It's been over a decade. He doesn't remember. I don't think about it anymore."

"Maybe he doesn't remember, but I doubt that. I think, deep within that nautilus he's alive, and he remembers and feels. I know that you remember what he did. Pain and disappointment don't evaporate with time, they just seep in deeper and deeper until they cannot be untangled from the essence of your being."

"Winston. I can't forget what happened. I will never forget that." It seemed her hands kept a rhythm with each phrase she said, like she was directing a choir of words.

"But Halem, no one is asking you to forget. Forgetting has nothing to do with forgiving."

"Why bring all of this up? Why does this matter to you! Is this really any of your business?"

"Halem, I care about you and oddly, I care about your dad even though we've never met."

"You only met *me* yesterday. How can you even care about me?" She gulped her coffee down in frustration.

Winston sipped his coffee gently, like a real Turk. "This is good, as good as the one I had in Istanbul."

"And stop looking at me!"

But Winston kept looking at her. Not the starry-eyed look that some of her male customers used to give her on Capitol Hill. Invitations to join these men for a concert… or a walk, always followed those looks. Winston's look was more intimate, like her father used to look at her when she was a little girl with a broken doll or had a friend who was not being nice.

Once Winston saw that she was calming down a bit, he spoke again, "I have this bad habit of liking everyone I meet and feeling concerned about them. I can't help it. That is my kryptonite." He gave her a little boyish look with his big dark eyes, now seeming bigger and rounder than before, as if he was looking out from a Margaret Keane painting.

She couldn't resist those eyes, "So, how does someone like me go about forgiving something that is so old?"

"There're two types of forgiveness and you just need the easier of the two. It's based on intent. The first type requires you to forgive someone who wanted to hurt you. That's hard to do, especially if they don't recant. The second type, however, requires you to forgive someone who meant you no harm. The latter type is much easier, even without an apology. The first step is figuring out which type you need. I'm confident that it's the easier of the two in your case."

"Are you sure my dad didn't mean to hurt me? I think he was just being selfish… getting me out of the way, so he could focus on mom."

"Maybe. But, in times of crisis, like your mother's suffering and eventual death, there is a gracious place for selfishness… and mistakes. There must be. The worst of us comes out when we are under stress. It's different than casual selfishness."

He finished off his last sip of coffee. "Hmm, that was really good. So Halem, this forgiveness will be easy. Just put yourself in your dad's shoes. Think about the fact that his soulmate, the woman of his dreams, the object of his total obsession was suffering, and there was NOTHING he could do about it. He was her protector, as he was yours, and he failed. He knew he was losing her. He was a desperate man. Reach down and feel that pain that's in your heart, the pain of you losing your mom and apply that pain to your dad. Her death may have hurt him even more than you. After all, he knew her much longer than you did."

Halem peered down into her, now-empty, demitasse and said, "That's not possible."

"Your forgiveness for your dad starts with you wallowing in *his* pain, just for a while, until you feel it and understand... not to justify it... but to simply understand why he acted the way he did. A lot of people try to forgive without making the effort to understand. I think that's a mistake. For a durable forgiveness, you must understand even if you find the perpetrator's reasons for doing what they did, shallow. Think too, that your father did love you and if he couldn't protect your mom from the awful, at least he felt like he could protect you."

They both sat in silence for what felt like ten minutes. Halem gave a tired sigh then stood and walked behind the bar, "I need to clean up and try to get home early tonight. I feel drained. All this emotional talk isn't helping."

Winston finished his coffee and put his cup in the dishwasher himself, along with her cup.

He asked if she needed any help. She didn't. He walked toward the door and stopped, standing on the rubber mat. Stomped on it. "Halem, it's time for you to lift up this mat and sweep up the dirt under it. It's starting to get lumpy." The two stared at each other. She seemed shocked that he had noticed her little cleaning idiosyncrasies. Then, just from the way he was looking at her, he felt that the metaphor had become apparent. Winston slipped out the door. She watched him walk past the front store windows until he was gone. This whole situation was going to get messy.

Chapter Seven

Kane

The next morning, Halem overslept, having forgotten to set her alarm. Sandra would usually wake her, but she did not return from Seattle the previous night. After Halem had texted her the shopping list, Sandra had messaged her back, "I think I'll stay in Seattle tonight. I bumped into an old friend. BTW, I had a coffee at the Emerald City Beans. Not as good as when you were there. Your friend, Matt, asked me if I knew where you were. I told him I did… and that you were safe but no details. I hope that's okay."

She wasn't sure who Sandra's "old friend" was but suspected it was one of her friends with benefits. It was not that unusual for her to stay in Seattle for a day or so. Halem just hoped that she remembered to buy the milk in Anacortes, so it would be as fresh as possible. She reflected on Sandra's last words. They were accurate. She did feel safe. She had not left Rock Harbor in over ten months. It was her womb… and her prison. Leaving was not logistically easy, but Sandra had offered to take her to Seattle several times, but she always declined.

Halem jumped up and looked at the time on her cellphone. Seven fifty-five. Five minutes to opening. She made a regrettable decision to forgo a shower and put on the same wrinkled tied-dyed gypsy skirt and black shirt, which she had worn the previous day. Unfortunately, the linen skirt seemed to always want to default to its crinkled state. She brushed her teeth and took off running toward the shop, sounding like a galloping horse in her wood-soled Birkenstocks.

As she came around the front of the coffee shop, looking through the windows toward the entrance on the southeast side, she saw someone standing by the door. She thought it was Winston, but when she came around the corner, where she could see him directly, she realized that it was Kane. He had his big briefcase in his right hand plus a small backpack strung over his left shoulder. He had his reading glasses on and appeared to be looking at his phone.

"Sorry," said Halem, words wrapped in a labored breath as she halted her run at the door. Her heavy breaths pulled in the smell of Kane's Brut aftershave. He always carried the scent as if it leaked from his holy pores. She felt her pocket for the keys. "Shit!" she said. "Oh... I'm sorry."

Kane smiled. "Yeah, you said that already."

"I was sorry for being late, and now I'm sorry for saying *shit* in front of you."

"Well, *shit* happens doesn't it?"

"I've got to run back and get my keys!"

She felt foolish and frustrated as she ran, *clippity-clop*, back down the stone terrace toward Sandra's house. Only then did she notice the brilliant tangerine sky above the North Cascades. That morning's sun was a simple saucer salaciously clad in sheer clouds. Seagulls circled in the low air, giving out their familiar squawk. Apparently, a fishing boat had just come in... or was about to depart with fresh bait on board.

She ran into the house, grabbed her keys off the dresser, and darted back out the door. She looked down on the harbor to her left, her eyes searching, penetratingly, for the small skiff among the yachts and fishing boats. *Was Winston gone?* Her eye caught the small white boat just as she passed back in front of the coffee shop, and it now was docked next to the *Molly's Miracle*.

She could not see through the windows of the shop this time. The reflection of the bright morning sky upon the large windows had grown in intensity, giving them a pink shimmer. She turned the corner, and there stood Kane, and... Winston. It must had been a dream during her night of brain-dead sleep, but she had a feeling that he had sailed out before daybreak.

As she approached the men, she slowed to a walk. She felt self-conscious, with uncombed hair, wrinkled clothes, and being flustered. It was Winston's presence that made the difference in her embarrassment. He glanced at her and flashed a kind smile. Then he returned his attention back to Kane. She got the door unlocked and walked in. She glanced up at the large round analog clock above the coffee bar, the fat hand on the 8 and the minute hand at the 25-minutes mark. The two men walked in behind her, Kane with his briefcase and backpack and Winston carrying a small duffle in his right hand.

Halem quickly worked on setting up the payment tablet and turned on her Lira. The shop still smelled of coffee from the previous day's grinding of beans. She knew Kane's morning drink, his perfect ristretto-based cappuccino. She set his cup up on the bar and finely ground his beans, enough for a double. Meanwhile, she was waiting for a breach in the men's conversation, so she could ask Winston for his order, as his taste seemed to fluctuate with his mood.

They were discussing religion. Winston was explaining that, while his dad was baptized into the Church of England, he later became agnostic. Winston had never attended a Church of England service, except for his grandmother's funeral in Brandon. His mother was Egyptian Coptic. He did attend special Coptic services with her, such as Christmas, Fast of Nineveh, and Easter, when they visited relatives in Egypt and when they found Coptic expatriate communities in Paris and Madras.

Halem was just finishing the last touches on Kane's coffee.

Winston asked, "Oh, are you waiting on my order?"

"I am."

"I'm sorry. I'll take a cappuccino, although that ristretto was excellent, and making it into a cappuccino would be great." He paused, reflective. "Did you notice that sky this morning?"

She nodded. "I'll be happy to make you a cappuccino out of a ristretto pull. I do that for Kane each morning."

Kane nodded in agreement as he stepped aside, giving Winston the space next to the counter.

She was working on grinding Winston's beans. Once the noise

died down, she asked, "The sky? Did you say something about the sky?"

"I asked if you had seen it this morning."

"Oh, yeah. It had a bit of orange in it." Asking her about the beautiful sky implied to her an emotional, if not a romantic connection to Winston. It would be odd for someone like Kane to ask her about seeing a sunrise. She felt warmth in her heart. But was that his intent? Still didn't like him sticking his nose into her personal life.

"As they say," said Winston. "'Red sky at morn, sailors take warn. Red sky at night, sailors' delight.' I think it means that the high pressure, which has been sitting over us and blocking our wind for a week, is moving out. I'm not sure if storms are coming, but for us who ride on sails, we would like to see the wind again. I think your California group will be heading out today. I spoke to them down at the harbor last night and they took me on a tour of their boats. I would call their boats as high end. But, compared to my humble wooden skiff, a fiberglass kayak is high end."

Halem continued crafting his cappuccino, pausing to ring up Kane's order. As Kane started to walk away with his cup and briefcase, Winston said to him, "Sit here with me at the bar and we can finish our discussion."

Kane appeared irresolute. Halem knew how much he liked to sit alone at his table and work on his reading and writing. But there stood Winston asking him to sit with him. Then Winston said something as if to bait Kane, to make his invitation to the pastor irresistible. "I would like to hear more about what you believe as a Presbyterian. Maybe I should consider your faith?"

Kane, as any decent pastor would agree, had no choice, took a seat at the bar. You can never ask a pastor to share more about their church or faith and expect them to decline, so it was something of a setup, a well-placed pastoral obligation.

Kane sat on the same stool that Jamie had sat on the previous morning, just over the Lira from where Halem worked. Winston got his drink, paid for it from a roll of dollars kept inside a red rubber band, in the front pocket of his denim trousers. When he pulled the roll out each time, an entourage of sand, pebbles, lint, watch, string, and sometimes a pocketknife would escort the money from his pants to his hand.

Halem wiped down the bar and pushed the crumbs into the clean utensil drawer. Hank came through the door and, behind him, the California sailors. Oddly, Jamie did not come in until later that morning. It took Halem back to the morning when Rob didn't appear and found out later that it was a tragedy. She was a bit worried about the boy until he arrived soon after the California group had left, at eleven. She then suspected that he was somewhere watching and waiting for their departure before coming in.

During the morning, she'd listened carefully to the conversation between Winston and Kane on the other side of her machine. She was hoping to discover Kane's little secret.

Winston asked Kane, "So, if you live in Eastsound, how and why do you come all the way over to Rock Harbor for coffee? From what Jamie told me, the road is treacherous."

Kane smiled. "I don't mind the road so much. Yeah, in the winter, when it's raining, it can get nasty. It can even be snowy on the higher elevations. But not only is traction a problem, it's very narrow and has no guardrails. It would be a nightmare to meet another car as there are few places to pass. I do have an old Land Rover Series with a winch. I've had to use the winch a few times to get out of the mud."

"But why do you do this to yourself?"

"I find the crossing an adventure. The coffee here is the best on Orcas Island or anywhere in the San Juans." Halem upon hearing those words, felt a sense of pride percolate up from her heart. She smiled.

"But most of all," Kane continued, "I have no peace in Eastsound. If I try to work from home or the church, I have constant interruptions. If I were to go to a coffee shop there, and there're only two, I would have people stopping to talk to me."

"Like what I'm doing to you right now?" asked Winston.

Kane felt a bit embarrassed and tried to weasel out of the comment he had just made. "Well, usually I sit here alone and get a lot of work done. I don't mind an interruption now and then."

"So, what're you working on?"

Kane pondered for a moment. "Apologetics."

"I assume that you studied that in seminary. So, why are you working on it now?" asked Winston.

Kane seemed a bit taken back. "Well, it's always good to brush up on these things."

"I think I know what apologetics are, but which part are you focusing on, the proof that God exist, or that Christianity, particularly, Presbyterianism, is the truth?" asked Winston.

"Well," answered Kane, rubbing his mostly bald crown, "certainly not that Presbyterianism is the only truth. I'm reviewing the arguments that support God's existence and that Christianity, in general, is uniquely true."

Halem looked across the coffee shop. It had almost filled up during, what she thought was a brief, conversation between Winston and Kane. She had been busy, but she was still listening. She was sure Winston could see the top of her head, with its messy mop of hair, above the machine, moving, making coffees, or cleaning up.

He looked back at Kane. "Could it be that you make this dangerous drive, over the mountain and here to the Rock Harbor Coffee Roasters, not because the coffee is savory, which it is, and not just to drive the dangerous roads, which I'm sure are fun, but, because you, you yourself, are having serious doubts about God's existence and are afraid of your perishers finding out?"

The color quickly departed from Kane's otherwise ruddy, face. His mouth seemed to be pregnant with words, which his lips held, suspended in silence... then he spoke. "Sir, I can see that you are a prophet."

Winston looked stunned. "What?"

Kane continued, startled that his personal thought had leaked out of his own mouth. "Oh, gosh, it was something the woman at the well said in the fourth chapter of John. You know, or maybe you don't, when Jesus told her about very personal things in her life."

Winston asked, "So… does that mean I'm right?"

Kane's mouth was gapped open, and the hollow space within was filled with quiet. He was staring into the back of the Lira, and the cherry red glow of the machine reflected off his reading glasses. Winston was sipping his coffee and waiting patiently for a response. He took his eyes off the Lira and looked back at Winston. "I'm a pastor. I'm the spiritual leader of about a hundred people. If I don't have confidence in my faith, where does that leave them?" He accented his question with two raised palms.

"So that's why you are here? To figure this out for yourself?"

Kane sipped his cappuccino again, repetitively, until he consumed it. Finally, he looked back at Winston and said, "I'll share my honest thoughts with you, but please don't speak about this to anyone. I am, as you have somehow observed, having a crisis of faith myself. I'm tired. I'm tired of twenty-eight years of ministry. I've seen some ugly things in the world, and even within my own churches. Bad things. People manipulating and hurting other people. Good, Christian people doing awful things. That whole world now seems to work on constant lying. Maybe I've grown a bit disillusioned. But when I was a young seminarian, I really thought the Christian faith had the corner on good, moral living. That we had a higher level of life than the rest of the world. Now, it all seems to be the same. The same evil, the same deception." Kane looked back over his shoulder, into the main area of the coffee shop as if to see if anyone was listening; however, he didn't catch Halem snooping on the other side of the Lira.

Winston finish his coffee patiently, as Kane watched him for some expression as to what he was thinking. But he sat in silence.

That's the secret! His mysterious behavior now explained. After ten months she had no clue… until now. Winston was able to pull it out of him and nail it in a matter of minutes.

Winston sat down his cup and looked out the window. The sun was now high, having discarded its obscuring clouds, its bright illumination had completely washed away the lingering tangerine twilight. He looked at the other customers, most of whom had to be familiar to him, and he had only been in town three days. In the backdrop, every few minutes the immediate space around them had been interrupted by the course hum of the bur grinder, and the sudden aroma of freshly ground beans as Halem continued to work her magic in coffee, just on the other side of the bar.

He turned back to look at the pastor. Kane was sitting erect on his bar stool, as if he were trying to figure out if Winston was completely ignoring his intimate confession.

Winston asked, "Why did you ever take this route to begin with?"

Kane, looking perplexed, asked, "Over the mountain?"

Winston laughed. "No, I mean, believing in God, and becoming a pastor... I mean, why?"

"There are two ways to answer that question," said Kane. "One is the honorable way, things about God speaking to me or calling me, almost supernaturally, into the ministry. That is my usual canned answer that I've found people want to hear. The other way was with candor. Since we are speaking in great frankness, I will continue with an honest answer."

"Great! I would appreciate that."

"I think it was expectant of me. My dad was a Presbyterian pastor as was my grandfather. I was raised in the church. I was just living up to the expectations set before me."

"So, your doubt isn't really about God so much as doubt about your path of oughts."

Kane seemed confused and a bit insulted. With his brow toying with forming a frown, he asked, "I don't think I know what you mean by oughts?"

"For me," said Winston, "I was raised outside the church and still am. However, I believe in God. I met him in my own soul during the long days alone at sea. I am self-aware, and I know that my being was not the sum of nothing. I've seen him in the faces and lives of all the people that I've met along my way. It was unintentional. However, I suspect, when the path is laid out for someone as oughts, enclosed in by your father's, and perhaps your mother's wishes, it's a deliberate course." Winston paused to allow his thoughts to catch up to him. "I'm sure my path of expectations was laid out for me too, but not so rigorously. I mean, my father wouldn't have been bothered if I had become a raging atheist or a devoted man of God. I think he didn't care because he, himself, was dubious."

Kane, seeming to be catching on to Winston's lucidity, then stated, for clarification, "So, you think my doubts are about my path in getting here, and not directly about my belief in God? Then what does a man like me do with this? It seems to be ending up at the same place, a lack of certainty that God is there, and that Christianity is true. Now that I'm reaching my middle years, God seems more and more silent."

Winston studied the interior of his empty cup. "I think that, for the first time, you need to look inside your own soul, the universe, and the creatures who inhabit it, and reach the best conclusion that you can. It must be an act of self-discovery, not inherited. This innovation is a simple choice. Ether you are a machine, made of blood and flesh, with no origin, no purpose, but a simple freak of nature, or you are real. If you're real, there must be more than the material universe that we see. Once you've reached your conclusion, you can build from there not the other way around."

"Really? That's it? That's the best advice you can give? I don't see how someone regains the certainty of their faith by the process you describe. There have been theologians, like St. Anselm and Aquinas, who spent their entire lives trying to prove God is there. They have written volumes on the topic. Surely they didn't overlook a simple plan like you just depicted."

The two men sat in silence as the heaviness of their conversation needed time to infuse into their comprehension. Halem was listening to every word, taking mental notes of Winston's mature style of inquisition, and giving insights.

Finally, Winston spoke. "Certainty? Is that your aspiration? Isn't asking our limited minds to reach certainty, the same as asking the cameraman to be sure and to catch the essence of the flower's fragrance? The cameraman can conjure up memories of a fragrance by the visual staging of the flower but not the full essence. Certainty is a perception that our flawed minds can't frame."

Kane pondered those curious words and then asked, "But Winston, you're leaving out the spiritual dimension. With the spiritual we can and should know, with great conviction that God is there, and the Christian message is true. That's the core of faith isn't it?"

Winston didn't respond but laid his head on his crossed arms, occasionally glancing up at Halem behind the coffee machine.

Kane continued, "The theologian Kierkegaard said that there are two types of truth, objective and subjective. That when objective truth is nonobtainable, what he called objective insufficiency, the Christian, then must rely on faith as a system for finding certainty, without the need for rationality."

Winston lifted his head. "Isn't faith or the spiritual a simple surrogate for the emotional? Are our emotions calibrated for finding truth, like reason is? Or is it for embracing truth, once found?"

Kane looked out the big windows. "Thomas Aquinas is my favorite theologian. He said this in another way, that knowing truth about God comes from two sources. The first is through rational demonstration, or simply our reason and observations of the universe, as you alluded to. But the other is through sacred teachings. So, maybe I have not been studious enough."

"I've actually read a lot of Aquinas and Kierkegaard, but I don't know St. Anselm. I like the other two a lot, meaning Aquinas and Kierkegaard. However, I think Aquinas gave our rational minds too much credit for figuring this out. He also tried to fill the gap of evidence with some Medieval mysticism. So, his Aristotelian view of reason could only carry part of the weight. At that juncture he gave into terminology such as sacred teachings. Then, Kierkegaard gave up on reason altogether with a new type of mysticism, a post enlightenment mysticism."

Kane shook his head. "Okay, how did you get to be so smart? I mean, the other day I heard you talking about boats. That I can understand since you spend your life in one. But I don't know many twenty-something... or thirty-something... how the hell old are you?"

Winston knew that even this simple question didn't have such a clear answer. "Uh... oh... I think I'm twenty-nine. Since I'm mostly alone, I don't celebrate birthdays and I'm not completely sure."

Halem thought that Winston was older than that. He seemed more knowledgeable and mature than the other men who were twenty-nine. Finn was twenty-eight; then she thought again, no, he would also be twenty-nine now, and was quite immature. The other thing that seemed to age Winston a bit was his face. While strikingly handsome as any as she has ever seen, it had more than its share of sun damage, at least that of a twenty-nine-year-old

Kane continued. "As I was saying, I haven't met anyone in their twenties who has read Aquinas or Kierkegaard, unless it was part of an introduction to a philosophy class in college, then the understanding was superficial at best. Of course, the pastors I know all have read the great theologians, but no lay people. Especially people outside the church, as you described yourself."

"Well," said Winston, "when you're holding the tiller of a sailboat for eighteen or twenty hours a day, with sails flopping so loudly that you think you will go nuts, and only water in your 360 degrees of vision, reading is the best distraction. I usually pick up a box full of books with each stop I make."

"There's no bookstores here. We do have a nice new and used bookstore over in Eastsound. Maybe, if you're here long enough, you can come over the mountain with me."

"Sure. If I'm here long enough. The winds are coming soon to blow me away."

Halem felt an acid dump in her stomach with those words. She shook her head to remove any thought of Winston's leaving from her mind, hoping for a reverse of the truism, out of mind... out of sight. If she didn't think it, it couldn't happen. Or could it?

Kane looked at his wristwatch. "Speaking of which, it's eleven thirty, and I need to get over the mountain. I have a funeral tomorrow morning and I need to make sure everything is set up this afternoon."

Winston shook Kane's hand. They heard Jamie, standing at the ordering bar, ask Halem: "Are you anorexic?"

He asked again, "Well, are you?"

"No Jamie, I'm not anorexic! Why would you even ask something like that?"

"Mother says you are."

She rang up Jamie's drink. "That will be four dollars and seventy-seven cents."

As he was paying with his usual five-dollar bill, he said, "Halem, are you going to answer me? If not, then I have to assume that you are."

Halem started to get upset—but not nearly as bad as the previous morning. "I *did* answer you Jamie! Why would she even think that? I hardly know her."

"She sees you around. She says that you are the skinniest girl she has ever seen, and that you must make yourself vomit after you eat."

Halem then said in a louder voice, "That's not even anorexia Jamie, that's bulimia! And tell your mother, no, I don't have anorexia or bulimia. My mother was also skinny, I guess I got it from her."

"I wish your mother would come to visit you. I would like to meet her."

Halem became teary. "So would I Jamie, so would I!"

Winston reached into his duffle bag and pulled out a folded-up paper map. "Jamie my good mate, good morning! Sit here with me again. I want you to tell me the best route up to Anchorage. I have a nautical map with me."

Jamie eased down at the end of the bar, sitting his mocha next to Winston's empty cup. Winston glanced at Halem. She smiled as one tear tumbled down her cheek. She quickly wiped it off with the wrinkled sleeve of her shirt. She mouthed in Winston's direction, "Thank you," and walked toward the back of the shop. It was the first tear she had ever shed for her mother, but maybe not her last.

Chapter Eight

Wind and Rain

The next day, the coffee shop was as busy as usual. The loud San Diego flotilla had sailed off riding on the previous evening's gales. But the winds also brought new sailors to town. The motorboats, Nordic Tugs, and others come and go whenever they want, but the sailors float in or out on the breezes like aquatic tumbleweeds.

She had always loved the feel of cool marine gusts blowing across her face on a summer's day. Now, they only brought dread. Those winds, so she feared, would eventually carry Winston away, like one of those tumbleweeds.

That morning, the coffee shop was full but felt vacant to Halem. Winston did not come. She felt nervous. She didn't have closure with the man yet. The next breeze coming down the mountain side could inflate his sail, and she would never see him again. Never, ever. You only meet a few remarkable people in your life, two or three if you are lucky. Winston was one of them.

Several times Halem exited the shop, walking out to the patio in front, to look down into the harbor. She felt the cool wind now coming in from the sea, and it was stirring up that salty-musty smell that Pugetians were well familiar with. She felt a wave of relief each time she saw his boat, still moored at the same spot, next to *Molly's Miracle*.

Jamie walked in, more subdued than normal. The only belligerent comment he made that morning was him saying to Halem that he told his mother what she had said that she wasn't anorexic. His mother's response was, "Well, she could gain some weight. She doesn't look good being so tall and walking around looking like a skeleton." Halem didn't respond to that comment, although it stirred up a fear that her lack of better looks may not keep Winston anchored in the bay.

Maybe if she were a five-foot-six busty blonde, the life of the party, he might stay longer... or who knows, take her with him. She chuckled to herself with that thought because she had just described the blonde, Diane, from San Diego, whom they all despised. But really, she would go with him, if asked. At this moment, especially with the fear of him leaving so pertinent, hell yeah, she would go with him even as an inept guide for a single leg. That additional intimacy of traveling together could earn her a farewell kiss. Maybe that was her greatest aspiration within the relationship.

Closing time seemed to never come. At the end of the day, Sandra came to visit carrying two gallons of fresh mainland milk. She walked up on Halem standing in front of the shop. "He didn't leave, did he?" she asked.

Halem turned her gaze from the harbor. "Nope. His boat's still here, but he didn't come to the shop today. Maybe he's getting ready to leave. What time did you get in last night?"

"Oh, it must have been three in the morning. I know I left the harbor in Anacortes at one-thirty."

"Isn't that dangerous crossing over at night and alone?"

"I think it's safer. There're fewer boats. No ferries, and the boats which are out there, are usually well lighted. My only fear, as I've said before, are the dead woods in the water or that vagrant boat with its lights out. It's hard to spot a log in daylight, and at night... impossible." She paused. "He wouldn't leave without saying goodbye, surely."

Halem began her last clean up. She started the dishwasher and stepped outside again. It was a minute after closing time, and there was no sign of Winston. As she headed back into the shop, her eyes caught a motion up on the fifth level of the village. There was a figure running across the small area of parked Jeeps and then to the escalator. *Winston!* Skipping down the stairs to her level and then turned right, rather than continuing down to the harbor, and was heading directly toward her. Her heart, now filled, was overwhelmed. She watched him closely. As she caught his eye, a big smile blushed across his face. He looked wonderful. She was caught in her smile, arms folded and leaning back against the front of the shop. She was staring at him, like his face was some type of tractor beam holding her, helplessly, in its grips.

Winston walked up and asked hastily, "Am I too late?"

"Too late for what?"

"Uh... coffee?"

"Oh, no. I was just closing but I can make you a cup." She turned to go back to the door. "I was worried about you."

"Because I didn't come in this morning?"

"Sure. I thought you had probably sailed off, but your boat was still here."

"I'm sorry. I told Jamie this morning where I was going."

"He was here but he never mentioned it to me. He doesn't have a particularly good memory when it comes to passing on messages," Halem said.

They entered the shop together and Halem locked the door behind them. Winston was the only late-comer she wanted to have. She came around the bar and put new beans into the grinder. She asked, "Cappuccino?"

"I'm still savoring the memory of that Turkish cup from the other night. I know that's a lot of trouble, but it was fantastic."

Halem shook her head, "That's alright. I don't mind." As she was changing the settings on the grinder to fine, she looked back up, "As you were saying about where you've been?"

Winston continued, "Oh, when you're cooped up in a small boat, sometimes for weeks, your lower body starts to atrophy. I do use my legs when I row. But when I make landfall, I must get some different types of exercise, so my legs don't get weak. So, I headed out before daybreak, and walked the logging road up to the top of Mount Constitution. Then I hiked around a bit up there. I was thinking my decent would be faster, but it wasn't. That's why I'm late."

"Was it pretty up there?" Halem asked.

"You don't know? Have you never been up on the mountain?"

Halem laughed, "Believe it or not, I haven't. I was never much of a hiker. I grew up as a city gal and did all my walking in downtown Seattle."

"Well, then, I'll take you up there for a picnic before I leave."

"You promise?" *Was this a date?*

Winston nodded.

Halem smiled.

She made two cups of Turkish coffee. She sat at the bar beside him and started rubbing her feet. "My feet are really tired today. I think I made thirty trips outside."

He looked at her feet. She had her thin slippers on. "Why do you wear those? They've no cushion for your feet or arch supports. Were you a dancer or something?"

Halem blushed. "Well, when you're a girl and you're almost six feet tall, you do everything you can, not to look any taller. And no, I was never a dancer. I would look like a clumsy giraffe on the dance floor."

"That must be why short girls wear those crazy high heels, to look taller."

"Yeah, and to make their asses look tight."

"Are you serious?"

"I am."

His coffee was too hot to sip. "Why so many trips outside?"

"Uh, well, to check on you for one. I was really worried that you had fallen into the bay."

Winston laugh. "What a story, I survived a capsize in the stormy Southern Ocean east of Cape Town, and then fell off the dock in the peaceful waters of Rock Harbor and drowned."

"Really, you capsized?"

"I did three times. Once in the Indian Ocean and then near Cape Town. The scariest one, was 200 kilometers east of the Fernando de Noronha Island, dead center of the Atlantic. That time it wasn't a storm but a rogue wave. The weather was calm that day, nothing like the thirty-foot swells east of Cape Town. But a fifty-foot wave came out of nowhere, and literally blindsided me. Maybe it was a tsunami or something. But there was no chance of rescue there. I wasn't even near a viable shipping lane. I was completely alone. After my first two capsizes, I had my boat modified in Cape Town to make it safer."

Halem looked puzzled. "How can you make a small boat like that safer? Seems like you would need something like outriggers."

"We added some weight to the bottom. The boatyard had done this before. They shaped a brass plate that bolted directly over the keel, adding one hundred pounds to the lowest point. Additionally, we modified my boat cover."

"How's that?"

"My original deck cover was made of canvas. It was okay when you were storing your boat in a harbor or dry docked. But it was worthless during bad weather as it leaked and flopped around in the wind. This was the type of cover they used in the nineteenth and early twentieth centuries. The famous Antarctic adventurer, Shackleton had a small boat, the James Caird, which was a lot like mine. It had the same type of canvas cover. He sailed it through angry and cold Antarctic seas for eight hundred miles... and survived! The boatyard in Cape Town created for me a modern neoprene deck cover that secures tightly around the boat, leaving an open space for me to sit and row or to hold the tiller. It was almost like the cover of a kayak cockpit. That modification was a godsend on that last capsize. I was lucky to have it on when the wave hit. It was morning and I put it on at night to sleep under it. I was even able to right the boat, because of it, and crawl back in. Without those modifications, the boat may have sunk, or I could have died clinging for weeks to the hull of an overturned boat, with nothing to eat or drink."

"I'm glad you're okay."

"Anyone at sea for long will have stories to tell." He closed his eyes and sloshed the coffee inside his mouth to savor the taste. Then he set down his cup. "Now, let's talk about you."

"I don't have many stories to tell. I mean, I've lived a quiet life as compared to you. I've had no adventures."

"Let's start with your dreams. What do you want to do with the rest of your life?"

"Well, my dream job would be a writer, a science fiction writer."

"Really? What do you write?"

"I've got a couple of stories I'm working on. One is about where the internet becomes conscious. It now has as many electronic connections as the brain has neurons. But the other story I've been working on here in Rock Harbor, is about a lady who develops a muscle twitch in her arm. It starts to drive her crazy. She's worried that she has some dreadful disease and goes to see a neurologist. Her tests all come back normal, and they tell her there is nothing they can do to help her. But the twitch haunts her day and night. She lays awake all night thinking about this twitch. Then she notices a pattern in it; there's long twitches and short ones. She's a clever woman so she starts to figure out that this twitch is sending Morse Code messages. To make a long story short, the messages are coming from an ancient ancestor from 300,000 years ago... a Neanderthal. You do know that most Europeans and some Asians have Neanderthal DNA?"

"Yes, I did know that, and your story is quite ingenious." Winston grinned. "But how does a Neanderthal know Morse Code? I don't think it was invented until the 1800s."

Halem rolled her eyes. "It's fiction, you know. How does someone walk inside a spaceship that is flying through space, where there's no gravitation?"

"I think you'll make a great science fiction writer. But, speaking of stories, let's get back to your personal one." After pausing, he added, "You have endured one of the most treacherous journeys any human can survive, as a child, losing a parent."

Halem sighed. "Do we have to go there again? I'm more than that. I'm more than a kid who lost a mother. As they say, I won't let that define who I am, and I don't want others to do it either."

"You're exactly right. You're far more than a grieving child. You've tremendous talents and things to offer this world. However, those gifts to the world are being held back. Your grief *is* defining you, whether you like it or not. I think it is the root to your unmerited low self-esteem. You don't know it, but you are much better than you think. Deeply inside your own shell there's a place where *you* take responsibility for what happened to your mom... and that's absurd."

"How can you say something like that! I'm not sitting around moping and feeling sorry for myself. Like I told you, I never even cried at my own mother's wake. I moved on. Some people would consider that very brave for a twelve-year-old."

"That *was* very brave." He sipped his coffee and looked out the front windows, leaning back against the bar. "Halem, if you'd cried for weeks or months and couldn't even find a way to dress yourself, after losing your mother, I would have no qualms with that. That would have been a healthy grieving process. It would be time to move on now. But, from what you've told me, you didn't grieve. Those facades of self-preservation must come down. You must grieve, before you can move on, and you can't just sweep those crumbs of pain into a clean drawer, or under a mat, so they are out of sight."

Halem stood up, walked around the bar, rinsed out her cup, and put it in the dishwasher. "Are you done?"

"With the conversation?"

"No, with the damn coffee!"

Winston took one last sip and handed her his cup.

"Who the hell are you that you think you can come into my coffee shop and tell me how to run my life?" she asked, voice rising. "You don't know me. I only met you a week ago. Haven't you heard that you should never tell someone how to grieve? I hope those southerly winds come soon to carry you away."

"I'm afraid that I cannot let this go. There's too much at stake, and I care too much about you. I saw that tear yesterday... you know when Jamie said he'd like to meet your mother. I sense a real potential here for you."

Halem slammed the bar top. "What do you want from me! It's been ten freakin' years since the wake. Do you want me to cry?

Would that make you happy?"

Winston stood up. "I want you to embrace your grief, head on. Open the drawer to the crumbs. Pull up the door matt and deal with the dirt beneath. Yeah, Miss Halem, you need to cry!"

Halem then yanked open the utensil drawer and dumped it out on the counter, utensils, crumbs, and all. She wiped up the crumbs in a dishtowel and into the garbage can beneath the bar. She slammed the drawer back into its place. She grabbed up the utensils and threw them back into the drawer.

She walked around the end of the bar, out to the window, and looked down on the harbor, her arms folded across her chest. She could see Winston's white skiff bobbing in the water, riding on the wake of a trawler making its way out to the rift. All day long she was hoping it was still there. Now, she honestly wished that it was gone, that Winston had sailed off with the group from San Diego.

Winston remained silent.

Who did she think she was that she would ever have a chance, romantically, with a man like Winston? What was she thinking? There was no future with the man, only agony. She wanted him to leave. But he didn't.

Halem saw her reflection on the inside of the glass. She felt ugly. Jamie's mother was right. She was too tall and too skinny. Her hair never looked good. Not grown out or chopped off as it is now. When she smiled her mouth crooked. The thought passed through her mind again that if she were prettier, Winston might not be talking to her this way. He may have been seduced into her symmetrical smile and working to bury any of her rough spots. That's what lovers do. That's what she did with Finn for over a year. She tried her best to bury his faults. He had no interest in hers, only her in bed with him in thoughtless love making, without conversations. Maybe if she had been in Winston's league, that's where this would be going. Not him seeing her as a pathetic stray puppy who needs help.

"What do you want from me, seriously?"

Winston gave her a warm smile. "Sit down beside me and tell me all about your mother."

She eased herself down onto the bar stool, one removed from his, facing the Lire. "I think I've told you everything. She was thin, beautiful, and full of music and life."

"Was she tall like you?"

"No. Not like me. Not six feet. No, I remember her being a good head shorter than Dad, and he's about six-foot three."

"What color was her hair?"

"I would call it auburn. Or, as some would say, a 'dirty blond, with a tinge of red.'"

"So, the same as yours? I can see your eyebrows and roots, and it looks like your natural color was similar."

Halem frowned and felt her hair. "I guess so. I've had mine so many colors that I almost forgot it was auburn."

"What was her favorite music?"

"She listened to all kinds. She, like everyone of that era, loved the Beatles. She loved the Mommas and the Papas. She used to sing their songs. I can still hear her singing as she did dishes, 'going to the chapel, going to get married.' Her favorite song of all songs was *Fields of Gold* by Eva Cassidy. They played that at her wake. Did you know that Eva died young from cancer too?"

Winston shook his head.

Halem continued. "But the music she performed with Dad was more folk music. Some Dylan and Seeger stuff, and a lot of stuff they made up. They were silly songs, that children liked." She smiled. "One song, Dad had written, was called 'Katie the Caterpillar.' It was about a caterpillar that loved its life climbing around in the trees and eating leaves so much that it, unlike her brothers and sisters, did not pause to build a cocoon. So, while her brothers and sisters came out as beautiful butterflies, she stayed in the caterpillar state. I can still remember the chorus, 'Katie, the caterpillar lady, didn't build a cocoon, because her schedule had no room, so she couldn't leave the leaves and fly to the blooms.' I know, that sounds corny, but with the music it was very catchy." Halem wiped a tear from her right eye. Then she flashed a big smile as to say, "all's well."

"What do you miss about her the most?"

Halem gave a soft moan, being disappointed that Winston was so damn persistent. Then she frowned. "Everything, I guess."

"How would your life be different now... if she had never died?"

Her eyes were turning watery. "It would be *totally* different. She wasn't just my mom... she was my best friend. She used to come into my bedroom every night and talk. When I was little, she would read me a story. But as I got older, she would talk about my day. I could tell her anything. If I had a crush on a boy. If girls at school were being mean to me, and when I had my first period; were all topics of late-night talks. She always knew exactly what to do. Dad wasn't bad at those talks either, in those days. He's so different now. He's gone and has been that way for a while. He's just a Cicadidae shell, long after the living insect has departed."

"You lost him too, didn't you?"

"Yep."

"So, in a moment, you went from this loving family, full of life, security and safety... a safety that seemed to never end... and, for no good reason, it was taken away from you."

Halem sniffed, "Yeah, and... if I had never been born, she might be a live today."

Winston shook his head, "Halem, you know that's nonsense. But still the loss is very real. No matter what you believe about an afterlife, you will never see, talk to, or hold your mother again in this world. You will never, ever feel her kisses, her soft cheek against yours, the smell of her perfume, see her creative touches to your house, and the world around you. You will never hear her songs again. You will never get to introduce your Prince Charming to her someday, or to help you pick out a wedding dress. She won't be there, when you give birth to your first baby or feel the joy of holding him, or her. A joy so strong that the two of you, mom, and daughter, are filled with tears. Halem, your life has been cheated. It wasn't fair and it sure as hell wasn't *your* fault."

"Stop! "If you are trying to make me cry, you are doing a pretty damn good job of it. But I'm afraid..."

"... Afraid of what?"

"If I ever start..." Tears were now streaming down her cheeks. "I'm afraid that I may never stop."

"The tears will stop, when it's time."

Halem wiped her face with her bare hand, and the tears continued to flow out. Her great force of resisting them was now exhausted. There was a continuous dripping from her chin and onto the floor. She looked down. Her wiping with her bare, impervious hand, could not keep up. The stream of unhindered water grew into sobbing. Her whole body was shaking as if in an epileptic fit.

Winston grabbed a handful of wadded-up paper napkins off the counter. She let the napkins fall to the floor as if she were suddenly overtaken by paralysis. She was shaking and crying. She began to bellow out loud. She cried uncontrollably for fifteen minutes and then a decrescendo descent into a quiet voice, "I'm so sorry, Mom. Why did this happen to you?" Then, in an almost desperate and angry tone, "God, why? I want my mommy back, God please! God please!" She raised her voice to a scream, "God, damnit why?" Her sobbing became a rhythmic snivel, purring, beneath her breath as the tears continued to fall. She could no longer sit, so she slumped to the floor, with Winston holding both her hands, to lower her gently.

"I never got to say goodbye! I never got to be with her when she drew her last breath! I had so much to tell her, about school, about my friends. I never thought I wouldn't see her again! But then it was too late! Goddamn you, Dad! You stupid man! So stupid!"

Winston slid down the front of the bar, beneath the Lira to sit beside her. She fell onto him, and he wrapped his arms around her, holding her like a baby. She was shaking so hard that Winston could not contain it. He too, was sobbing too hard to speak. He held her tight. Her shaking was so intense that the whole bar was rocking, and the cups on the top of the Lira were clinking together in the rhythm of her sorrow. She could feel the drops of his warm tears on the back of her head, as she succumbed into his lap. *Why would this stranger be crying over my loss?*

They laid in that position, her laying across the floor with her head buried in his lap and Winston stroking the back of her head. "I'm here," he said. "I'm with you."

They kept this position for over two hours, Halem sobbing the entire time. Winston had his back to the bar facing the big windows and watched as the shadow of Mount Constitution meticulously slid down the side of the village, until it overtook the harbor itself. Sandra came up to the window, pressed her face up to the glass, and shielded her eyes above with her hand so she could see inside. She looked horrified when she spotted them, on the floor, beneath the front of the bar. *Was Halem injured? Was this a rape?*

Winston smiled and flashed an okay sign with his hand. This did seem to dispel her concern enough that she eventually walked away... but her face carried the worried look with her.

It was late, a little after ten. Halem drifted in and out of sleep, only to awaken and start sobbing again. She looked up at him, her eyes so swollen that they could barely open beyond mere slits. He got a cup of water from the bar's sink. "Here's some water. Can I get you something else?"

"Milk," she said, barely audible. He drank the cup of water himself and went back behind the bar and opened a jug of the fresh milk and poured a glassful for each of them. He helped her to sit up on the floor so that she could drink hers. He drank his quickly and returned their glasses to the dishwasher. He sat back under the bar and she laid her head on his shoulder. She stared into his eyes and he, hers. She moved closer like she was about to kiss him on his lips. He pulled away—but not with a shock but rather a soft smile. "Halem, this is not the time for that."

"I'm sorry," she said, raspy. With a tone of embarrassment, "I don't know what I was thinking."

"It's okay," he said. Then, as she was trying to pull away, he pulled her head back to his broad shoulder. At four in the morning, she woke again. Winston was still seated on the floor with his back to the bar, her head back on his lap. He said, "Let me walk you home so that you can go to bed."

"I need to open the shop in three hours."

"I don't think you can. You're in no shape for that." After a couple of minutes, he asked, "Didn't you tell me that Sandra was a good barista in her own right?"

Halem didn't answer.

"I'll talk to her about filling in for you."

He walked her home, arm around her waist. They got to the door of Sandra's house and he helped her in. She looked at him and said, once again with tears dripping out of the slit of her engorged eyes, "Please don't leave me. I don't want to be alone."

He helped her to her bedroom and promised that he would sleep on the couch just outside her door. Her hand slipped gently out of his, and she closed the bedroom door between them. That night, the grief that had been chasing Halem for over ten years... finally caught up with her.

Chapter Nine

Winston

Winston was in a deep sleep on the couch when he heard a noise and started his rise to the surface of slumber. He felt the presence of someone standing over him blocking the window's light from the morning's sun. He eased open one eye and saw Sandra above him in a white terry cloth bathrobe with its belt tied into a big bow at her waist.

She said to him, "I thought I smelled a man in my house." She pointed to her nose. "I have a keen sense of smell. What's going on here? It's almost seven and Halem's still in bed. I'm confused. Why are you sleeping in *my* house? Did you two have a lover's quarrel or something last night? Did you say goodbye and you're leaving today? What is it?" She reached over and turned on a pole lamp behind her to illuminate his sleepy head.

He dropped his feet over the edge of the couch and slowly sat up, looking up at her, shielding his eyes from the lamp. She studied him, from his bare hairy-toed feet up to his unkept bushy hair, which framed in his rustic morning face. A face that carried impressions from the couch cushion buttons like fossilized imprints. The impression on *her* face was one of concern, if not frank annoyance at his presence.

"No. None of that," he said, rubbing his eyes. "I'm sorry. I meant to talk to you before now, but I guess I didn't wake up in time." He coughed, clearing up the morning mucus. "You see, Halem's had a rough night. It's about her mom."

"Her *mom*?"

"Yes. You know she lost her mom, didn't you?"

"Last night?"

"No, no, no, it was more than ten years ago."

"Oh. I was confused about that. But I never inquired as it seemed too personal." Sandra paused. "But that was ten years ago?"

"Well, I don't know if you can understand this, but she never really had the chance to mourn over losing her mom. Now she is."

The muddlement on Sandra's face seemed to thicken. She asked, "Why now? Did something happen to bring this up?"

Winston rubbed his eyes again. "Yeah, it's all my fault."

"But why? How? Why in the Sam Hill would you bring that up?"

"Because she needed to mourn, and I brought it up to her because she needed me to. Now she's very distressed. She's in no shape to work today."

"Are you serious? Who's going to run the shop?" Then, after another long pause, she stepped outside and looked up at the coffee shop. She stepped back into the house. "Damn, there's people lining up already. Are you messing with her? She's a sweet girl and has been through enough."

"I guess I *am* messing with her. But what I'm saying is that she needed it. Regarding the shop, well, I was hoping that you could manage it today. Halem said you were a rather good barista in your own right. Can you?"

"Well, I guess if I have no choice, but I had other plans for today. I guess they'll just have to wait, won't they? But I need to shower and clean up. There's no way in hell that I'm going down there looking like this."

"I can help. I know how to make coffee. I can run down now and open up while you get ready... if I have a key."

Sandra took a group of keys on a chain off a peg. She removed one brass key and then handed it to Winston. He put on his dirty sandals. Went into the kitchen and gulped a glass of water. Ran the tap again and splashed water into his sleepy eyes then put a handful on his hair. Paused at a hall mirror near the door to try and shaped his black locks with his fingers. Then he went out the door and took off running in the direction of the coffee shop.

Hank and Kane were already at the door plus a trio of what appeared to be fishermen standing between them.

"Good morning gentlemen," said Winston as he pushed through the group. "I'm sorry the shop's still closed. Halem's ill today and Sandra's coming, but I can let you in and start making coffee." He fiddled with the key, trying to get it to go in one way, then another, until the lock turned, and the door popped open. He let them all in.

Winston went behind the bar and looked around. He certainly wouldn't mess with the money tablet. But he did know his way around an expresso machine. He turned on the boiler.

He looked up at Kane, who was first in line. "Kane, can I get you something. Don't you drink a cappuccino?"

"So, Halem's not coming at all today?"

"I'll be surprised if she shows. But, if you are doubting my abilities, I will say that, while I may not have Halem's touch, I do know what I'm doing. I've made many espressos in my time and Halem just taught me about how to make a ristretto, the best of the bean, and I know that's how you like yours."

"This morning, I'll have a regular cappuccino."

"Really?"

"My ristretto is precise. and I'll wait on Halem for that. But you do know how to make a cappuccino with regular shots?"

Winston smiled. "So, I'm giving you empirical, historical evidence that I can make you a good cappuccino. I seem to be an honest guy that you can usually trust. I report to you that I'm skilled at making cappuccinos and have made many in my life and that I know how to pull a ristretto shot. You're standing there and can observe how I work to confirm my abilities as I make it. However, that evidence cannot guarantee a certainty that it will be a good cup. Even the best barista can have a bad day, or something like bad milk [Halem told him the story about making coffee with soured milk]." He winked. "However, it will be enough evidence for you to accept and to enjoy the cup by trust."

Kane remained silent, just nodding. Hank was oblivious to the conversation, but the fishermen in front of him, stared at one another and flashed the pulled-back frown to each other, as to say,

"What the hell?"

Winston took out a scoop of beans and put them into the grinder. Kane spoke up, with what seemed to be a sudden change of mind, "Set it to fine and see if you can pull ristretto shots like Halem does."

Winston noticed that his scoop hit the bottom of the coffee bean bin, under the bar. It worried him if they would have enough beans for the day. He ground the beans with a finer grind and sifted out fifteen grams to fill the portafilter. He pressed and turned the hand tamp a quarter turn. Then he repositioned his hands and pressed and turned the tamp another quarter of turn.

Kane spoke, "Uh, Halem doesn't twist it twice like that."

Winston smiled. "Well, some believe that the twisting sets the grains of coffee to expose more of their surface area to extract additional flavor. However, some don't think it's necessary. If you want, I'll be happy to start over."

"That's okay, go ahead."

Winston set up the portafilter, locking it on the brew head. Kane watched carefully. "Uh, try pulling the cup away at thirteen seconds. That's what Halem does."

"I know, and I can certainly do that." Then he looked at the clock on the machine and pulled the cup away just like Kane had requested.

Winston apologized to the pastor that he was not good in drawing a fern with the micro-foam but assured him that it would not affect the taste.

Next, he served the three fishermen. They had just finished their spring salmon trolling season in Alaska and were coming to Rock Harbor to re-tool their boat for Dungeness crab season in Puget Sound. Keeping their boats in Rock Harbor saved at least a day in their turnaround by avoiding the larger mainland marinas.

Then he served Hank, the quiet man. Tall and lean, always donning a few-day's growth in beard. He had dark, thinning hair on top with a bit of gray in his temples. His eyes were the darkest that Winston ever remember seeing, even in his dark-skinned friends. He too, wanted a cappuccino. While he was working on Hank's drink, Jamie came in along with a couple, a man and woman—apparently tourists, as Winston had not seen them before. He looked at Hank, as he continued to work on his drink. He had a large black headset around his neck. Carried in his right hand was his steampunk laptop inside a wooden case.

Winston asked, "Did I hear that you're a famous drummer?"

Hank said nothing.

"Is that not true?"

"What does it matter? Who cares?"

"I care, or I wouldn't have asked. I think it's fascinating. Did you really play with Nirvana?"

Hank said nothing. Winston finished his cup and set it on the bar in front of him. He smiled and explained to him that he would have to pay when Sandra arrived.

Hank picked up his cup and turned to find a table.

Winston realized that it was now eight-thirty, and Sandra had still not shown up. "Some morning," he said to Hank, "I would love to hear your entire story."

Hank said nothing. Just walked on to his usual table.

Jamie was then standing at the counter. He looked worried. "Where's Halem? Is she alright?"

"She's fine, Jamie. I can tell by the look on your face that you are worried about her."

"I am. Did you do something to her?"

"Well, maybe it was my fault, but she's feeling sad about things we talked about last night. I shouldn't say anything else, but that she feels ill today."

"Did you molest her? My mother warned me about strangers who come through town, and that some could be evil and even molest girls or children."

The tourist couple standing just behind Jamie looked at each other with raised eyebrows.

"Now Jamie, you know that I care a lot about Halem and would never do anything to intentionally hurt or disrespect her. I can see your concern in your face, and I'm showing you the same concern. See those wrinkles on my forehead, that's because I'm concerned and worried like you. Feel your own forehead and you'll feel the same wrinkles. It's like you can tell a purse seine from a gillnetter by the net skiff sitting on the stern."

The tourists continued staring at each other, as if they had stumbled into a most unusual place.

Winston finished serving Jamie and the tourists; then, he took a breather, leaning back against the bar with Jamie sitting quietly at the end of it.

Sandra walked in the door about quarter past nine, looking like she was ready for a night on the town. "How's it going?" she mumbled as she walked past Winston. She looked quite different than when he had seen her standing over him in her bathrobe. She was "made-up" with a smooth brown face, highlighted pink cheeks, and well-outlined eyes. She smelled of honeysuckles. She had combed her hair and teased a bit to look fuller and less tangled. You could easily have mistaken her age as ten years younger than she looked ninety minutes earlier, which was her goal.

"Fine," said Winston and started cleaning up around the bar. "Looks like I have all the first-comers settled. They do need to pay up when you get the chance to ring them up."

"Oh, if only I can remember the log-on password," said Sandra as she started punching screen buttons on the tablet.

The rest of the morning was busy as Winston worked to clean up the Lira and grinder and put away the dirty dishes customers brought up to the bar. He found a small quantity of beans in the sack, which remained after Halem filled the hopper.

Sandra focused on taking payments. A few stragglers came in. Jamie's father, Dale, came in for a black coffee, carryout. He was a rough-looking man, wrinkled and leathery face with kinky gray hair and cobalt-blue eyes. His teeth were brown. He smelled of tobacco.

"Are you Winston?"

"I am." Winston shook his hand across the bar.

"Molly and I are grateful for the kindness you've shown Jamie. Not all people do."

"Oh, he's a great kid," said Winston, loud enough for Jamie to hear him.

"Really? I mean, Molly and I think so, but he's our boy. He can't help what he says to people."

"Yeah, I know."

About that time, Sandra came back through the door. She poured herself a glass of iced water with a slice of a fresh lemon and walked back to the roaster and sat down. "I'm exhausted," she said. "I didn't sleep well." She took a sip of her water and rested her head back against the iron roaster itself. Then she closed her eyes.

Before giving her time to doze off, Winston asked, "Do you mind if I make myself a coffee."

"Oh, please do, and on the house," said Sandra, eyes closed.

He made himself a cortado in a small shot glass and came back to the back of the shop. There he sat down near Sandra. Even though her eyes were closed, she habitually reached for her glass of iced water and sipped.

Then Sandra opened one eye and said, "I'm worried. Halem's still in bed. I had to change her pillowcase because she had soaked it with her tears. She's lifeless."

Winston sipped his coffee. "She's gonna be okay."

Sandra opened both eyes. "How do *you* know that? I had a friend who got depressed like that and eventually took an over-dose. That's what scares me."

"She's not depressed."

"How can you say that? Are you a shrink? She can't get out of bed for Pete's sake. She's as limp as a wash rag. She has cried so hard that she can't talk anymore. Not that she is just choked up, but she has laryngitis, maybe aphasia."

"She's fine. She's grieving. This is what raw angst looks like. Imagine that she just found out this morning that her mother had died. We wouldn't expect anything less than how she's behaving. Depression is grief without an external source. Halem has a reason to her sorrow, a good reason. A child losing a parent, especially a girl losing her mother, is the worst heartache imaginable, except maybe... for a mother losing a child."

"But what if she gets stuck? What if she never comes out of this?"

Winston smiled. "She will. I promise."

Sandra just shook her head.

He kept the same poised smile, adding, "Halem will be fine, but not until after the anguish has finished its term. And Sandra, the reason that I'm snooping into people's personal lives is because I live alone, in the middle of nowhere, confined inside the hull of a five by seventeen-foot space. When I do eventually find people, I have an insatiable curiosity to learn about them, to listen, and to help them in any way I can. That's just who I am."

Sandra and Winston kept the shop open. On the fourth day, Sandra hardly came in the shop at all as she was confident that Winston knew his way around. He was even running the payment program on the tablet after Sandra had shown him how. She left the harbor, going out through the rift in her boat that morning, Winston didn't know where she was going. During those days, when he wasn't in the shop, Winston gave Halem her space, only visiting her each morning to bring her a Turkish coffee. He didn't talk, just made sure she was eating and drinking, picking up the old cup, leaving the new full one.

Sandra pulled into the harbor about the time Winston was closing the shop that evening. He recognized her boat coming through the rift. Once the shop was empty and the door locked, he sat at the table in front, Kane's favorite table, with a good view out the window. He had something on his mind, and he needed to talk to Sandra about it. He had expressed concern to her that they were out of roasted beans. Their only choice was to close until Halem was able to roast more.

Sandra had encouraged Winston that morning to roast the beans on his own. After all, he had watched Halem doing her last batch.

But he wasn't so sure. Sandra had pulled a thick spiral-bound book from the cabinet and handed it to him to study. It was the user manual for the roaster. Her last words, before leaving was, "I don't care if you can't produce good beans, but please don't blow anything up or burn the place down."

"Really, you think I can do it?"

Sandra smiled, heading out the door that morning. "I'll try to get back to help you."

But as Winston was watching Sandra, she got out of her boat, retrieved the harbor cart, and placed several bags of groceries into it. Winston thought it would be a good idea to help Sandra carry the bags from the fourth level stop of the trolley, down to her house. As they walked, he hoped to find out if she was going to help him with the roasting.

Winston walked toward Sandra's house and then past it, down to where the escalator and trolley terminate. Sandra was still working her way up the steps. The tub, with the bags, arrived first. He took two of the bags in his arms. Sandra was looking down at her phone as she reached the top of the stairs and hadn't noticed him yet.

She looked up just as she reached the last step. "Oh, hi. Are you here to help me?"

"Yes ma'am, and I was hoping you could help me too."

"Uh, I don't know. You mean with the roast?"

"Yes ma'am."

"I'm tired, and I really need to check on Halem. She needs a good cooked dinner. I'm sure you can roast without me."

"Have you seen Halem today?" he asked.

"Not since I brought her breakfast this morning. I'm worried about her. I know you're not, but she's fragile."

"I beg to differ. She's a remarkable girl... maybe too tough."

Winston followed her into the house, setting the groceries on the counter. They both looked around the kitchen and living areas and didn't see Halem. Her bedroom door was closed. Winston stayed in the kitchen while Sandra knocked on Halem's door and walked in.

Then he went over next to her door so he could hear the conversation and peak between the door and its frame.

"How are you doing?" asked Sandra.

Halem said nothing at first, then after a deep breath, "I don't know."

"Aren't you feeling any better?"

"I don't know." She sniffled and became teary. "I miss my mom... and my dad. I just feel this ache inside that I cannot subdue. I'm so disappointed in life. Is it really going to be like this?" She reached for a Kleenex, blew her nose, threw the tissue into the pile on the floor. "I don't see what's the point."

"Now Halem, you must shake this off. You can't talk like that or who knows what will happen. I mean, I'm just worried about you girl."

Halem closed her eyes. "I'm really mad at that Winston. I think he meant well. He has a gift of finding lost feelings hiding inside someone's hollow shell and using words to bring them to the surface. I didn't want to do this grieving process... now or ever."

"Winston's gifted for sure," said Sandra. "He's like me, an artist. But he paints with his tongue, words his medium, and letters his strokes. Some people use charming words as cover for their real, foul intent." She paused. "I don't know, Halem. I just don't trust him. I don't understand how a stranger can come into town, and suddenly he's meddling in everyone's personal affairs. I'm afraid before he leaves, he's going to swindle somebody out of something—or possibly all of us out of everything. I also don't believe his damn stories about crossing the Atlantic in that tiny rowboat of his. That's not even possible. My ex, he did a crossing once in his forty-nine-foot Nordic Tug when he was in his twenties. He said it was a complete nightmare with thirty-foot waves washing over his bow. So, don't tell me that he did it alone in that little boat that he's in. I can smell a liar, and I think Winston is one of the biggest."

A brief smile came to Halem's puffy face. She scooted up in bed. Put her pillow behind her back to support it in a sitting position. "I don't know, Sandra. He just seems genuinely nice and like he really does care. I don't know if bringing up my mother, like he did, was the right thing to do, but I don't question his motives. I know I've been mad at him, but maybe he's right. Maybe I'm long overdue for a hard and lengthy bereavement."

Halem teared up again and continued. "But I just hurt soooo bad. I feel physical pain in my heart, like something is being torn from me or stabbed into me. Didn't you ever lose anyone?"

Sandra embraced Halem. "Now, don't cry, hon. It's okay. Just stop crying. Everything will be okay... Yeah, I lost someone alright. I lost an innocent fifteen-year-old girl. No, not my daughter, but my-self. It's a story best left untold."

Winston left quietly.

He returned to the shop and made himself a pour-over with the last cup of remaining beans. Then he sat at the bar with his coffee and studied the spiral-bound instruction manual for the roaster. He periodically walked back and study the machine itself to make sure he understood the instructions properly. When he completed his re-view of the manual, he finished off his last gulp of coffee and laid the book down. Walked back to the roaster one more time. Tapped on the touch screen to wake it up.

Winston punched buttons to test the burners by turning then them on and then off again. He saw the full sack of beans. He dragged the sack toward the roaster and cut the string with his pocketknife. He tried to imitate Halem's tender care in the way he spread his fingers and pulled them through the beans. He took out a couple of small twigs. Then he took a deep breath and programed the machine to repeat the last roast. He waited until the roaster was at 398 degrees Fahrenheit and poured them into the top shoot. As soon as the beans were in, he heard the shop door open.

Halem.

Winston flashed her a big smile. She smiled back. She'd show-ered, put on a little pink lipstick. Looked like she was back among the living. She was wearing ragged jeans and a gray sweatshirt with an oversized neck hole that exposed her entire shoulder. He could smell her herbal shampoo, which overtook the sweet smell of roasting beans.

"I thought you might need some assistance," she said. "But it looks like you have everything under control." She peeked into the roaster through its port window. She quickly grabbed the handle of the coffee tryer and pulled out a sample. Just like before, she picked one dark bean and, while replacing the tryer, blew on that bean to cool it. She then tossed it into her mouth and crunched it. She hastily pulled the handle to dump the entire load of beans into the cooling tray.

Winston stepped back. "Did I over-roast?"

"Almost. I think if I hadn't come in when I did, distracting you, you would've been fine. But they are roasted slightly beyond perfection."

As the beans cooled, they sat at the bar.

"What're you staring at?" she asked.

"Are you okay?"

"I don't know. Everyone keeps asking me that! I don't even know what it means to be okay anymore. Maybe I was never *okay*."

"It's good to see you out of the house again. I know that Sandra's worried about you."

"And you."

"Me? Am I worried about you? Not so much. I'm sure you'll be fine. You're a strong woman."

"No! I mean that Sandra is also worried about *you*."

Halem realized that she had probably said too much, not understanding that Winston already knew of Sandra's suspicion from his eavesdropping.

Winston looked confused. "Why would she be worried about me?"

"Never mind, it's not important, but try to get back on her good side, if you can." She paused. "What am I saying? Here you are running her coffee shop and doing it for free. I guess you're doing the best anyone can."

Winston closed his eyes, gathering his thoughts. He walked to the front windows. Could see the shadow of Mount Constitution once again moving down the mountain as the sun was dipping in the west behind it. The harbor was like a giant sundial, where you could tell the precise time by the leading edge of the shadow of the mountain coming down the different levels of the village. You just had to know the season.

He looked at Halem. "Is it time to put the beans away?"

"Not yet. I usually wait until they're room temperature."

"Would you like to taste them? I mean with a pour-over or anything you want?" asked Winston.

"I would die for a doppio. I can't remember when I've had this little coffee over three days. If you hadn't brought me that Turkish coffee, I think my head would have exploded by now."

"I would love to make you a doppio."

He returned from the bar with a scoop of beans, ground and weighted them, and then set up a doppio cup. He pulled a double shot and handed her the cup. She blew across the brim to cool it down. "Not bad, especially for unrested beans. Maybe a very slight bitter aftertaste but I'm doubtful if anyone would notice... except maybe Kane."

His eyes lit up. "I would like to make you dinner. Not tonight, as I'll need to buy supplies. But what's your favorite meal, something you would consider a real comfort food?"

She smiled. "Really? Anything?"

"Anything... anything that I can find in this neck of the woods."

"Well, I've only had lobster once in my life. Delicious! I have never forgotten that meal. Here, the locals are always giving me their excess Dungeness crabs and shrimp. Those are great and fresh. But I still think about that lobster. It was silly, but a friend took me to the senior prom and out to a nice dinner at Anthony's restaurant on the waterfront."

"Why was that silly?"

"Oh, I think this friend was feeling sorry for me and took me to the prom. You know it was a few years after Mom died. After the prom, he kept calling, but I never picked up or called him back as I knew it was just an act of solace."

"Hmm. I think if a high school guy paid for a dinner like that, it was more than just pity. That was probably a week's salary for that age, on burger-joint wages."

"Is that what this dinner is, the one you want to prepare, pity?"

"Of course not!" He seemed disappointed with that comment.

"A date?"

Winston gave her a forced smile. "No, I wouldn't call it that, either. Sandra's welcome to join us. It, the meal, is just a friend who cares about you, who wants to give you some comfort. But that's different from pity. With pity, you have sorrow for what has happened to someone else. Certainly, I feel pity for young Halem who lost her mom. But I don't feel pity for you now. You're not pity-worthy. I feel joy. I think you are finding yourself and you're in the process of finally becoming that beautiful butterfly your mother and father had imagined."

She smiled, not sure what to say.

"So," said Winston, "Where would I find them?"

"Them who? My father and mother?"

"Lobsters? I don't think they live in Puget Sound, do they?"

Halem chuckled. "I don't know. For lobsters, maybe the market in Eastsound would have them in their frozen food case. For certain the bigger grocery stores in Anacortes. But getting there is the problem."

"Remember, I do have a sailboat, and we've had good winds of late."

"I know. You could sail the five miles to North Beach. From there, it is at least a mile walk each way into Eastsound. Anacortes is just ten miles by water. If you sail around to the east side, to the Cap Sante harbor, then you'll be right in town when you dock and fifty yards from the larger grocery stores."

"Okay. If you're able to take over the shop in the morning, I'll leave early. From what the mariners tell me, the westerly winds should persist tomorrow. The winds would favor my trip east to An-

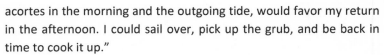

acortes in the morning and the outgoing tide, would favor my return in the afternoon. I could sail over, pick up the grub, and be back in time to cook it up."

Halem looked into her cup, saying nothing.

"Can you?" added Winston.

"Can I what?"

"Take over the shop in the morning?"

She nodded.

The next morning, just as the sun was making its way back over the serrated mountains of the North Cascade Range, in the east, Winston stuck in a bottle of potable water and hoisted the sail. Laid his chart down on the seat and then sat on it. It was the only way to keep it from blowing overboard.

He untied the bow line and let the sail pull the bow away from the dock and pointed out into the bay. Then he released the stern line and moved out into open water. With the steep walls of the harbor blocking the breezes, he had barely enough power to pull him out of his mooring. He considered his oars, but he loved the feel of the wind. It was magic to him, to harness such an omnipotent force for his personal use.

The gentle gusts picked up as he neared the rift, but then died again once in the deep channel. He used one oar to push him along the southern wall, until he exited into the main sound. Once there, the winds picked up dramatically and the canvas inflated fully and billowed out. The edge of the taut material quivered in the escaping air releasing a rhythmic hum into the space around the boat. The wind pulled the bow toward the deeper waters.

The boat leaned sharply to the portside, and Winston scooted to the starboard for a counterbalance. He was picking up speed to the point that he could hear the water tearing apart at the cut of the bow. He loved that sound too, wood cutting water, and the feel of the wind across his face, his bushy hair floppy about. He loved the feel of the power of the gales being transmitted down the wooden mast into the boat and into his body. He could feel the bite of the rudder through the wooden tiller in his hand. The rudder's tug felt like he had tamed the ocean, as if he had put a bit in the mouth of a stallion. A harbor seal tried to keep up, but then either tired out, or became bored and retreated to the dark underworld.

As he came around the southern edge of Cypress Island, Winston kept his nautical chart in view down between his legs, so he could understand the complex dance of the islands and navigate through them. He had learned the hard way in the intricate fjords and islands of the southern tip of South America, how easy it was to become disoriented to the landscape from the seat of a small craft. That's why he took on a local to help him find the way through that convoluted course. At that moment, he regretted that he had not thought to have invited Jamie on this day trip. It would have been perfect for him. But maybe the next time he sailed he would.

He entered the Guemes Channel with a vigorous tide washing out, slowing his passage so much he thought for a while he was at a standstill. Fortunately, with a stiff wind still at his back, he was able to penetrate the escaping surf once it started to slow down. He swung around and entered Cap Sante Harbor.

Since he didn't carry a radio, he put down his sail and methodically rowed his way around, until he found a slip and tied up. The harbormaster was quick to point out that someone had reserved that slip; there were no available ones. The owner of a large sailboat was sitting on his deck drinking coffee and reading the paper. He had overheard the conversation and invited Winston to bring his small boat over and tie it up against his boat, in his slip.

In town, he picked up a couple of rope stays to reorganize his lines. Got a haircut, just a trim, and then ventured into the grocery store. American stores overwhelmed him with a feel of excess. Too many choices tell of a spoiled population. He loved the simple markets in other parts of the world, those along the coast of West Africa being his favorite. They were untainted by the pleasures of tourists, who dominated places like the Caribbean with cheap island trinkets, made in China.

He returned to his boat in the early afternoon with four live lobsters wrapped in wet paper, a bottle of wine, and a loaf of French bread. The sailboat owner was still sitting on his deck, now with a short, stubby bottle of brown liquor. Watched Winston, with great curiosity, as he pumped water into his boat with his hand bilge-pump. Once it filled with three inches of water, Winston liberated the lobsters. The man chuckled when he figured out his intentions.

Winston gave the sailor a shout of gratitude and left the harbor, sailing back, his treasures aboard.

A brief spring rainstorm passed over him. He could see clear skies in the west, so he didn't bother pulling out his neoprene boat cover, besides, his boat already had a puddle of water. He didn't even don his rain jacket, which he'd stowed away in the bow. He allowed the cold drops to hit is face, even looking up directly into the sky, inviting them to strike. For him, something about being in a boat alone at sea was a place of repose. While on land, he could not resist the alluring draw of people's lives. Each person to him was an unexplored cavern full of ancient paintings, such as at Lascaux, holding unimagined beauty and intrigue. For some, as he had described to Halem, those secrets were labyrinths, whose painters had become lost in the shadows. He did regret Sandra's cynicism, which put a damper on a task that was already difficult. Would she now investigate his own past? Would she find a dark grotto full of secrets?

Chapter Ten

Halem

Winston arrived back in Rock Harbor at four in the afternoon. Halem was working in the coffee shop and spotted him through the rift. It was reminiscent of just two weeks earlier when he came rowing into town for the first time. This time, his mast was erect, his sail engaged with the wind, and his oars at peace, as he hitched a ride on the breezes, pulling him in, from across the outer waters.

As Halem served her customers, she'd pause now and then to look out the window to check on Winston's progress. Once, she stood motionless looking above her Lire as he entered the rift. The first time she saw him, two weeks ago, as just a dot on the sea, she was curious. Now, with so much water under the bridge, or in this case *boat*, she felt sad, angered, but at the same time, enamored by the mysterious man. Her worse fear was that Sandra was right, Winston was preparing her for his dark side to emerge.

It would happen just like it did with Finn. She adored Finn... for the first few weeks. But this time she was confident that she would notice the insidious rise of the deceit earlier. Her heart was on-guard. She also felt a part of her, maybe a lot of her, falling in love with the enigmatic man from the sea. She didn't want to think in those terms as Winston had warned her that he would certainly leave again. Even if Sandra's conjectures about his darkness were wrong, he would still leave. Maybe it was just her fantasy that he would be good, purely good, without a tinge of malevolence. But all men, all people, have dark sides, don't they?

But if Winston is the exception, so she thought, and takes her with him, out to sea and away, that would be the sonnet in which she could write her life. That's what she would dream if she were twelve, before the tragedy had quelled her dreaming ability.

Finding a rustic cabin in Rock Harbor, or an old sailing yacht to restore and live on forever in their bay, would be another acceptable aspiration. However, he must have been in a thousand beautiful harbors with girls more desirable than herself, at least that was her thought at that moment. But she knew that she was just ordinary at best. Too tall and skinny. She had no merits to offset her looks, beyond making a damn good cup of coffee. She was messed up. Depressed at times and now was one of those times. She had nothing to offer the man… that's if he turned out to be good or even mostly good. *Was it really an issue of low self-esteem? It didn't feel like it.*

Still, another part of her was angry at him. If he were a conman, she would be really pissed at him for what he had put her through. Undergirding all those feelings was a deep sense of sorrow. It penetrated and made bisque of her marrow. It was a sorrow for her loss. Winston had hit a weak spot in her soul when he had her think about how things could have been, if her mother had lived. Before, she could not go there. Now she could not leave. She had intrusive thoughts of what life would have been like with her mom and a healthy dad, of a career, maybe a husband, or a sober man in her life. The tears came again.

Halem's meandering thoughts were interrupted when Jamie asked, uncharacteristically, "Are you alright? I know that when I cry, I feel sad." Jamie was sitting just on the other side of the Lira, a place that Winston had asked him to sit and now was his new spot.

She was embarrassed that he had seen her tears. Forced a quick smile. Wiped her tears quickly away with the sleeve of her sweatshirt. "I'm okay Jamie." Then she thought that this breakthrough of him being so perceptive must be rewarded, so she added, "It was so kind of you to notice." She stood on her tiptoes, leaned over the Lira, and kissed Jamie on the top of his head. His hair tasted like sweat. He blushed.

She walked to the side of the machine so that she could look directly across the bar at the boy. The look on his face was a look of being left wanting. She felt that he deserved more than what she had given him in the past. But it was always risky, saying anything to Jamie, with the fear he would shout it out to everyone. But she was willing to take that risk. "Jamie, I'm feeling sad about losing my mother. She died ten years ago, but I'm just now being sad about it."

He seemed confused. "Why weren't you sad then? I would be very sad if something happened to Molly."

"Jamie, it's hard to explain, but sometimes things are so awful that your brain sort of decides to file it away. It's a kind of survival." Fishing is something she knew Jamie could relate to, so she said. "Like the salmon swimming upstream to their certain deaths, just so that they can spawn. If they thought about it, they would never do it. It is too awful for them to think about the suffering of swimming in fresh water, and then dying as their skin molts off."

"I didn't know that you knew so much about salmon."

She smiled. "You can't live around here very long until you become an expert in fishing, crabbing, and boating." She laid her hand on Jamie's. "I'm indebted to smart people like you."

Jamie just stared at her and finished off his mocha with a straw, then he said, "I wished they all would fear for their lives and not come back to spawn. Then there would be no salmon, and I would never have fallen into Bristol Bay trying to catch them."

"But Jamie," Halem said, "if there's no salmon, and some day there may not be any left, your dad would lose his livelihood."

Jamie never ceased to surprise her, and this moment was no exception. "Can I kiss you back?" She wasn't sure how to take that question, then his follow up question confirmed his intent, "On the lips this time. You kissed me on my head." He rubbed his hair. "So, can I kiss you on your lips now? That might make you feel better. I know it will make *me* feel better." Then he started to lean toward her.

She stood up straight. "No Mr. Jamie, you may not kiss me on my lips. Not you or anybody else."

"Just Winston then?"

"No Jamie, not even Winston... not anybody."

Chapter Eleven

Dinner

Winston was comfortable in a kitchen. It came from his younger years, when he helped his mom prepare gourmet meals for dignitaries and other foreign service families. She was an expert on Egyptian cuisine, but she loved Greek, Italian, and Indian almost as much.

But, on this night, this was going to be a rather simple meal as compared to his mother's Indian lamb curry and garlic naan. He bought a salad kit at the supermarket, which saved him a lot of time in chopping and mixing kale and cabbage. He warmed up the baguettes and sliced cheeses. He steamed asparagus in a kettle, and then scattered smoked-cheddar flakes across them.

He kept the lobsters alive in the sink full of salted water while he worked. As it was nearing time to cook them, he chose the least cruel way to kill them, as taught to him by a spiny lobster diver in South Africa. First, he cooled them down by adding trays of ice cubes to their water. Then he sat a large pot on to boil. When the chill had penetrated them to the point of arresting their muscle movements, anesthetizing them, he took them out of the cold water. They were still alive but limp. Then he thrusted a sharp knife into their brains, behind their eyes. Only then did he drop them into the boiling water.

When Sandra walked into the kitchen she asked, "Why are there four lobsters?"

"I invited Jamie. He said he had never been in your house before."

Sandra shook her head, "Good grief. Don't know if I can handle the boy through an entire meal."

She went to the back of her house to start a load of laundry but returned to help Winston set up the tables, as he would be clueless about her storage arrangement of dishes and silverware. Halem was in her bedroom. Door open. Listening. She meandered out to the couch so she could read their body language and not just their words.

Sandra asked Winston, "So, how long are you going to be here?"

He answered with a look that suggested he thought it was an odd question, "I guess two to three hours. I want to clean up before I leave. I bet you wanna to turn in early don't you?"

"No, no... I'm not talking about tonight. I'm asking about how long you'll be in Rock Harbor?"

Winston arranged the now-drained lobsters, one on each plate. They were golden-orange and smelled of the sea. He wiped his hands on a towel and looked at Sandra, "I'm not sure. It depends on when I feel I'm finished here... and the winds."

"Finished what?" She then asked in a more impetuous tone. "What are you here for anyway?"

He leaned back against the wall and looked down at the floor, as he was searching for the best words. "You don't trust me, do you?"

"How could I trust anyone I just met a couple of weeks ago? I don't know you enough to trust you and you don't know me," she answered with assured tone.

"That's true that we just met. But I trust you. I start out trusting people until they lose that trust."

"Then you must be someone's sucker a lot," she said with a sneer.

"Not really," answered Winston as he returned to setting the food dishes on the table. "I honestly don't remember ever falling for a con or deception. But, Sandra, I sense that someone has betrayed you in your past, and for that reason, it's hard for you to trust anyone again."

She started shaking her head and smiling big, then she pointed her index finger straight up in front of him, shaking it to the left and right, "No, no, no pretty boy. You're not pulling that psychoanalyzing bullshit on me. Everyone else is falling for your games, but not me, not now, not ever!"

About this time, they noticed Halem sitting on the couch, looking much better. She had applied touches of makeup and was wearing a beautiful lapis blue skirt and a white blouse. She didn't say anything about overhearing their conversation, but you could see the marks of it on her facial expression, which looked serious.

"Hi Halem," said Winston. "I hope you are feeling as well as you look."

She blushed. "I'm sure I don't." She paused. "Oh, I don't mean I think I look good."

Winston answered quickly, "Of course you don't."

"Can I help in any way?"

Sandra handed her the bowl of salad and, between the three of them, they finished carrying everything to the table.

Halem asked, "Four plates? Who else is joining us?"

"Mr. Winston here has invited Jamie." Said Sandra, expecting Halem to cringe.

She didn't. She just smiled and said, "Okay."

As soon as they had arranged everything, they all took a seat. Winston asked, "Speaking of Jamie, I wonder where the bloke could be?"

Halem answered, "He will be late for his own wedding… or funeral, whichever comes first."

Sandra mumbled, almost inaudibly, "I can't imagine that boy married, and if so, I would pity the girl."

Winston's dimples reemerged around his broad smile. Resting his elbows firmly on the table, he said, "I think everyone can find at least one person whose right for them."

"So, like a soulmate?" asked Halem.

"Not really a soulmate, if you mean only one person in the world for that individual. But someone that fits right, like a proper fitting shoe on an oddly shaped foot. There may be many shoes that fit, but only one that is obtainable at that time."

"But the boy's an idiot," said Sandra.

Sandra's harsh words surprised even Halem. Sandra was usually a kind woman and saying something like that was not her normal tone.

"Idiot?" asked Halem. "I can't believe you said that. He has his problems, but he's no idiot."

Nodding his head, Winston added, "I agree."

About that time a knock came at the door. Jamie. He had a new haircut and had slicked it back like he was part of the Sicilian mafia. He was even wearing a sports jacket, although over a white tee with a red and yellow Superman logo on the chest and black jeans.

Halem said, "Well, look at you Mr. Jamie. You look very handsome."

Jamie's face turned pink. "I know you don't mean that because I'm too fat."

"Yeah, and I'm too skinny, so what?" Everyone turned to look at her.

Winston motioned Jamie over to the table. "Have a seat right here beside me, Clark Kent."

Jamie took a seat, speechless, and stared at the lobster.

Winston asked, "Have you ever had lobster before?"

"I have eaten hundreds if not thousands of crabs of all sorts, but I don't think I've eaten a Maine lobster before. It looks like you killed it with a stab to the brain."

"That's right Jamie."

"You're a kind man."

"Oh, please," said Sandra. "Lobster taste best if you drop it alive into boiling water. I've eaten a lot of lobsters, some at the finest restaurants in the world, and they all do it the same way. The lobsters feel nothing."

Winston looked at her. "Were you a lobster?"

Sandra rolled her eyes. "Let me pour all of you a glass of wine."

"Halem," said Jamie. "You look gorgeous, like a movie star."

She flashed him a grin. "That is so thoughtful for you to say Jamie."

"It wasn't me being thoughtful. I was just saying what I saw. I thought you looked ugly at the coffee shop this morning, I told you that too."

"Jamie, what Halem meant is that when you say nice things to people, it makes them feel good," said Winston. "Like when I say, honestly, you're a boat genius. By saying it, I was trying to be thoughtful. You didn't have to say anything, even if you thought she was gorgeous, but you did and that shows your kindness."

Sandra mumbled, "Oh, pleeeease! For God's sake."

As they started to eat, things got quiet around the four full mouths.

"This lobster was even better than the one I had on the night of my prom. The melted garlic and butter are a perfect dressing for the sweet crab-meat taste."

"King crab is even better, especially when eaten on the boat, within thirty minutes of bringing it up from the bottom of the Bering Sea," added Jamie. "My dad said the best way to cook crab is to do it in the same sea water from where they came. It only needs a little lemon."

Winston asked him a series of questions about those experiences at sea with his mom and dad. Jamie told several fascinating stories, and Winston appeared to hang on every sentence.

Jamie was rather funny this evening, causing both Winston and Halem to laugh so hard that wine came out their noses. This was a side of the boy that none of them had witnessed before. The chain of adventurous fishing seasons in Alaska, however, concluded with the summer that Jamie fell into Bristol Bay. Of course, that story wasn't so amusing. A line to a fishing net wrapped around his right ankle and pulled him overboard, at least that's what his father says.

Jamie told them that he didn't remember anything but lots of crazy dreams and waking up in a hospital, feeling like he was suffocating from a tube in his throat. Halem and Sandra had heard that story too many times to count. As Halem watched Winston, she realized that he, himself, must have incredible stories to tell too, but he, kindly, was focusing on Jamie. Sandra seemed uncustomary incurious.

Once there was a pause in the conversation, as Winston went

back into the kitchen to create his surprise dessert (hot fudge cake) Jamie looked at Halem. "Are you still sad?"

"Jamie, I'll always be sad. I loved my mother and father very much and have lost them."

"Your father's dead too?" he asked, surprised.

"As I've tried to explain before... In a way, he's dead."

Jamie laughed out loud as if she was trying to be funny. "You either have died or haven't. I died but came alive again, but I never really died... at least not completely."

"My father vanished, after my mother passed, he withdrew into himself and we hardly ever talked again."

Oddly, Jamie thought that was funny too, and he gave a single burst of a loud laugh.

Winston calmly looked at him and asked, "What's so funny about that Jamie?"

"You can't disappear and still be here."

"You've seen turtles pull their heads into their shell when they are frightened?" asked Winston.

"Yeah. I had pet turtles when I was a kid."

"Humans can do the same."

Again, Jamie laughed. Winston realized that Jamie may have a hard time grasping the figurative, so he added, more literally, "Well, they don't pull their heads into their chest, and humans certainly don't have shells that you can see. But they do have invisible shells that you can't see or feel, but you can hide within them. You hide by not talking or speaking to others. When we stop communicating, we're pulling into those invisible, but sound-proof shells. That's what Halem's father did. We do it to avoid pain. But the pain eventually finds us one way or the other. It has a way of seeping in through the cracks."

Sandra, who had been silent, took a long drink of her red wine, set it down and glared at Winston, "I find it odd that you know so much about so many people. Let's turn the table and pry into your personal world. Why are you sailing around the world? Is it for the adventure, or are you running from something? Maybe the sea is your shell?"

"Well, I never thought about it like that. I could be wrong, but I don't think I'm running from anything. My parents are living in Dubai now. They were in Singapore when I left four years ago. Dad is working only part-time as a consultant. I had a rather healthy family, although Mom and Dad weren't as close as I had wished. I think it was the cultural differences. Dad was formal and dignified. Mom, being a typical Egyptian wife, gave him his space. He wasn't a close father, but Mom more than made up for this distance."

Winston paused, seeming to ponder his next words, then he spoke. "I did lose my little brother, Nigel, a few months before I took to the sea, and I'm sure that has something to do with why I started this journey, although I don't think it's correlative now. But no one has ever done me wrong or anything like that. I really, honestly, fell in love with people. I think it was the result of living all over the world at such a young age. I had to learn to make friends quickly and deeply and to embrace their personalities, cultures, quirks, and all... as well as their cultures. There was no time for weeks of small talk or superficial games. I think that's why I am the way that I am."

Halem looked at Sandra and said, "I think Winston has an uncanny gift of seeing people's hearts." She turned and looked directly at Winston. "I remember the very first night we met, you spoke of your brother in past-tense. I wanted to know more but forgot to bring it up. So, while you were focusing on my losses, I had completely ignored *yours*, and now I feel bad about that."

"That's okay," said Winston.

Sandra sat, her chair pulled out from the table, her legs crossed and her top leg bobbing up and down. She gave Halem a stern look. "You're so naïve." Then she looked at Winston. "I'm sorry about your little brother. But imagine if you're wrong about Halem."

Sandra looked back at Halem. "What if it's doing you no good to go back and rehash your mother's death?" The inflection of Sandra's voice intensified. "What if all these tears were better left unshed, and that you won't be a better person on the other side of all of this shit? Some things are left bottled up until you leave this earth for good."

Teardrops began to run down Halem's face once again.

"See," said Sandra. "I never saw her cry before, and now she cries at the drop of a hat. You can't go through life wearing your feelings on your sleeves or you'll never make it. Life is damn tough!"

Halem pushed away from the table with a screech of her chair's legs on the tiled floor. She ran back to her bedroom and slammed the door shut. The three remaining dinner partners sat in silence.

Jamie stood up. He started walking toward the door.

"Where're you going mate?"

"I don't like to be around people who are arguing. I'm going home."

Sandra looked up at him. "Oh, for Pete's sake Jamie. No one is arguing here and don't run home to tell your mommy they were. She is the biggest gossip in town."

Jamie said nothing but went out the front door, methodically latching it behind him.

Sandra mumbled something about Jamie's mother being the gossip queen of not only of Rock Harbor but of the entire Pacific Northwest.

Winston stared at Sandra, who was now looking down at the floor. Finally, she looked up, "What? What's on your mind pretty boy?"

Halem, laying on her bed clutching a Kleenex could hear every word, at least those spoken in a normal volume.

"Sandra, you're a strong woman. You came to this rough harbor town and made a success of it. You set up the coffee shop. You took in Halem, and that was very risky. I don't know much about it, but Halem mentioned that you're in charge of several big business projects in Seattle. You have the right to be proud of your accomplishments."

Winston paused to sip his water.

"But Sandra, I sense cynicism within you that must have started somewhere. People are usually born optimists but only become cynical through experiences." He then paused to see if Sandra wanted to respond.

She poured herself a fourth glass of wine, finishing off the bottle. She sipped it and her foot continued to bob as in time to an imaginary source of music.

Finally, she turned to him and said in a sudden change of tone, "Thanks for helping in the shop for the last two days. I'll pay you for your time. Is eighteen an hour enough?"

Winston nodded.

Sandra continued but with yet another abrupt change in tone, "But for now, get out of my house and leave Halem the hell alone!" She added, almost as a postscript, in a lower tone that Halem could barely make out, "You've done enough to her and now she tells me that you think it's her responsibility to save her dad. That's bullshit and nothing but a guilt trip for her. He's an adult. He can save himself if he wants to be saved. Now, we must all work to get her better."

Winston stood and said, almost metaphorically, "I can't leave my mess for you to clean up. So, let me quickly work on the kitchen, and I'll be gone."

Sandra continued sitting at the table, sipping her wine ignoring Winston's presence. Meanwhile, he worked cleaning up the dishes and the pots in the absence of gratitude from the host. He slipped out the door and into the dark hush of the night. Halem watched him from her window. As he walked toward the escalator, he paused. On this night, he looked down on the boats, now resting in the inky shadows of the surrounding bluffs. Penetrating that darkness in places were small lights leaking out from a few boat portholes onto the water. It was beautiful. The faint alpenglow of Mount Baker was still dominating the eastern sky, and the cool breeze was coming down Mount Constitution. There was no place on earth with more numinous glory.

Halem continued studying Winston through her bedroom window, peeking between her blue and white-plaid curtains. He walked to the landing where the stone stairs intersected their shelf. Double-rail metal fences framed in the landing. He stepped on the bottom of the metal rail and leaned onto the top one. He smiled and closed his eyes as if he was listening to something or just soaking up the moment. The gusts were tossing his neatly trimmed hair gently around the edges of his face. He rubbed his fingers along the top pipe of the railing.

Halem slid open her window to listen for what Winston might be hearing. Heard the squawk of a seagull high overhead. Looked up to see it, but the sky was too dark. In the forest above the town, she also heard the three hoots and then a pause of a Great Horned Owl.

Winston heard the owl too, as something was drawing his interest into the otherwise silent night air. Down below in the village, she heard faint voices. They were too far way to understand. One, however, she identified as Jamie's. He always spoke loudly and rapidly. The stone surrounding the bay held in the sounds at the harbor and magnified them like an amphitheater designed with acoustical perfection. From Halem's viewpoint, Winston was fading into just a shadow himself, but, when he turned his head, she spotted his trademark dimples, assuring her that he was in good spirits. Despite all the negativity brought to the dinner party by Sandra... it had been a good night.

Chapter Twelve

Hank

Over the next few days, everything was returning to normalcy, or so it seemed. At least Halem was back in the shop. Her disposition, while customarily quiet, seemed even to garnish fewer words than before. She didn't smile much either. The usual customers were still coming in, including Winston. There was, as always, the scattering of strangers, tourists, fishermen, and maritime vagabonds.

Winston was kind to Halem, always asking how she was doing but abandoning his typical inquisitiveness, when she offered nothing more than, "okay." He turned his penetrating focus on other customers.

Hank seemed to be the one most impervious to Winston's dialogic gestures—but Winston was persistent. He had an uncanny talent for allowing his curiosity to push him to the edge of causing hostility. Then he would back down, and the next day move the line a little deeper into the person's soul. His questions were always poignant, striking a chord within the interlocutor and it was no different with Hank.

Winston had asked Hank to join him at the bar several times, and each time he rejected the invitation. One morning, Halem served Hank's coffee at the bar in her usual fashioned, and as he was paying for it, she commented, "I think I need to remake your cappuccino.

"What's wrong with this one?"

"It didn't feel right when it came out. I was a bit distracted (she didn't share that she was distracted by Winston's presence sitting at the bar) and I don't think I knocked out the portafilter completely after the last pull."

The puzzled look on Hank's face didn't abate. She added, "In other words, I'm afraid that there were still old grounds in the portafilter when I sifted yours in. But never mind, I'll make you a perfect cup and bring it to you."

When Halem finished Hank's new cappuccino, she started around the bar, heading in his direction. Winston waved his hand to get her attention and asked quietly, as he stood up, "Can I do that?" She handed him Hank's cup. She had an intuition that it was Winston's attempt to get into Hank's head, and she was right. Winston walked over to Hank's table with the new cappuccino in hand. Fortunately, it was a close table so that Halem could listen to the conversation.

With the big earphones and watching his computer screen, the gamer was unmindful of Winston's approach—or anything going on. Rather than just setting his coffee down, like Halem would have done, Winston pushed the coffee across the table within Hank's view. Hank didn't take his eyes off his screen. Winston waited patiently for him to look up.

Hank eventually lifted his fingers from the keyboard, pulled his headset down to around his neck. "Thanks for bringing my coffee. Is there something else I can do for you?" It was a rather cold tone.

"Sure," said Winston.

Hank rubbed his eyes and sipped his steaming hot coffee softly. "So, what do ya want to know today?"

Winston reached into the front pocket of his canvas pants and pulled out a small device wrapped in the cord of earbuds. It was an old MP3 player.

"I know," said Hank. "You want to know if that's me playing the drums in *Love Buzz* or *Blew*. W*ell it wasn't. It was Chad Channing."

Winston frowned. "Oh, no. Not at all. I wanted you to hear a drum beat that I recorded in west Africa. I've never heard anything like it before. I don't know a lot about drumming, but I thought maybe you knew what this was."

Winston handed the earbuds to Hank. He inserted both buds in his ears with purpose, and then reached for the MP3 player itself. He then turned up the volume so loud that Halem could hear it from ten feet away. Hank's head started to nod, and his right foot softly tapped on the stone floor, both in time with the beat. Hank closed his eyes. Then he spoke, rather loudly, apparently not noticing the level of his voice with the music in his ears turned way up. "This is a version of Mali Bobo drumming." He paused, looked up at Winston, and removed the ear buds. "They're quite good. You recorded this *yourself*?"

"Yeah, I was in a tiny fishing village in Senegal. I think the name is Djiffer. In a way, it reminds me a lot of Rock Harbor. Geographically, it couldn't be more different. Djiffer was flat, sandy, and hot. It sits on a long spit of land, quite isolated from the rest of Senegal. I had come ashore just at the end of Ramadan. Everyone insisted that I waited until the Eid al-fitr, which is a big Muslim party, before I cast off again. Holy cow! It was a festival that went on for days. Since they rarely have outsiders, every single family requested that I be their special guest. Then, they took me up to Palmarin, a larger village on the mainland, to meet their extended families. We had this two-day celebration, and these incredible drummers were there the whole time."

Hank flashed Winston a rare smile. "It's funny, but I got my start with drumming after hearing Paul Simon's *Graceland*. I think I was about seven or eight. I fell in love with African music. Mom got me a set of bongo drums at a second-hand store. It wasn't long until I graduated to a Djembe, which she picked up at a street fair in west Seattle. Then I got my first complete drum set for my birthday when I turned ten. As they say, the rest is history."

Halem noticed Winston's face light up. Then he asked Hank, "When did you start performing, I mean really performing, in front of people?"

"I've always hated performing. I just played in my basement. I wasn't very social; coming straight home after school and drumming for hours was my escape. I loved it! But then my dad encouraged me to enter a talent contest as a freshman in high school. I was terrified. I couldn't sleep for weeks leading up to the contest. My mom and dad assumed that it would help me socially. I think it did the opposite. It was traumatic."

"Didn't do so well?"

Hank started typing on his computer, apparently logging out of the game. "I think I played horribly." He paused to sip more coffee. "Yet, I won."

Winston looked perplexed. "Won what?"

"The damn talent show! The whole thing. This was a big deal for a freshman to win, and we had a lot of talent in that big Seattle school. I had many garage bands from my school and around Seattle start contacting me, asking me to join them. I do love music, but I never wanted to perform in public, anywhere."

Halem was still at the bar, watching the two men and listening to every word they said. Her captivating glare was interrupted now and then when customers came in.

Hank sipped his coffee again. Halem realized Winston was engaging Hank in a deeper conversation than the man probably had in months, if not years.

It had started to rain with the essence of one of the Pacific Northwest's light summer squalls. Over the sound and over the foothills on the mainland, Halem could see patches of blue-gray rain forming tight patterns of parallel lines reaching from the cumulus clouds, angling down and into the sea or shore.

Hank looked back at Winston. "But I did end up joining a band. I only joined them when they told me that we were just going to play for our own enjoyment. However, we got surprisingly good. Then one night the founder came in and..." Hank paused to finish his coffee. Turned the cup upside down and slammed it on the table like a shot glass in a bar.

"With a great deal of excitement, this guy told us that he had scheduled a gig... for money. It was at a local night club. I hated it. It wasn't just for one performance but a gig every Friday and Saturday night for a month. I thought I was doing a terrible job and that the fans didn't like us, or at least, didn't like me. But toward the end of the engagement, the owner of the club pulled me aside. He told me about this young guy Kurt and his friend Krist, who were from Aberdeen, but they were performing in Seattle. They were looking for a drummer. This dude, Joey I think was his name, wanted to introduce me to them. I said no. But, without my permission, he invited Kurt and Krist to our last show. I didn't even know they were in the crowd. Of course, I'd never met them and wouldn't have recognized them. Immediately the two came up after we were done playing, about one in the morning, and pulled me to the side. They asked me, then and there, to try out for their new band. This was around '87 or maybe it was '86. Do you want to hear more?"

"Absolutely!" said Winston.

"A couple of weeks later," he said. "I took Amtrak down to Aberdeen... well to Vancouver, Washington, and Kurt picked me up in his stepmother's rabbit. We jammed for the entire weekend, literally in his dad's garage. I loved it. Those guys had a unique talent as lyricists and music writers. I was never a good writer or even a reader of music, but I could improvise anything, once the basic music score was created. Anyway, by Sunday morning, Kurt and I went out for coffee, in Portland. There he asked me to join their band. I told him I would think about it, but I was worried about public performances. The three of us drove over to the beach and spent the rest of the day playing around with kites and bottles of Tequila." Hank smiled. "I had never been a big drinker, but it did seem to calm my nerves and foul my judgment. Kurt had started drinking after his folks divorced, around age ten. I missed my return on Amtrak and missed work the following morning at a restaurant. But on that day, and I think it was while I was intoxicated, I must have told Kurt yes, that I would join them... Are you still interested?"

"Yes, yes, yes! It's an incredible story."

"Well, we started to perform around Seattle and then spending many hours in practice, and eventually at the recording studio. I didn't mind jamming or even recording, but the live performances scared the hell out of me. The boys kept me supplied in liquor, which helped with my nerves. But it was difficult to find the right amount to quieten my anxiety, without influencing my performances. Then, the demand for our concerts began to skyrocket, so much that I was having to drink heavily, almost every night. I was twenty and heading for alcoholism."

"I understand that most alcoholics end up that way because they were using liquor to self-medicate their anxiety... or depression."

"Well, that was certainly true for me. I think Kurt's demon was depression, while mine, anxiety." Hank started typing.

"Is there more?"

"Not really," said Hank without looking up.

"There has to be. So, what happened between then and now? How did you end up here?"

Hank glanced upward and sighed. "I think the whole world knows the rest of the story. I failed horribly and ran away to Rock Harbor."

The rain became more intense, ricocheting off the big clear windows.

"Blast it!" Winston cried. "I left my boat uncovered. I'll have to bail water when this storm is over."

Hank, the earphones around his head again, was plunged back into his computer screen. Winston tapped him on the arm.

"What?"

Hank looked angry. He pulled down his headphones away from his ears. The sounds of war were emanating from it.

"I just want to know more," said Winston. "Halem told me that Kurt Cobain, himself, said that you were the best drummer he ever had. So, why do you see yourself as a failure?"

Hank yanked the headset down completely around his neck again. Now he seemed quite angry. "What do you think asshole? I screwed up. I had to be so drunk to play, and the crowds were becoming enormous, that I couldn't keep a level beat, or, without the alcohol, I would be shaking so hard that I would screw up. There was no hope for me, and I had no choice but to quit, because I wasn't good enough for that level."

"Do you blame yourself?"

"Hell, yeah!" Then made a sarcastic chuckle, "Who the hell am I supposed to blame? The fans? The drums? Kurt? Fate?"

"Oh, of those, I would choose fate."

"Fate? I'm the one that couldn't handle the crowds. I have no one to blame but myself."

"I'm not so sure about that. When did *you* choose to have stage fright? When did *you* order social phobia from the personality trait store?" Winston flashed him a smile. "I suspect that you were the bravest guy on stage. You had to try despite enormous fears. The others performed with no anxiety. I bet they were just having a ball, while you were going to war with these terrible demons."

Hank said nothing, just dissipated back into the cyberworld. Winston's words still lingered in the air around him, like a lost musical note... looking for a score.

Chapter Thirteen

Ms. Van Dijk

Winston came into the shop just two days later sporting a bandage around his left hand. It didn't look like gauze, the type from a pharmacy, but more like strips of sailcloth and duct tape securing the edges. Yet, there were some blood spots soaking through, suggesting that it was clearly meant to be a dressing. Halem paused as she was frothing milk for a customer's cappuccino. The coffee connoisseur was a young woman with blond curls in natural long tight twists, giving the illusion of dreadlocks. He did not recognize her. She was getting her coffee in a paper cup, with an obvious intent of taking it with her.

"What happened to you?" Halem asked, speaking over the customer's shoulder.

"Oh, not much. I had a little accident with Billy Brown's saber saw while helping him fix his fishing boat. It'll be okay."

The customer smiled. "I'm a nurse and could look at it. Maybe you need a stitch or two."

"Oh, I've had much worse without stitches, and I'll be fine."

"Whatever you say." Picked up her cappuccino and exited the shop.

"Who was that?" Winston asked Halem as he moved up next to the ordering bar.

"I think her name is Lindsay. She stops in here now and then, coming and leaving on the water taxi from Anacortes. I don't know what her business is in Rock Harbor, and I don't ask, but I think she's a friend of Ms. Van Dijk; you know the older lady who sits at the very center of the shop."

Wiping down the steaming wand, Halem asked, "Do you think she's pretty?"

Winston raised his eyebrows. "Ms. Van Dijk? Yeah, for a woman her age, and I would guess she's at least seventy. She looks beautiful."

"No, silly! The girl who just walked out the door. She's your type. She's quite beautiful." Halem smirked.

"Maybe Ms. Van Dijk's my type?"

"You're funny. But speaking of the devil, here she comes."

Winston looked to see Ms. Van Dijk turn the corner in front of the shop. She was wearing leopard patterned leggings and a fuzzy, almost fur-like, yellow sweater. She was also donning her big pearl necklace. Sensing the need to hurry up, he said, "I'll take a flat white this morning."

"Oh, mixing it up a bit I see."

"My mom always said that variety was the spice of life. Besides, I could use a little more milk this morning as my stomach is upset from the ibuprofen, which Billy gave me for my cut hand."

"Good morning, Ms. Van Dijk," said Halem.

The lady said nothing.

Winston watched as Ms. Van Dijk gave Halem a five-dollar bill. She then walked over to her usual center table and took a seat.

Halem was working on Winston's flat white when he asked in a soft voice, "So, what's her story?"

"Oh, she's somewhat of an enigma. She comes in here Monday, Wednesday, and Fridays like clockwork, always at 10:30 a.m. She almost never speaks, and if she does, it's usually a grouchy tone. Jamie calls her 'the bitch,' after she lectured him one morning about wearing pants that were sliding down to his knees. She sits and drinks her hot cocoa, come rain, snow, or the heat of summer. She stares out the window; sometimes she brings a fashion magazine to look at. According to Sandra, she's very wealthy and well-known in the fashion world. She has a nice but simple home here. We think she comes here to design clothes without someone interrupting her. Maybe she does. I've seen her drawing on a sketch pad at times. But otherwise, she keeps to herself."

"Why does she need a nurse?" asked Winston.

"Who said anything about needing a nurse?"

"Lindsay, who was just here, you said is a friend of Ms. Van Dijk's and Lindsay just told me, and I think you heard her, that she's a nurse. She comes here on a regular basis. I don't think, with her Scandinavian complexion, that Lindsay is related to Ms. Van Dijk, who is dark-skinned, and I suspect is of either Jewish or Arab descent... or maybe Armenian. So, that leaves me to think that she's here to visit Ms. Van Dijk for professional reasons, and a nurse wouldn't be here to talk fashion. It would have to relate to Ms. Van Dijk's health."

"You're incredible, a regular Sherlock Holmes. I mean, seriously, you're one of the most observant men I've ever met. Maybe you should think about going into law-enforcement. You would make a great detective."

Winston shook his head. "Never."

Halem handed him his flat white and then turned to work on Ms. Van Dijk's hot cocoa. Halem heated a frothing pitcher full of whole milk and poured in a dark cocoa powder.

Winston stared at the lady from across the room while Halem continued working on her beverage. Then she asked, "Not to change the subject, but what does this cut on your hand do to your rowing?"

"Well, that's a good question. It was cut deep, but we cleaned it well and put an antibiotic ointment on it. If I took off across the sea rowing now, it would open, get salt, sand, and who knows what kinds of germs in it and for certain I would get a nasty infection. So, it looks like I'll be here for a little longer, until it heals up enough, that I don't have to worry about the constant grinding and twisting of the wooden oar handles against my palms."

A broad smile swept across Halem's face. She finished the cocoa and started to walk around the bar to hand-deliver it to Ms. Van Dijk. Winston grabbed her wrist. "Let me do that," he said.

Halem handed Winston the hot cocoa. "Don't waste your time with her. She doesn't talk to anyone but keeps to herself."

"That's what puzzles me. I'd like to know why."

He sat down across from Ms. Van Dijk and slid the drink in her direction. Her eyes were fixed on the morning sun in the distant North Cascades.

Halem was dying to hear this conversation, so she grabbed the spiral manual to the roaster and took it to the table just next to the lady. She sat down and pretended to study the manual, while she was really studying Ms. Van Dijk and the conversation, she, unknowingly, was about to embark upon with Winston.

She was a thin, dark woman, maybe five-foot-six with an aquiline nose. Her hair was dyed coal-black with gray roots starting to appear. She wore well-proportioned and tastefully applied makeup and eyeliner with eyelashes enhanced with black mascara. She had just a touch of pink on her cheeks, Portofino Red lipstick, and she smelled of rose pedals, reflecting a high-end perfume. Halem had always wanted to ask her for advice in her own makeup.

Ms. Van Dijk looked at Winston. "What do you want?" Her voice was stern and loud enough that Halem could have heard it from the bar.

"Uh, hi, my name's Winston." He reached across the table to shake her hand.

She did not reciprocate. "Yes, everyone knows who you are, but what do you want from me?"

"I just would like to know more about you."

She sipped her cocoa, wiping the sticky remains of a marshmallow off her red lip with a napkin and resumed her stare out the window

"I want to hear all about your cancer," he said.

Halem felt shocked that he would say something like that. Was he right?

Ms. Van Dijk's cup rattled on the saucer in her hand. Her mascara-thickened eyelashes batted. "So, you're a damn reporter. I told them in New York I wasn't having this conversation."

"No, I'm not a reporter. I'm not here to do a story about you or your cancer."

"No one here knows about that." She pointed to his nose. "Not

Halem, not Sandra... no one in this damn town. So, if you're not from New York, how do you know?"

"It's simply a deduction. I just met Lindsay, your nurse..."

"What did she say? She can't talk about my health to anybody!"

"Oh, no, no, no Ms. Van Dijk, Lindsay told me nothing, except she was a nurse. She wanted to look at my hand." He held up his bandaged mitt. "When she left, I asked Halem who she was, and she mentioned that she had been seen with you, but otherwise no one knew who she was. So, I just figured she comes here to check on you as a nurse. She certainly doesn't look related to you. A nurse wouldn't be coming here to talk fashion with you, not unless you're now designing fancy scrubs." He smiled. "So, I reasoned that you must have some serious chronic illness. I thought that it might be dementia, however that didn't make sense. You are so punctual, at least according to Halem. You are so well-groomed and dressed, like you were ready to walk the catwalk. I knew that you had all your mental facilities. So, it must be cancer. I thought about which type... and I arrived at leukemia. Am I right?"

"No, you're dead wrong! It's colon... stage four and incurable."

Winston drew back with a deep frown on his face. "I'm so sorry."

"That's it? No big advice about how you know some great doctor or nutritional supplement that can save me?"

"No, I would never say that. You would have found such on your own if one existed. I just feel your pain, the pain of your suffering, which I can't begin to imagine."

"Hell, no you can't!" She paused and sipped her drink. "You're wasting your time here, son, you're talking to a dead woman. I'm no more than a walking corpse... a fucking zombie."

"I beg to differ. The Ms. Van Dijk that I'm talking to seems very much alive to me."

The two of them then sat in silence, watching the sunlight dance over the clouds. Halem turned to look at what they were looking at.

"I would imagine that if all your cancer cells were cut out of your body," Winston said, "it would weigh, what? A pound? And how much do you weigh?"

"My weight? I'm down to one hundred and five pounds. I was one hundred and thirty before all this shit."

"So, your cancer is less than one percent of your weight, leaving ninety-nine percent of you as a very alive and healthy, Ms. Van Dijk, no different than you were fifty years ago."

"Bullshit! It's just an illusion, a damn delusion. I've checked out. I'm gone. I'm just sitting here taking up space and oxygen. I have no meaning to this fucking world anymore, just decades of old moth-eaten clothes in old women's closets... clothes that their grandkids play dress-up with, but which never appear at parties anymore."

"Kids playing dress up isn't so bad."

She just rolled her eyes and sipped her cocoa.

"Are you done fighting this?"

"Hell, yeah. I've clocked out of this life. I've come to Rock Harbor as my Aokigahara, my Sea of Trees, you know, the forest on the flanks of Mount Fuji, where people go to die." She wiped her lips with the Portofino red-stained napkin. "But don't worry, it won't be messy. No one here will have to know. Lindsay will take care of everything. The private hospice group that she works with have even given me the drugs I need to kill my pain—and my body if I want, what's left of it. They will zip me up in a black, plastic bag and take me by boat to Seattle, where I'll become compost for a redwood sapling. That'll be my contribution to this fucking world, a beautiful redwood tree that will rebreathe the oxygen I've taken. So, I'll owe no one nothing."

"How did you come to this decision to quit fighting? Did your doctors give up too?"

"No, they offered me the opportunity to enter some new trials... but I turned them down. But you've got to understand why I did. I asked my husband, Azrael, what he thought. 'Should I enter a study?' I asked him. Do you know what he said?"

Winston shook his head. Ms. Van Dijk touched his hand. Her finger felt ice cold. "My husband said to me, 'Do what you like, dear. I'll leave it up to you, dear.'" She turned back to the window.

"What did you want him to say?"

She sat up. "I wanted him to fall down on the damn apartment floor, crawl to me, grab me by my ankles, cry into my socks, and beg me to try anything that might add a few more days to my miserable life… but no, he didn't. He just said what I said he said and walked out of our bedroom."

"Did that make you feel like he didn't care?"

"Oh, he cares. He cares a lot, just not about me. I mean, when I was still in the hospital after my bowel obstruction, and the doctors had just told us that horrible news that I had metastatic colon cancer, Azrael started to take these long drives into Connecticut or out to Long Island, just to 'clear his head' about the fact that I had life-threatening cancer. So, I was thinking it was an empathetic suffering, but… it was more narcissistic. He was mourning his own loss of me and how that would interfere with the big plans for *his* life."

Winston sipped the last of his coffee and asked, "How do you know what he was feeling."

She laughed. "Well, do you know where Azrael is right now?"

Winston shook his head.

"He's somewhere in Tuscany," she went on. "We bought an old stone ruin of a farmhouse there twenty years ago. A long and narrow road crosses the hills leading up to it, lined on both sides with tall Lombardy poplars and past vineyards all in neat rows. We had a plan to restore it and to live there in retirement. It's perched high on a hill with incredible views of the countryside and an ancient olive grove on its northside. One old gnarly tree next to the ruin has the diameter of a wagon wheel. A neighbor guessed it was over a thousand years old. It appears that he's in the process of restoring the house now… and has a lovely Italian woman as his personal, and I assume 'very personal,' assistant helping him. Do you know how I know?"

Winston shook his head again.

"You see, I have two daughters," she continued. "Hannah and Leah. Hannah manages our Milano… I mean Milan, Italy, store and Leah manages our Manhattan shop. A few months after I moved to

Rock Harbor, Hannah called me and told me that her dad had been there, and that he was living in our old farmhouse with this woman. He'd moved on already. So, you see, I don't exist anymore."

"I bet your daughters adore you. They're in the same profession as you, aren't they? So, they're following in your footsteps."

"I'm not so sure," said Ms. Van Dijk as she gulped her last bit of hot cocoa. "Within months of getting my shocking news, they started to call me and to say, 'We need to have a meeting.' I assumed it was for them to tell me how much they loved me and would stand by me no matter how bad the suffering got. It wasn't about that. It turned out that they wanted to have a meeting to discuss the business because I'm still a majority owner, and that we needed to transfer the ownership before I 'became incapacitated.'" She made air quotes with her fingers. "When I realized what the meeting was all about, I stood up and said to them, 'Screw you! I'll write in my will that my whole enterprise will be liquidated, and the proceeds given to the Wildlife Foundation,' and then I walked out the door. I went back to our midtown apartment alone. I don't remember where Azrael was, maybe he was already in Italy or on one of his fucking drives, I can't remember. But that wasn't the last straw. The last straw came later that day." She puckered her lips as if she were done speaking.

"And then what?"

"I went out to the Whole Foods Market to buy myself something really nice to have for dinner, and some good wine. I had been on a terrible diet for weeks, having to have part of my bowels hanging outside of my abdomen, like a freak show star, and a stinky collection bag taped over it. But as I got to the market, I saw my best friend, Elizabeth, going in the door ahead of me. She was the first person I had called months earlier when I got my diagnosis. Once inside, I couldn't find her. I was going to invite her to come home with me to share dinner. We have eaten together countless times over the years and had always loved being with her. I think she loved being with me when I was alive. Anyway, I was at the frozen food locker, with my hand on the chrome handle, ready to open it when I looked up and saw Elizabeth's reflection on the door, as plain as if it was a polished mirror. I saw her walk up behind me and then suddenly stop in her tracks when she realized it was me. Then she slowly backed up and walked away. She didn't want to talk to me. But she wasn't the first. I had noticed that since my diagnosis, people stopped seeing me. They would look past me. They would walk up and talk to Azrael as if I were his briefcase or umbrella by his side. They saw and cared about him and how my disease was affecting him, but I was a ghost already. I was the milk jug with an expiration date stamped on the neck, a day that had already passed."

She paused, closing her eyes. "I went home after the experience at Whole Foods, and I think it was a cumulation of all those things, that I cried my eyes out for hours, realizing that I was all alone in this journey, and in the world's eyes, I was dead already. I finished off a $1000 bottle of Château Pape Clément Red. I declared myself dead that night; it was more like the realization that the world had already declared me deceased, and I haven't looked back. There's been no more tears and no room for self-pity. When I'm finally gone, Azrael, Elizabeth, and my daughters will all read about it in the paper in the same way the stranger will, down on the Lower East Side. Fuck them all!"

Winston put his hand over hers. She grasped his fingers within her fist, showing a return to his gesture of sympathy. Halem walked back to the bar in disbelief of what she was hearing. She got herself a glass of water and returned to her table.

"I've got to go," said Ms. Van Dijk. "I'm tired."

Winston smiled. "Ms. Van Dijk..."

"Call me 'Ronnie.' That's my first name."

"Okay, Ronnie. With my injury, it looks like I'll be sticking around another week or two. I would love to meet you here or come by your place and listen to all the details of your life. I want to hear about your diagnosis, your treatments, and mostly how you feel. I want to know about your previous dreams and how those have been interrupted. I want to hear about the pain it causes you to pull your colostomy bag loose from your sensitive skin. I want to hear about the pain in your bones that keep you awake at night, the nausea from the chemo, and I want to hear how you're feeling, emotionally. I want it all, and I've no time limits."

Ronnie smiled. "You're a sweet boy."

"Listening is the occupation of the companion of those in grief... and we'll all eventually have loss."

Tears filled Ms. Van Dijk's eyes.

"If you could have anything right now, what would it be?" asked Winston. "Any wish... besides the obvious of being cured?"

"If I could have anything," she said, thinking. "I would bring my dear mother back. She was a survivor of the Nazis. She was taken first to Amersfoort in The Netherlands. She watched her parents being shot in the head in their home in Jodenbuurt when they resisted their arrest; her nine-year-old brother thrown into a bonfire of kerosene-soaked Hebrew books, alive, in the street in front of their house. He crawled out, screaming, and engulfed in fire, and the Nazi SS guards picked him up again and threw him back on the fire like he was a worthless piece of wood. His crime? Becoming hysterical after watching them shoot his parents. She was only eleven when she witnessed this horror."

Ronnie paused, thinking again. "But she was cursed in other ways too. She was a very pretty girl, dark black Semitic hair, and blue Dutch eyes. For that, they raped her in the back of the truck on the way to the camp, those filthy animals did. She was raped again at the camp by the nice Lutheran guards. She eventually was transferred to Herzogenbusch camp, which was run by the SS.

"Mom was a very strong woman," she went on. "I would bring her back and clamber up into her big warm lap, smell the jasmine that incessantly hung in her black hair, and let her hold me. She would stroke my cheek with the back of her tender hand and promise to protect me. She had stood up to the worst monsters this planet has ever produced, spitting in their faces when the Russians liberated her camp. So, I knew that nothing could get to me while on her invincible lap. She knew pain so she could feel mine, even a skinned knee. She loved me unconditionally. She told me many times that the only reason she survived was so that she could pass life on to me."

She paused to gather her thoughts and then continued, "Somehow, that woman came out of the nightmare with her faith intact. As soon as I heard her stories—while still a little girl—I lost mine. What god could have allowed this? It would be either a god who is cruel, one who is impotent, or one who is ignorant. So, God makes no sense to me, not then, not now."

Winston took her hand again. "I'll come to your house," he said. "We can sit on your porch, and you're welcome to climb upon my lap, and while not as brave as your mother, or as empathic, I will hold you as long as you want to be held."

Ronnie chuckled. "Now, wouldn't we be the talk of the town?"

Winston met her laugh. "I don't care. We'll both be leaving this town soon and who cares what people think. I understand completely how difficult it is for you, to imagine a god who could let these bad things happen. That's exactly how I felt when I lost my little brother to an avalanche in a mountaineering accident in Indian Kashmir. It is for that bottomless grief that I took to the sea. My going to sea was an act of suicide. But I survived the Indian Ocean, the pirates of Somalia, the stormy Southern Ocean, the intense crossing of the Atlantic, and even the drug cartels of Central America. But it was during the weeks of profound solitude on the water that I came to terms with God. It became for me a quandary. While the idea of a god presents the problem of evil that you have so clearly alluded to, but to live without God means that all of us... " he looked around the coffee shop, "are nothing but walking corpses. This entire planet Earth is our Aokigahara, where we've come to die. We're made up of protoplasm wrapped in a cellular membrane but assembled from chunks of lifeless chemistry. If there's nothing on the other side, then there can be nothing on this side... just an illusion of life... a mirage of meaning. That made even less sense to me than a god who allows evil."

Ronnie let her right hand fall out of his. "Here's something you could do for me… if you really want. You could take me sailing in that little boat of yours. Can you take me out to be with the sunset?"

"Absolutely!"

She smiled. "When Azrael and I were first married, we were so in love. It was 1970, and there was so much hope in the air… despite that awful Asian war. I had just returned from fashion school in Paris, and we were married in New York. I hardly knew him as our parents had done the matching. My dad wanted a good Jewish boy for me, one that could guarantee me a life free from want. Azrael was just finishing law school at Columbia, and his parents wanted a pedigree of not just a Jewish girl, but one with a Dutch-Jewish descent. But we fell in love anyway, one with the other." She cleared her throat. "After the wedding we took his father's sailboat and sailed down to the Caribbean, for three whole months. Who has the luxury of a three-month honeymoon these days? Now, they just take a long weekend." She chuckled. "But it was magic for us, more than any fairytale that I'd ever imagined. We swam in the turquoise bath-warm waters. We laid on the oiled teak deck under the buttery sun. We had no worries, but it was endless love making and passion. We ate fresh fruit from the harbors; we ate fish and shrimp, which we caught. That woman, that signora, maybe she can give him pleasure now, that this dead body of mine can no longer give, but she can never love him like I did… or like he did me. He was totally in love with me and a woman has a way of knowing that. We can see it in our men's eyes and feel it with their tender touches. I just don't know what the hell happened to him now."

Winston responded in a soft voice. "I don't know, either. I always say that people in times of crisis often make mistakes in their choices and, considering the crisis, deserve extra grace. But I also feel angry at him… and those daughters of yours. I think they still love you, but within their own pain, they've made some bad, insensitive choices. I will take you in my sailboat and wrap you in my arms and a warm blanket, and we'll sail into that Salish Sea's dusk. We'll touch that buttery sun and let it melt and run through our fingers, dripping into the watery abyss."

"Azrael, you know he was a lawyer, used to say about sunsets… that it was the sun's closing arguments about a glorious day." She paused, looked around the café. "I really must go. I don't feel well."

"Maybe you should invite Halem to take this journey with you."

Halem felt shocked.

Ronnie looked perplexed. "Why would you say something like that?"

"You would be surprised. I believe it would be good for you… and for her. I think she could be that daughter that you don't have close right now. She may be that person who might fall at your ankles, cry into your socks, and beg you to fight this horrible disease a little longer. But I'm certain, if you give her a chance, she will grow to love you."

Chapter Fourteen

Sandra

Sandra was sitting in her red Adirondack chair under the disk of the yellow sun suspended in an impeccable sky. She sipped her morning coffee. Oddly, while she was truly a coffee elitist, she relied on her Keurig rather than facing the public at the shop for a world-class, hand-crafted brew from Halem's artisan hand. Sandra was not a morning person and enjoyed the peace that Rock Harbor afforded her. She was watching Winston work on his boat with her bird-watching binoculars. She observed him methodically move from side to side, inside the boat and out. He mentioned at the dinner party that a hole had opened beneath his portside gunwale. He was bending over, shirt off, with his sweat-drenched back facing up the bluff.

Winston shifted back and forth under that bright morning sun. At times, Sandra found him to be quite attractive. *What woman wouldn't?* Even though he was a little more than half her age. But, for reasons she didn't fully understand, she had no interest in moving closer even as a friend but preferred going to battle with him. She realized that it was a bit Freudian to feel this sexual attraction to the man she wanted to fight with. She was drawn to fight with him as a strange, sensual-social tango. While mysterious, handsome, and with a constant demeaner of kindness, something about him pissed her off. For one, she really was angry about what he had done to Halem. Before he had dug into her past, Halem was quiet and serene. Sandra had this growing feeling that he was up to something no good. He seemed too good to be true. Her father, a navy captain, used to always tell her, "Anything that seems too good to be true usually isn't."

When Winston tried to bring up Sandra's own past and connecting that to her distrust for men, she batted away the comment as soon as he said it. She realized this morning that deflection was for a reason. She did have her own secrets, that only her little sister knew about. But she asked herself the honest question, is this why she feels attracted to Winston and hates him at the same time?

The event in her life, at age fifteen was undeniably a defining moment. But it was so private that she never spoke about it to anyone, save her sister.

Sandra was seeing a shrink as she was preparing to ask Bret for a divorce. It was a hard move against a powerful man, and—while being a strong woman—she knew she needed the emotional support that a shrink could offer. This psychiatrist tried to dig into her past, but this secret was impermeable to his snooping.

She didn't want to remember the painful experience, even to herself. Yet, it was constantly haunting her like an unwelcomed friend. This morning she chose to reminisce over those painful events, to take this out of her soul for a rare walk in the light. Part of that reflection was because she wanted to know, herself, if those things were linked to her present distrust of Winston. It would be most unfair to him if her distrust stemmed from another man.

And it *was* another man, much like Winston, but with golden blond hair. Like many fifteen-year-old girls, she had a crush. Hers was on Wayne. At seventeen, he was big for his, or any age. He was their school's quarterback. He had never given Sandra a glance and certainly didn't know her name... until that infamous day. Maybe he didn't even know it then?

Sandra was showing her rabbits for 4-H at the Snohomish county fair. To her shock, Wayne came into their barn. His family were dairy farmers and were in another barn with their animals. She remembered her heart fluttering when she saw his tall, curly-haired head in the crowd. What would she say? Her father, the Captain, always taught her to be brave and tough. She decided to speak to Wayne.

"Hey Cougar [their school mascot] want to see the world's best Flemish Giant?"

Wayne walked over and looked at the rabbit she was holding on her lap, her in a rocking chair, blue ribbon pinned on the cage beside them. Sandra remembered holding her rabbit up and saying, "Lilly's twenty-five pounds and champion. She's from a strong pedigree. Her father won the state and her mother was a runner-up. I bred them myself."

Wayne snickered as he padded Lilly's head. "How'd you know I'm a Cougar?"

"Cause, I'm one too!" She smiled big.

Sandra reflected on how she explained who she was, and he admitted then that he recognized her. But in her confident nature, she decided to say something flirtatious, and to not waste such a moment. Looking back, she realized how corny, and naive it was.

"I would give *you* a blue ribbon for your fine pedigree. Do you have a football poster of yourself that I can hang on my wall?"

He just stood looking at her. Then he said something incredible, "Wanna go for a picnic?"

A soft smile came across Sandra's face that sunny morning as she thought about how euphoric she felt at that moment long ago.

"Yes," she said to Wayne. "But I have to stay here until noon."

She was coasting on moonbeams for the next hour. *Would Wayne Jenkins really come and take her on a picnic?* She could not wait to tell all her friends. They wouldn't believe it. *Was this the beginning of a relationship? An eventual marriage?*

He did come. She packed two sandwiches and pieces of rhubarb pie, which her mother had made for the fair. She put the pieces of pie in two small boxes and then into her bag. He led her through the fairgrounds, then by the racetrack, her carrying the sack with their lunch, and up a path to a large wooded hill; at the top of which, they came to a clearing. She remembers a circle of large rocks enclosing ashes and a few pieces of garbage. While she was still soaking in the atmosphere of this secret spot and without any provocation, Wayne knocked her to the ground. Hard. The sack flew out of her hand. Immediately he was on top of her like a wild wolf. He ripped off her shirt and buttons went flying. He pulled her bra up to her neck. With his brute force he pinned her against the dirt, and she can still feel the rocks cutting into the skin of her back.

This all happened so fast that her fifteen-year-old mind could not process it. Was it some type of joke? A trick? A roughhousing? A rape? It couldn't be... or could it? It came so quickly, yet it seemed like an eternity. She barely grasped what was happening to her until it was over. With her pants ripped open and pulled down, her laying in the dirt feeling devastated, Wayne did one last cruel thing. He reached over, grabbed a piece of glass from the fire pit. He held it to her throat. "If you breathe one word of this to anybody, I will ruin you. I will cut your damn head off. He stood up, fastened then dusted off his jeans. As she was scrambling to cover herself for modesty's sake; Wayne looking down on her, said something like, "You don't get a ribbon for *that* performance Susan... you pathetic little rabbit fucker." Then walked away, eating the rhubarb pie, which he had picked off the ground on his way out of the clearing. She remembers whispering, "Sandra... my name is Sandra."

The only reason her sister was privy to this horrible event in her life was because she was home when Sandra came running up to her bedroom, her flannel shirt barely able to stay on because it was so torn.

She decided then that this horrendous experience would never leave her heart to anyone else's ears. That she would be strong and endure.

Is that why she doesn't trust Winston? Tears were forming in her eyes, so she quickly let the memory go back to its lead-clad vault.

As Sandra studied the man, him working on his boat under the beat of the sun, she had a flight of ideas, mostly centered around the question, "What if?" What if Halem becomes so swept away with Winston that she is devastated when he leaves. What if he takes her with him? What if he does something bad to Jamie? What if he steals all the money from the coffee shop... or from Halem... or from a coffee shop regular? What if he rapes Halem with brute force? That was her fear when she first saw them laying under the bar on her tearful night in the coffee shop.

On impulse, she went into the house and turned on her laptop at the kitchen table. She first searched for "Winston in a rowboat." The only thing that came up was a novel, *The Rowboat Robbers*, by Winston B. Philpott. Halem passed through the kitchen, on her way to work, she said her "Good morning." Sandra indiscreetly turned her laptop to shield her screen. "Halem, where did Winston say he was before coming here?"

"Roche Harbor... why do you ask?"

"Oh, I was just curious." She paused as Halem stood in silence then opened the refrigerator and poured herself a glass of orange juice. "I mean, before that. Before Roche Harbor, where was he?"

Halem finished her juice and washed out the glass in the sink. "I think he came to Roche Harbor from Victoria. He had sailed from Port Townsend to Victoria the week before. Then before that, he spent several weeks in Port Angeles. Do you need more?"

"No, that's helpful."

Halem looked angry. "Helpful for what? Are you spying on him?"

Sandra closed the laptop.

"You don't trust him, do you?" asked Halem

Sandra didn't want to engage further in the conversation. She simply gave Halem a glance and then her eyes moved to the window. She studied a faint double rainbow forming over on the interior until she heard Halem leave.

Sandra searched for a Facebook page for Port Angeles. She found several for independent businesses and stumbled onto the "What's Happening in Port Angeles" page. She hesitated then typed: "Does anyone know a Winston who came into town on a skiff a few weeks ago? Then he sailed or rowed on to Port Townsend. I'm a friend and trying to find him." She felt bad for lying, so she typed, "He left something valuable here and I need to find him to return it."

She posted a similar statement on Craig's List.

Sandra let the requests "soak" for a few days before returning to Facebook and Craig's List. On Craig's List she received a personal message from a girl, who went by the name "Blossom." She said that she met Winston when he was in Port Angeles and wanted to know what Sandra wanted with him.

Sandra typed back, "He left a box of documents that I think he needs. What did you think of him? Was he nice? Did he con anyone out of anything?"

It was five days before she heard anything from Blossom. "Do you mean, was he good in bed? If so, yeah, he was. He was very charming and then he conned everyone."

This didn't sound like Winston, but, then again, he had only been in Rock Harbor for a few weeks. Yet, at the same time, her worst fears were that he was a con-man and maybe a womanizer. But now she regretted asking such a blatant question, "Did he con anyone?" because it was leading. But now she wanted to know more. She typed back, "How did he con everyone?"

Blossom replied a few days later. "He took our money, a lot of it. Do you know where he is? Can you help us get our money back?"

Several good winds had come and gone, and Winston's hand appeared to be healing well, yet, for some reason, he kept hanging around. Sandra felt that his tardiness to get back on the sea could mean he was up to something... something not so good.

Sandra felt like she was standing where two opposing currents meet, one warm and one cold. She would feel sick if there was a chance that Winston was about to con them all. It would break Halem's heart to pieces, at least what was left of it. Yet, Sandra would feel vindicated if indeed Winston wasn't the man he seemed, as most men aren't.

Blossom continued to correspond over the following week, sharing more details with each message. Sandra felt the time had come for her to confront both Halem and Winston, before he left town, and that could be soon.

Chapter Fifteen

Downfall

Ten days had passed after the morning encounter in the kitchen between Sandra and Halem about Winston's previous stops. Halem was getting back to normal with no visible signs of mourning for her mother, although her demeanor was more subdued. Winston had been busy getting his boat ready for departure, taking more hikes on the mountain, and doing odd jobs for other villagers. His rowing hand had healed up nicely. He had taken a two-day trip with Kane to visit Eastsound and their bookstore. He came back with a box of old classic novels and one nonfiction book about a woman, a "Barnacle Betty," from Anacortes, who had canoed all the way to Ketchikan. He seemed more aloof, spending more time with Jamie, Kane, and even Hank than her. She had to eavesdrop to hear all that he was up to and the way he was planning for his trip north.

His boat was now fully refurbished, and the crack patched. He had packed in about 10 pounds of smoked salmon, a couple of tubs of peanut butter, and salted peanuts in the shell. The mariner's weather forecast predicted steady westerly gales for the near future, riding in on the prevailing winds of late August. Halem knew that Winston was long over-due to escape, to be reclaimed by the sea. The sea had brought him to her, and now she had to give him back. She felt the grief rising, slowly percolating upward within her chest with each gust of wind or each time she saw Winston put his boat out in the harbor for a local trip. It was different than the previous mourning period but no less intense.

After work one evening, Sandra was waiting on Halem at the kitchen table with a bottle of Italian wine. Sprinkles had driven her inside from her outside chairs. Halem was late. At a quarter past six, she came through the door with wet shoulders. Sandra looked outside. The raindrops had become intense. Sandra's solemn presence at the table startled Halem. She felt like it was an ambush.

"I thought you must be roasting. I was waiting outside for you with some wine, but a few raindrops started to fall, and I came inside."

"No, I needed to do a thorough cleaning. I had left a lot of dirt under the mats, in the drawers, and under the flowerpots."

"Really?"

Halem nodded. "Uh, what's up?"

"Sit down girl. I have something to tell you."

Halem took a seat at the table, and Sandra poured her a glass of wine. Then she leaned back in her wooden chair and tossed her white bangs out of her face.

Halem had never seen Sandra so serious-minded. She stopped making eye contact with her and looked down, studying the checkerboards of the kitchen floor.

"Halem, I've contacted someone in Port Angeles who met Winston. It appears she was intimate with him."

Halem frowned. "Really?" She could feel her heart skipping beats. That news hurt, and she wasn't sure why. She had no claim on Winston whatsoever, and his private life was none of her business. If this was true, Winston apparently did not oppose a relationship with a woman after all... just with her. She had never expected more, nothing outside the dimensions of a contemptible dream.

"Yeah, sounds like it. They had a sexual relationship at least. He was there for a few weeks."

Halem's eyes grew watery, which embarrassed her. She quickly wiped her eyes with her shirt sleeve. She used to never cry and now tears came so easily.

"That's not all, Halem."

"I'm sure you had more to tell me than trivial facts about Winston's personal life."

"I do. It appears that Winston swindled her and several other people out of a lot of money."

"Really? I can't believe that. He's never asked for money from anyone. Are you sure?"

"But you told me you haven't been with him as much as before. Who knows what he's talking about with Kane or Hank or, may God forbid, Jamie? But the other thing is that I spotted him taking Ms. Van Dijk out through the rift in his boat the other night. It was bizarre. She was all snuggled into the bow, wrapped in a blanket, and Winston with his arm around her like two young love birds or her a cougar and him her prey… or more likely, him a fox and she *his* prey. The only thing I could think of was that he was putting the moves on her. She's worth millions and would be an easy target for swindler. It just didn't look right."

"I don't believe it. I mean I don't know why he was with Ms. Van Dijk, except that he had coffee with her a couple of weeks ago and they seem to have gotten along very well. But Winston gets along with everybody. She has cancer, so I overheard, and I think he was going to take her sailing. I just don't believe that he's up to something cunning."

Sandra flashed a cynical smile. "Well, the lady in Port Angeles seems to know what she's talking about."

They sat in silence until Sandra looked out the window, down on the harbor. "Look at that rainbow," said Sandra. "I just saw a double one the other day."

Halem gave a quick glance to the harbor and said nothing about it. The rainbow was beautiful, arching off the mountain and down into the sea. But it was meaningless to Halem. The whole, external world was completely meaningless.

After a couple of minutes, Halem asked, "So, how did he do this? How did he swindle people out of their money?"

Sandra shook her head. "I don't know the details. It's complicated, and Blossom said it had something to do with an investment in his father's African gold mine, with a promise of a fifty percent return on their money within a couple of months. Once he got the money, he sailed off in the pitch of dark."

"Blossom? That's the lady's name? You must be joking."

"Yeah… or at least that's her online name."

Halem shook her head. "Sounds like a hooker."

"No, she's a twenty-eight-year-old business owner. She has a pet sitting service and owns a small vintage clothing shop. I think they started calling her Blossom when she was a florist."

"How do you know all of this? Have you met her?"

"Not yet. We corresponded online, and then we talked on the phone. I'm going over this week in my boat to meet her. She wants me to bring the two grand that Winston took from her."

Halem gave Sandra a stern gaze. "I know that Winston doesn't have that kind of money on him. I just can't comprehend him making up a story about a gold mine. Are you sure it's not Blossom trying to swindle *you*?"

"Well, I doubt if I could get the money from him, unless I had a brute that threatened to break his rowing arm. So, I've decided to take her two thousand dollars of my own money and tell her it's from Winston."

"Why?"

"Why what?"

"Why would you give a complete stranger two thousand dollars, with no proof that Winston had taken it from her?"

"Halem, I don't need proof. I've been around this world a lot longer than you have, and there's no man that's that good, who meddles in other people's lives without some foul intent… believe me, I know. Besides, two thousand dollars may sound like a lot, but really, it's chump change to me."

Halem shook her head. She looked up at the rainbow again. It was starting to fade as the expanding sunlight bleached out the brilliant colors. She remembered when she was still a little girl and her father would read her books about rainbows, pots of gold, and unicorns. Life seemed magical to her then, filled with so many dreams and hopes. Now, life was covered with dread, a long line of hardships, disappointments, and grief about what could have been.

Before Halem had finished her thought, Sandra said, "That's not all, Halem."

"What else could there be?"

"I also talked to Bret, he told me that there was no way that Winston rowed and sailed that little skiff of his from Singapore, around Africa, across the Atlantic, around South America, and up the Pacific coast. He said that there has been a handful of people who have rowed or sailed skiff-like boats across the Atlantic, but it's a big deal. They have sponsors. They're in the news and set records. He is one hundred percent confident that Winston is lying about that. Bret certainly is an expert when it comes to men lying."

"But Winston's not a proud guy. He would never seek the limelight. He doesn't need sponsors."

Sandra touched Halem's arm. "Halem dear, wake up. Finn fooled you and so has Winston."

Implying that Halem was a sucker for lying men made her angry. She didn't want to talk about it anymore and left. Went down the walkway to the escalator, climbed up to the fifth level and continued walking up the mountain road. Headed up the side of Mount Constitution alone as dusk was sweeping down the mountainside to greet her. She stumbled home later in the pitch of night.

As the next few days passed, Winston only warmed up to Halem slightly. She felt like she had disappointed him. She let her mind meander through the possibilities. Maybe he was just busy with all the other "project" people he was working with, now that he was successful in getting Halem to mourn for her mother. Maybe, just maybe, Winston was starting to feel something romantic toward her, and it was his way to prepare for his departure, by pulling back. But she knew that was just her wishful thinking. Most likely, there was something inherently wrong with her, something offensive, that would make him not want to spend time with her now that he knew her better. She always felt she was too ordinary both in appearance and personality. That had to be it.

Halem feared that Sandra would confront Winston and that would seal his departure and doom their relationship. He had been known, according to his own travel tales, to leave a place in the middle of the night to avoid too many painful goodbyes and to catch the shifting breezes at sunrise.

Even though Sandra had been successful in sowing doubts within her, Halem knew too, that she had fallen in love with the man, and the thoughts of Winston infused her every waking thought. More so than with Finn or anyone. This was totally different. She thought Finn might be as good as it gets. But Winston, at least up until this point, had been a man far beyond her greatest aspirations for a soulmate. It was the stuff of fairytales like her father used to read to her. But if what Sandra said was true, that he had at least a sexual, if not romantic relationship with this Blossom girl, then clearly the reason he didn't pursue Halem wasn't because of his mission of completely circumnavigating the globe without romantic entanglement, but because he found her to be too plain. She hated her mundane-ness yet feared taking the risks required to escape it.

The next morning, Halem watched Winston rowing out through the rift. Her heart sank and tears began to flow. But then, as he was deeply into the rift and the morning sun was piercing the outer entrance, the silhouette made it clear that the rower was not alone. The bulky frame beside Winston had to be Jamie. Surely, Winston would not row or sail away with Jamie on board... or would he? Maybe he was heading to Alaska with Jamie as his guide.

Later, she learned from Dale that the two men had gone out only to fish. Winston did carve out time for Halem after his return late in the afternoon. He came into the coffee shop after all the other customers, save one, were gone.

He brought Halem a large chinook salmon on a string through its gills. She thanked him but did not want the smell in the coffee shop, so she ran it down to Sandra's house and dropped it in the sink, washed the slimy scales off her hands, and quickly returned. Being a fishing village, it certainly wasn't the first salmon to inhabit Sandra's stainless-steel sink.

While walking back to the shop, she reflected on how she was in a place of emotional purgatory, not knowing what to do. Beside feeling that Winston's departure was imminent, she also feared that any moment Sandra would confront him, and he would pull away—at least figuratively—for good. He wouldn't even want to be pen-pals after that.

That evening, he was in an unusually talkative mood. He seemed as pleasant as always. He asked about how she was feeling and if she had given a visit to her dad any more thought. She hadn't. Then Halem decided to bring up Sandra's claim to Winston.

She was cleaning the Lire one last time for the day. Winston was in the middle of talking about Jamie and the progress he had seen him make as he tried to be more empathic. He added that Jamie was a brilliant fisherman and could easily be a sport fishing guide. Only Winston could find such potential in the boy. Halem had noticed that Jamie had not said anything offensive to her in at least two weeks. But then she changed the topic.

"Winston?"

"Yes?"

"Did you know a girl named Blossom in Port Angeles?"

He looked puzzled. "No," he said with confidence. "That's her real name? I would remember a name like that. Why do you ask?"

"I'm not sure if that's her real name. Maybe it's a nickname or social media name. But did you borrow money from her or from anyone?"

Winston looked stunned. "No, I'd never do that. There's been a couple of times I had to borrow a few bucks for a day or two while I'm waiting on my money. I have my own money in my bank back home. Now and then I stop at an ATM and withdraw cash. But I didn't borrow even a dime in Port Angeles from anyone. Did this Blossom say I did?"

"Yeah. She said that you were good in bed too."

For the first time, she saw Winston recoil into a sour mood. He didn't speak. Just shook his head.

Halem asked, "This didn't happen?"

Winston sat his coffee cup on the bar. "Thank you for the coffee, but I must be going."

Tears started to well up. Had she made a dreadful mistake? Rock Harbor was hanging on to Winston by only an unravelling thread. He walked toward the door and exited without another word. As the door re-latched behind him, a single tear ran down her face. She wiped it off with her dish rag. She had wanted to ask him how he felt. Was he angry at her question because it was so untrue? Or was he upset that they had found out about his previous exploits in another town? She may never know. But now, at that moment, she felt angry at herself for asking him such a question. But she wanted him to say it wasn't true, and she would have believed him if he had. She said to herself in an audible voice, "Halem, what the hell's wrong with you?"

She watched Winston walk down the side of the building. As he turned to walk in front of the shop, he stopped. Stared down the walkway as if something had caught his eye, something Halem couldn't see. Then Sandra appeared walking into view from the left. The two of them stood face to face as a lively conversation suddenly erupted. If Sandra was bringing up Blossom, the timing could not have been worse. The conversation ended as fast as it started. Then Winston continued walking in the same direction, slowly toward the staircase, with his head hung low, and quickly out of Halem's view.

Sandra spun around to watch him walk away with her arms folded. Then she walked in the same direction, back toward her house, until she was—likewise—out of Halem's view.

The next morning, Winston walked into the coffee shop with Hank. From overhearing their conversation, it sounded like Winston had been at Hank's log cabin playing video games the previous morning... and the drums. Winston flashed Halem a smile and paid for his coffee without extraneous words. But she found the quick smile reassuring, as she was willing to grasp on to anything as a positive sign that Winston didn't hate her. Winston and Hank took a seat together over next to the window, not a typical spot for Hank. It was beyond Halem's eavesdropping range. She wished that she could read lips, but she couldn't make out a single word.

Halem didn't like the feeling of disaffection that hung in the air between her and Winston. As short as their relationship had been, still shy of six weeks, she felt closer to him than any human in her entire life, save her mother. Now, the relationship had been reduced to a conjured smile across an aimless room. Did Winston despise her, and the smile was no more than a reflex? If she had just kept her big mouth shut, Sandra was going to confront him anyway, then she could have spoken up in Winston's defense. Part of her felt like talking to him first would help him prepare for Sandra's confrontation. But apparently it didn't.

Sandra then walked, more like marched, in front of the shop, then turned down the side and directly through the door. Terror filled Halem as she anticipated what was about to happen. She had never seen Sandra so upset. What had she and Winston started earlier? Was this the culmination to the argument?

Sandra passed the bar without making eye contact with Halem and walked directly to Winston and Hank. Winston awkwardly twisted in his chair to look up at her. She then looked around the shop and said in a loud, community voice, "People, Mr. Winston here, or whatever the hell his name is, is a con artist!"

Halem felt like she was falling down a bottomless well, where she was only hearing echoes funneling down from the awful world above. Sandra was making a huge mistake by being so public about something that she has so little evidence to support, but there was nothing Halem could do to stop her. Halem held onto the Lira to keep from fainting. Then she sank to the floor, both hands gripping the machine.

Sandra continued. "I've found out that he has never sailed across the Atlantic in his little boat. He has only been around Puget Sound ripping off people that he has befriended. If he has asked you for money, don't give it to him. If he has tried to mess with your head, ignore what he has said. He's a cult leader."

Winston stood up slowly and walked methodically from the window seat toward the bar, while Sandra, and the entire room were caught up in the wake of his silence. He sat down his empty cup on the bar as every eye in the room was on him. He looked at Halem and smiled. She was looking up while hunkered in the most unusual position below the bar. From behind his sober eyes, he mouthed, "Thank you, Halem." Then he exited the shop, walked up the side, across the front windows, and disappeared into the gray of the afternoon.

Suddenly, there was a loud crash and Halem turned to see Ms. Van Dijk dropping her dishes, forcefully, into the plastic dirty dish tub. She then turned and looked at the shop full of regulars, then at Sandra and said, "You're the real phony!" She then went out the door and up the side of the building. Halem threw down her dishcloth in the floor and ran out the door behind her and passed her before she turned the corner in front of the shop.

Winston was already fifty yards ahead, not running but walking at a breakneck speed. Halem was trying to catch him before he reached the cold metal railing of the escalator. "Winston! Stop!"

He paused and looked at her. Tears were running down her face. "Where're you going?"

He flashed his kind, dimpled smile. "I'm not sure, but I feel the tide has turned."

"Winston, Sandra isn't right, is she? If you're innocent, why didn't you defend yourself?"

He shook his head. "Nope, she's not right."

She held onto his elbow, so he would not begin his descent down the lichened-covered stairs. She asked again, but more emphatically, "Why in the hell didn't you say something? Why didn't you defend yourself?"

He smiled again. "Halem, it doesn't matter. What's been done is done. Somehow, as strong of a woman as Sandra is, someone, maybe Bret or someone has hurt her. Once I've lost credibility, I have no foundation upon which to mount a defense. There was nothing I could've said that would change her or anyone's doubt, if others do doubt me. It is best if I let it be. She has a trust problem, and neither I nor anyone can help her with it if she's not willing. Time has a way of correcting these types of errors, something I cannot do by persuasive talk in a span of a few minutes."

Halem was aware that Winston was poised to leave Rock Harbor, and this moment together could be their last, forever. But she felt tongue-tied. No words came to her mind or maybe it was so many words that she could not choose the most correct ones. She wanted to scream, "But I love you!" with all her strength, but that would only make things worse. She kept sobbing. She reached up to hug him, and he hugged her in return. "Winston... you mean the world to me," and with that, she lost her ability to talk.

"And you to me." He kissed the top of her head.

Winston's eyes seemed moist. "I gotta go and tend to my boat." He turned and descended the steps. Part of Halem wanted to run down after him. The words were starting to come to her, words such as, "I'm so sorry. Please forgive me for not trusting you," but it was too late as he was quickly out of earshot.

Her eyes followed him, until he disappeared into the shadows of the lower levels. Down, down, he went, descending from the coffee shop, from Rock Harbor, and from her life. Her spirit crumbled.

She sobbed and walked directly to Sandra's house and then to her bedroom. She closed the door and locked it. She climbed beneath the comforter, but it gave no comfort. Her grief was even worse than that she had felt for her mom during her season of mourning a few weeks earlier. But maybe it was that her sense of grief had been set free by the experience of her mourning and now she could feel it deeper than ever before. Was she really going to lose him?

Chapter Sixteen

The Departure

Halem did not hear Sandra come home. She did not know where she had gone, but, after confronting Winston in the coffee shop, Sandra had left in her boat.

The first light of dawn was inching over the mainland's mountains. Halem sat on the side of her bed. Disorientated. She walked to her bedroom door and opened it. She listened carefully and could hear Sandra's familiar snore coming from her bedroom down the hall. She walked into the kitchen. She looked out the bay window where the rosemary and basil grew from a row of tall beer mugs. The stars still adorned the western moonless sky like a jeweler's case. She saw the swaying of the rose bushes—still in bud, awaiting their autumn bloom—which Sandra had planted beneath the windows in half-cut whiskey barrels. Surely, the trade winds had returned. Her heart sank. Tears propelled by fear began to well up in her eyes. She stumbled to the outside door. She knew the only way she would know if Winston was still in town was to go out on the walkway and to look down into the harbor.

She stepped outside and noticed that the coming daybreak was coloring the sky with a soft tint of Congo pink as a backdrop to the North Cascades silhouette. As pale as it was, it was still breathtaking, but she was in no mood to savor it. On this side of the skyline, the small clusters of cumulus clouds gave the sky a clay, cobblestone appearance, surrounded by the sea of stars still above her in the darker sky. She could not see the harbor and stood, chilled to the bone, as she waited for the edge of the lazy sun to lift itself up and over the horizon. Over the next hour, the sun did just that, being subdued by the filtering of an early morning fog over the costal lowlands.

She felt as though she was walking through a jungle of poisonous snakes. She hated snakes. She pushed herself closer to the rail as she braced for the bite of the loss. Her eyes were fixed at the sunrise, being fearful to look down at the now-delicately lit harbor eighty-feet below. She felt the cool breezes across her face and that familiar smell of seagrass. The wind was not her friend this morning. She whispered to that wind, "Damn you. I hate you!"

Halem looked down at the array of floating docks. No Winston's boat. The empty slip stood out like an absent incisor in an otherwise, perfect smile. Her eyes searched the harbor, and there was no trace of the white skiff... none. She sighed. Tears started to flow down her rosy, wind burnt cheeks, and she mumbled out loud for her own ears and the seagulls sitting on the railing below her, "Oh God, he's gone... he's gone for good."

Tears poured down her face, and she stumbled back toward Sandra's house. She wanted the shelter of her bed but couldn't bear the thoughts of seeing Sandra, so she lingered outside. Her bed had become her womb during the days of crying for her mother, and she wished that she could crawl into it through her window. She sat in the red chair and stared straight up into the sky to watch the stars melt away. It took almost an hour as the nocturnal shadows softly submitted to the flowering sun. About that time, she glimpsed Jamie walking down the walkway toward her, from the staircase. "Oh God, not Jamie," she mumbled. She wanted to get in the door before he reached her, but she was too late.

"Halem, are you okay? You're crying again. You're always crying. Did someone hurt you? Are you still sad about your mother?" Then he put his arms around her. "Halem, it's going to be okay. We all love you."

She cried harder and buried her face into Jamie's soft shoulder. He held her tightly. She could barely stand up, so both eased back down into the Adirondack chairs that were perched in front of Sandra's house. One crimson red and one sapphire blue. She sat in the blue one this time and Jamie in the red.

After several hard sobs, Halem molded a few words out of her feelings, "He's gone, Jamie. Winston's gone." She cried harder with her face in her hands and Jamie rubbing her back. If empathy was uncharacteristic for the boy, maybe he had matured under Winston's watch. If so, it would mean that Winston wasn't a fraud after all.

"Oh, that. Yeah, he left in the middle of the night. I heard noise down at the dock and went out in my briefs to check on him. He had his mast up, and he was just capturing enough wind in his sail to pull him away from the dock. I yelled to him, 'Where're you going?' Winston yelled back to me, 'Take care Jamie. You're a smart and caring man. I'm heading north. Say goodbye to Halem and tell her that I'll miss her.' If he said anything else, I didn't hear him for he was already far out in the bay."

Halem continued to snivel.

Jamie added. "I feel sad too. Winston was the best friend I've ever had. I like him a lot, even though Mom said he was a bad guy. But I returned to my cabin on my boat and cried too."

With red eyes above a gentle smile, Halem looked up at him. She pulled his head toward her and kissed him on the cheek. "Jamie, you are a real sweetie, and *I* want to be your best friend now."

"Really?"

She walked to the railing and looked once more at the empty slip, thinking maybe Winston had returned. Maybe he had forgotten something. Maybe rowing was hurting his injured hand.

"I feel faint and I want to go back to bed," she told Jamie.

"Who's going to open the shop?"

"Haven't a clue."

Halem went to her bedroom, pulled the plaid curtains closed and locked her door. She rolled up in her comforter like a burrito and withdrew into a deep sleep.

She awakened to noise in the kitchen. She had been sleeping for a long time—how long, she wasn't sure. The years of insomnia left her with such a deep deficiency, for which it would take months of solid sleep to fill. But, for now, it had just been her escape and the peace that comes when you know of nothing else you can do.

She heard the beeping on the refrigerator, which sounds off when the door doesn't close tightly. *Sandra can't hear that high-pitch sound—she doesn't even notice it.* Halem looked at her-cell phone on the night table. Three in the afternoon. Forced her eyes to fully open. Sat on the side of the bed. Re-oriented her brain to the vertical world. Walked out her door into the bright lights of the kitchen.

Sandra was fixing herself a sandwich. Halem pushed the refrigerator door closed. Gave Sandra a hateful stare. The irritating noise was only the catalyst of her anger toward the woman.

Sandra glanced up at Halem and then back to the block of cheddar cheese, which she was carefully slicing. She seemed irritated too.

What right does she have to be in a bad mood? She got her way and now Winston is gone.

"So, how long are you going to be away from the shop this time? I hope shorter than when you got in your last crying spell."

Sandra took a big bite of her sandwich. Then she started to speak again with her mouth still full, crumbs falling out. "Don't worry about today. I went up and got everyone's coffee set up. I just came down to quickly eat, leaving the customers in the shop alone. I'll go back to clean up and close up… unless you're up to it now, Sleeping Beauty."

"No, take your time and eat your damn sandwich! I'll go shower and run up to close the shop. I'll stay and roast tonight too, as I'm going to be gone for a while." She walked to her bedroom to get a change of clothes.

"So, where're you going… or are you just going to stay in your bedroom and mope for a while?"

Halem shouted, "No, I'm going to go visit my dad… that's if that is okay with you! You know, I haven't seen him in almost a year."

"Go see your dad! You really should! We'll just close the damn coffee shop down. The villagers can drink Sanka. Maybe they'll appreciate you more when you return."

Halem walked into her bedroom. Slammed the door. Sandra

shouted through it, "That's *if* you're coming back!"

She was met with silence, so she put her ear to the door to make sure she didn't miss anything. Heard nothing. "Halem, someday you'll thank me for what I've done. I was just thinking of you."

Suddenly, the door opened, so abruptly that Sandra almost lost her balance. "You... you, you're not my mother!" Halem cried. "Leave me and my personal affairs the hell alone!" Then she slammed the door.

Chapter Seventeen

Father

Early the next morning, Sandra came into the kitchen in her bathrobe. Halem was tying her red tennis shoe with her foot on a chair. "Oh, I hope I didn't wake you," she said.

Sandra looked at the clock on the microwave. "It's six-thirty. I should be up anyway, especially if I need to take care of the coffee shop."

"Well, you've got plenty of beans roasted. I went out last night and roasted enough for a couple of weeks."

"When? The last time I saw you was when you went to bed around ten. You went back out?"

"Yes, I packed and then went back to the shop at midnight and roasted, coming home at three."

"Where're you going? Are you really going to see your dad?"

"Yeah. I'm catching a ride to Anacortes with Jamie's mom. She's taking their runabout over to get groceries. She had planned on going later in the week but agreed to go today."

"And, going where once you get there?"

"I told you I was going to see my dad."

"He's still in Seattle, isn't he?"

"Yeah. But there's a bus to Mount Vernon from Anacortes and Amtrak from there to downtown Seattle. Don't worry, I'm a big girl and can find my own way."

Halem picked up her backpack and started for the door. Sandra grabbed Halem's wrist. "Halem, are you okay?"

"Yes, of course."

"I'm really sorry about our argument yesterday. I can understand why you'd be upset... I mean, losing your hopes in Winston. He certainly was a fine specimen of a man... if he were only honest."

"Whatever…"

"And you're coming back… right?"

Halem flashed her a big smile. "Most likely. I've unfinished business with my father. I'm coming back when he's ready for me to leave. I think I'm coming back… but again, who knows." She pulled away and left.

Halem's trip to Seattle was uneventful but long and tiring, especially with so little sleep the night before. She kept nodding off on the train. Then she would catch her head sliding down the window and her butt sliding out of her seat. She went from sea, to bus, to train, arriving at the King Street Station around nine in the evening. She felt torn. Her father wasn't expecting her. She hadn't seen him in almost two years. She ran into him once, on the streets of Seattle, and that was after she had moved in with Finn, but they had exchanged only a shallow greeting. He didn't ask her where she was living or why she had left. *Had he even noticed?*

Halem considered giving her old co-barista, Matt, a call for a couch to sleep on. But she just stuck the phone back in her pocket and started to walk in the direction of her father's apartment. She did have a key, but if she just barged in like that, who knows what she would find.

Her worst fear was that she would find her father's decomposed body. She didn't think his coworkers at the library would miss him all that much. He had no friends to report him missing. No cats that would devour his flesh like in a story she read in a tabloid at Walgreens.

The other worst images were that her father would be naked, which was possible. But then he could have a girlfriend—both naked in the apartment. She let that last thought settle in for a moment, as she came out of the train station and turned onto 3rd Avenue. But then she realized the possibility of that last notion as slim to none, and it would be more likely if he had bought a cat, and the cat had eaten his lifeless body. If it were true, finding her dad and a naked girlfriend together, she would feel her mission was no longer needed, and she could turn around and head right back to Rock Harbor.

Halem would have called her dad, but he didn't have a cellphone. If he had purchased one, she wouldn't know the number. She didn't even remember the land-line number. It started with two threes, then a two, but then it had fives and a couple of sixes, but she couldn't remember the order.

She turned on Bell Street. As she approached the building, something looked different. She didn't recognize the change at first, until it dawned on her that a matching building next door, built at the same time as their building, was gone. Torn down. Nothing left but a huge crater and a boarded fence, with photos of a new high-rise that was coming in that space.

She walked up the three flights of stairs and knocked on her old apartment door. Someone had painted it a drab brown, with brass numbers, *327,* in the center top. The edges of the numbers had brown paint on them, as well as many other old colors, including a bright red, hunter green, and royal blue from the work of previous careless painters. She never remembered a time when one of those bright colors don their door, as it must have been when she was quite small, and her parents were in more joyful times.

She knocked again. Nothing. Maybe he wasn't home. But that didn't make sense. She remembered her last days of living there, almost two years ago, and by this time of night her father would be passed out in his easy chair, with an aluminum remnant of his TV dinner, or pot pie, on the folding TV tray stand beside him. She never knew, in those days, if he was passed out from alcohol, just fatigue, or chronic grief. She never remembered seeing more than two cans of Rainier Beer or two bottles of Alaskan Amber beside his chair, so it couldn't have been the beer, unless he was drinking somewhere else, before he got home.

She knocked again. Louder. She used the rigid edge of her knuckles and knocked more forcibly on the old hard door until it hurt. Still nothing. She imagined finding her father's skeleton, covered with dust. She was about to turn away when she heard a crash.

The door unlatched. She turned and stepped closer, squaring

herself up to the anticipated opening. The door creaked, and then suddenly her father's face came up to the vertical gap, looking older and heavier than she remembered. His grayish hair still looked full but unkept, sticking straight up in places. He was wearing his khaki pants, with his unfastened leather belt. She could have assumed that his pants were down when she knocked, perhaps him sitting on the toilet, but she remembered that he often unfastened his belt when he sat down in his chair. He didn't seem to recognize her.

"Yes?"

"Dad, it's me."

The confusion on his face did not let up but intensified. The smell of beer breath meandered into the dark hallway. He wiped down his face with the palm of his hand, as if to remove the lingering sleep.

"Dad, it's Halem."

He rubbed his face again and then wiped down his wild hair with his spit-wetted fingers. "Halem? Oh, my," he opened the door, "are you okay?"

"Yes dad, but can I come in?"

He stepped back. "Of course, but the place's a mess."

The apartment seemed even darker, dingy, and smelled like burnt fish. He was wearing dirty tube socks, each one pulled away from his toes by a couple of inches, like they were coming off as he walked. He had on the same khaki Dockers that he always wore to work, previously owning four pairs and rotating them between washes. She knew because she did the laundry. But these pants seemed dirty with food stains on the front of his thighs, like he had dropped a meatball or something and never wiped it off. Had on his typical denim buttoned-up shirt. Seemed like the same one he'd worn every day when she was living there.

They walked from the dark entry way into the kitchen. Her dad flipped on an overhead florescent light. Her father squinted and pointed at the table, "Have a seat."

Her father sat at his usual place at the end of the table. She removed a stack of old wrinkled newspapers and she sat to his left. She studied him, stirring up memories. His unruly hair appeared thinner under the bright, overhead florescence than in the dim hall-way. His beard stubs still looked thick but were clearly whiter than she remembered. He was tall, at least six-foot three inches, and he was heavier in his face. He used to be thin, with narrow hips but broad shoulders. No doubt he was her biological father with such a resemblance. Now had a bit of a stomach too, but it was well confined to his belly, in the same way a pregnancy would drape the slender body of a petite girl. His darker tone surprised her because he, unless things had changed, never spent time in the sun. But his father was Croatian. She had only met her grandfather once, when she was young, and she remembered him being dark as well. Her father never made eye contact, even when he was talking to her. He was always looking down. She wasn't sure, but she didn't remember that as a trait before her mother died.

She looked at the table and remembered it as the old black, and white, linoleum table with tubular chrome legs that she grew up with. She had short flashes of a long-forgotten reminiscence of sitting in a wooden highchair at this same table. She looked around the kitchen, at the old plastic clock that adorned one of the olive-green walls, featuring the Space Needle in the center of the dial. An old faded photo of the three of them—Mom, Dad, and a five- or six-year-old Halem sitting on her mom's lap on the adjacent wall, just above the table.

Her dad looked even more weathered under the brighter light, with a few days, if not a week's worth of beard growth on his face. Looking like a drifter whose been sleeping under a bridge. "Were you sleeping?"

"Oh, I must've been. I don't remember anything until I heard the knocking." He paused. "Halem, where have you been? Did you move out?"

She smelled the beer breath. Rolled her eyes. "Oh Dad, I moved out almost two years ago. Did you think I still lived here?"

"I didn't know. You never said goodbye." His eyes watered.

She reached over and put her hand on his. "Dad, has anyone else been in this apartment since I left?"

He thought for a moment. "Yes, about six months ago, a plumber was here for two days fixing our drainpipe as wastewater was backing up in the bathtub."

Halem giggled. She kissed the top of his hand. It tasted like dish soap. "Oh, Dad, that's it? No one else?"

He looked at her sternly, as if the giggles were mocking him. "No. I prefer to be alone."

She studied his unkept face. *Surely, he's not going to work looking like this.* "Do you still work at the library?"

His head started shaking before the words came out, "Yeah, of course I do."

"They let you come to work unshaven?"

"Oh, I don't know. I doubt they would care. I've not been at work this week, but I'm going back tomorrow."

"Why not?"

He rubbed his face, still looking sleepy. Halem had forgotten how deeply blue his eyes were, and she noticed how long his eyebrow hairs had become, like they were two giant caterpillars crawling across his forehead. He must have been a very handsome man when he first caught her mother's eye. She felt like her mother was inside her head at that moment, looking at him with admiration.

He continued. "They made me take some days off because I've accumulated so much vacation time that I was going to lose it."

"Why don't you take a trip rather than spending your vacation in this stinky apartment?" Then she immediately regretted saying the word *stinky*. She could have gotten by with calling his apartment stinky when she was living there, but now it was just his apartment, and she was just a guest, so she had no right to be critical. "Dad, that's why I left. I couldn't live like this anymore. It wasn't because I didn't love you, but this place's so gloomy."

He looked around the kitchen. "So, you're staying here tonight? You know. It's getting kinda late."

"Please, Dad, if I could. I don't have a place to stay in Capitol Hill."

"Is that where you are living?"

"Yeah, it was, but now I'm living in Rock Harbor, up on Orcas Island. I've been there for almost a year."

"Really? So, I guess you'll have to stay here." He paused, then added. "I haven't been in your bedroom since you left, so I assume that you left bed sheets and blankets on your bed."

"Dad, you've not been in that room in almost two years? Really?"

"Why should I've?"

"How did you know I was even gone? How did you know that I wasn't laying in there dead?"

"I didn't know you were gone. It was quieter than normal, but I don't know when you stopped living here. Just one day I figured it out." He stood up. "If you had died, there would have been a stench." Then he winked.

Her dad always had an unorthodox sense of humor, which at least reassured her that her old dad was still conscious.

The next morning, Halem got up early. She dressed in old jeans and white T-shirt, which she found in her pink, glittered dresser. Her father added the multicolored glitter when she was a little girl. She looked the apartment over, and it was more depressing than its previous state. There was nothing to eat or drink, except for a box of Jimmy Dean breakfast sandwiches in the freezer. It looked like some cryogenic experiment.

She grabbed her coat and backpack and went to the basement. Her old yellow bike was still hanging in their apartment's storage area, covered in grime. Each storage area was like a prison cell, with a door and walls of heavy-gauged painted metal mesh. Her key still fit the padlock. She pulled the bike down, creating a grime cloud when the tires bounced on the concrete floor. She couldn't find her helmet.

Halem rolled the bike up the stairs to the street level and then headed to Pike's Place Market. At the market, she found fresh fruit, goat cheese, eggs, smoked salmon, and lots of flowers. She hurried back before her dad left for work at nine-thirty.

She heard humming from down the hall, and she smelled sausage penetrating and supplanting the previously burnt-fish smell in the air. She walked into the kitchen to discover the microwave running, indicating her father was up. He was in the bathroom and had apparently decided to heat up one of the Jimmy Dean breakfast sandwiches.

Halem had left the box of sandwiches on the kitchen counter because she was going to throw them out, but the garbage can was overflowing. She had to first carry the garbage bag out, which she did on the way out of the building. However, apparently her father found the box of ice-encrusted, uneatable hockey pucks, and now one was riding the microwave carousel like a kid at an amusement park. She hit the "End" button and threw the soggy sandwich, along with Jimmy's frosty brothers, into the now empty garbage can.

She then set the bouquet of beautiful red, purple, and yellow tulips in a vase. She hurried to make a goat-cheese omelet, fresh slices of fruit, and hand-squeezed orange juice. Her dad shuffled in from down the hall in his brown corduroy house shoes. His hair was all wet and combed to the side. He didn't notice what she had done, and he opened the door of the microwave, finding it empty. "Did you eat my sandwich?"

"Dad. Your breakfast is over here."

Her dad looked stunned. "Wow... why? My sandwich was fine."

"Dad! The expiration date was nine months ago. Why would you eat garbage like that?"

"I found them in the cheap bin at the Grocery Outlet. They were about to expire when I got them. They weren't that bad."

"Dad, you deserve better than this. You ought to have a good fresh meal each morning. Are you that hard-up for money?"

He shook his head and sat down to eat.

"Actually Dad, it doesn't cost any more to eat fresh and unprocessed, just takes a little more time."

"Wow! This looks like a restaurant's breakfast. That's something I don't have a lot of."

"Time?"

He didn't answer.

"Dad, what do you do besides work and come home to eat and sleep? Do you go anywhere?"

He still didn't answer. Finished off the orange juice.

"What do you mean you don't have time?"

Still didn't say anything.

"Dad, hey you with the wet hair! I'm talking to you."

He got up, walked to the bathroom, and brushed his teeth. He came out in a hurry and grabbed his black raincoat.

"Dad, it's not raining today. I was out earlier. It's looks like it's gonna be a sunny day."

"I guess what I mean is that I don't see the value of making something fancy like your breakfast."

"It's because you don't see yourself or your life as valuable anymore. But it is! You're valuable to me and you could contribute to lots of people."

"I've got to go."

Halem wanted to start a major cleaning project on the apartment. But the task quickly became daunting. She decided to start with her own room. Precisely, it had to begin in the small closet. Not the big one that still stowed her clothes, which was on the opposite side to the outside windows. The small one was her "vault," as she called it. The place where she put everything that reminded her of her mom. *What would she find in there?*

Chapter Eighteen

Mother

Time and weather had jammed the small closet door. It had not been opened in a decade. A time-capsule. The changing seasons in Seattle, from winter monsoons to summer drought and back to wet again, seemed to have caused the fir framing to swell and warp. She walked back into the kitchen and found a large butcher knife. It too, seemed like a relic or archeological artifact with spots of rust around the handle.

She used the large knife to pry the door open, bit by bit. Wherever the knife contacted the wood trim of the door frame, or the veneer of the door itself, it came loose in chunks. Finally, it opened. She could not have done this just a year earlier, but now the pain seemed more objective than emotionally all-encompassing.

The first thing she saw was a long purple dress, which her mother had made for her fifth grade's *Little Mermaid* play. She put it on. It still barely fit, but it was tight around the ankles, her mother having designed it that way. She was much taller now, and the straps, meant to go over her shoulders, would not reach. She spun around in front of her mirror. Only then did she remember that her mother sang a couple of the songs during the play. She sang, *Part of Your World*... and, of course, *Under the Sea*. The memory made her smile.

She had to stay focused. Had to tend to her dad. She decided to pack her mom's memory closet up into four garbage bags and put them in the dumpster. She did save photos of her mom and some poems her mother had written her when she was a little girl... but that's all.

Next, she took down her old faded posters. She couldn't remember ever being a Nirvana fan, but she had a poster of them on her wall. It was the three band members with a much younger Hank standing in the middle. She giggled, never realizing she slept under a photo of Hank for years... and now serves him coffee. She thought she put it up to impress her girlfriends... but, once her mother was gone, she had no friends, except for Kasey. Kasey stuck with her but always commented that her "apartment was so depressing." But, unlike her other friends, she did keep coming back.

By the time her room was clean, it was noon. She could see her dad as a vestige of the man he once was, now deeply withdrawn into the "curl of his shell," as Winston had described him. She carefully contemplated the task before her. *How was she going to do this? How could she find her dad again?*

When she had asked Winston, he said that the answers would come. He told her to just let her love for her father guide her, like a torch in a cave. But, if Winston was a fraud, then nothing he said really mattered. This whole trip could be one of futility.

She walked through the apartment, meditating on the love and concern that she really did feel for her father's lost soul, even though she had spent the last two years trying to forget it. Then the words of "beauty, color, and music," came to her mind. She looked at the dingy walls, covered in old dull photos. Most were prints of scenes around Seattle, at least Seattle in the 1970s. They all needed to find a new home... in the dumpster.

She imagined the walls a brighter color. Maybe yellow or robin-egg blue. She imagined new paintings and photos of the family—her father, mother, and herself. She wanted to bring music to the rooms once more.

Halem jumped back on her bike and headed downtown. She had some shopping to do, but nothing was on her mind. She found the old Goodwill store, where she'd bought all her clothes after her mother was gone. Her father never took her shopping. He rarely gave her money as if the notion of needing clothes, or even food for that matter, was never in his indifferent mind. She had to stretch her money to its limit.

She was not disappointed in the Goodwill store, as she found several beautiful paintings, some original, for about five to ten bucks each. She bought more than she could possibly put in the basket on her bike. She asked the cashier if she could leave her goods there, thinking she would have to come up with a new plan.

At the other end of the block was a True Value Hardware Store. While keeping the thought that she was on a bike in the back of her mind, she still bought way too much in the hardware store. She bought cans of canary yellow and robin-egg blue paint, then masking tape, brushes, rollers, and drop-cloths. She had so much that it would barely fit in a car's trunk and never in a bike's basket. On top of that were the paintings and other things from the Goodwill store.

On an impulse, she flagged a taxi. Explained to the driver, "I know this might sound strange, but I need a lift for my stuff, and I will follow on my bike."

He shook his head. "Sure, how far are you going?"

"Eight blocks."

He jumped out of the car and opened the hatchback. "Where's your stuff?"

She went back into the store and rolled the shopping cart outside, then put her painting supplies in the little Prius' trunk space. She then directed the driver to stop at the Goodwill store, pointing the two blocks up the street. She beat him there, able to dart through traffic faster than he could in his car. As she finished loading up her things, it dawned on her that she will pay handsomely for this "ride"; therefore, she should make the most of it. She said to the driver, "Can you meet me at the brass pig?" All Seattleites knew that was at the entrance to the Pike Place Market.

The dark-sinned driver, wearing the gray "newsie," answered in his Middle Eastern accent, "It's your dime, Miss."

She then took off toward the market. This time the cab beat her and double-parked near the brass pig. She rolled up on her bike and asked, "How long can you wait?"

"As long as you are willing to pay; the meter is running you know."

"Yes, of course. But I mean how long will the police let you sit here?" Halem asked, still out of breath from the ride over the hills.

"They're pretty lenient, as long as I'm in my car."

Halem bought a bouquet of sunflowers, which her mother loved. She also bought roses for the kitchen table and daisies for the bathroom. She bought king crab legs, chocolates, and bags of fresh vegetables. She had been craving crab legs ever since Jamie talked about how tasty they were a couple of weeks earlier, saying they were better than even lobster. She would not be able to cook them in seawater, but that didn't matter. When her arms held as much as they could, and another twenty-five minutes had expired on the cab's meter, she returned. The driver said, "I think we're full."

"Do you think I'm crazy with this much stuff?"

He smiled. "No, ma'am. I do this at least once a day. A dime is a dime, and as long as my meter is running, I really don't care."

"I'm done." She gave him the address. "I'll meet you at my apartment." She took off on her bike, and he pulled out right behind her, turning at the next block to go to 2nd Avenue.

When she arrived back at her father's apartment, the cab wasn't there. She started to get a little worried but then considered that he would rather have her seventy bucks for the time than all her stuff. Then she thought that maybe he had taken the long way to add up more dimes.

After a few minutes, the cab emerged from the alley across the street and pulled up in front of her father's building. She carried five loads of things up the three flights of stairs and set them in the hall. When she finished hauling her things up the narrow stairs, the cab driver, Ahmed from Somalia, said the bill was eighty-five dollars. She gave him a hundred-dollar bill and told him to keep the change. He then said, "I can do this again," and handed her his business card.

Her time was running out. It was two in the afternoon already. She contemplated what to do next, before her dad got home at six. She thought that maybe she could paint the kitchen and then cook a wonderful meal. However, prepping the wall took much longer than she had imagined.

Halem filled many small holes with spackle. The walls were so dirty, she washed them too, thinking that paint would not stick to greasy grime. She observed the marks of a ruler at the corner of the kitchen and hallway. In a variety of pen colors, some in pencil, were the lines and numbers marking her height and her age. Her father was the one who use to measure her, but the marks stopped abruptly when she was eleven. Her growth no longer mattering to him, as nothing did. She took a deep breath, closed her eyes, and painted over the marks with a brush just so the idea of preserving them wouldn't tempt her.

Five-fifteen. She taped around the woodwork and cut in with a brush around all the edges. She was washing out the brush when her father walked in the door.

He seemed to have a complete loss of words and just glared. He looked at the clean and partially painted walls and studied the stack of new pictures, now on the table, waiting to be hung. "What are you doing?"

"Dad, your house needs rehab. It's old and dingy. I want to brighten it up."

Her father didn't seem happy. He shook his head, opened the refrigerator, and grabbed a beer. Popped the cap off with a bottle opener mounted to the kitchen cabinet. Walked past her into the living room and flopped down in his recliner, as he had done for hundreds if not thousands of times. Halem followed him but holding to her silence. He picked up his remote and clicked on the TV. "I can get free pictures for the walls at the library, when they throw them away."

"I know Dad, but I wanted something fresher. Besides, you could have brought those old ones from the library a long time ago but haven't."

After taking a long hard drink, he looked up at her. "What? What do you want from me?"

Halem knelt beside his recliner. Took his big hand and held it between hers. His nails were overgrown, ragged, and torn. Tears came to her eyes. "Dad, I forgive you for taking me to Grandma's when Mom was dying. I do love you, and I want to save you."

208 J. Michael Jones

"Save me from what?"

"From your grief. I want to save you from this tomb."

He kept watching the TV. She held his hand. Started to feel shaking come through his fingers and into hers. She saw the tears starting to flow down, dripping from his chin. He took another drink of his beer.

Halem pulled his head into hers. He didn't resist. Their foreheads touched. She held his head tight against hers. His sobbing became more intense... until he was shaking out of control. In a high-pitched squeal, he said, "I love her so much. I loved your mom so much!"

"I know, Dad. You did, as did I. But you must let her live on in this world through you... through us. I know that's what she would want, for you to be full of life, to go out and feel the breezes on your face again, the gusts that she can no longer feel, and for you to feel the bright sun in your squinting eyes. How, she loved the sun!"

She wiped the tears from his cheeks. They sat, her kneeling at the side of his recliner and him leaning into her, now his head on her shoulder. Finally, Halem said, "Let me make us something for dinner. I bought some fresh crab legs at Pike Place."

Halem spent the next week painting, decorating, cooking, and bringing as much good cheer into the apartment as she could. *How do I approach my father?* Not sure if they should sit around and reminisce about her mom or avoid the topic altogether.

She avoided the topic, except for a casual mentioning when necessary. In her mind, at least, her father had dwelled too long and too much on her mother, and it was time to focus on him and the world around him.

Halem didn't think she could save her dad when she first got there. The task seemed too intimidating. *Was I too late?*

After that first week, it seemed to be working. After dinner each night, the two of them took long walks down to the waterfront. With each passing day, her father seemed to engage more with the external world. He began to see things, things that he hadn't noticed before. Whole buildings had gone up, just down the street, but completely out of this previous narrow field of vision. He didn't even know that Seattle had built a tunnel under downtown.

It was the tenth day, and Halem was finishing painting her father's bedroom. A tone of purple that reeked of the spirit of Prince, one of her dad's favorite musicians. The color was the perfect choice, as it brought him to tears when she showed him the sample from the hardware store. A shade of purple dedicated to the singer called, "Love Symbol #2." He knew immediately what it represented.

Halem sat in the kitchen, looking out the one window with a view of downtown Seattle, and made herself a cup of pour-over Ethiopian blend. Wanted so much to go up to the Emerald City Roasters. She was afraid that, if her old friends found out she was living in Rock Harbor, Finn would pull that information out of them. It would be even worse if she accidently bumped into Finn himself, on the way to the shop. Regrettably, she stayed away.

Halem held the mug of coffee in both hands to soak up its warmth. She let her mind replay the previous two weeks since she last set foot in Rock Harbor. The transformation in her father had been real. She wasn't confident that it would stick, but certainly she had been able to enter her father's shell, take him by the hand, and escort him into the light. *Would he stay in the light or retreat again if she leaves?*

But it was clear, it had worked for now—and it was Winston's idea! Winston's method had worked on herself as well. She knew, beyond a shadow of a doubt, that she was better off now, emotionally than before her clash with grief. Her brow furrowed with that thought. She whispered to herself, "How can it be that Winston was so wise and yet a complete phony? Can something good come out of a bad person? Can sweet water also come out of a poisoned well?" An epiphany. A smile swept across her face, as she realized that it was not possible for Winston to be so wise and yet a fraud. He was real. He was good!

The thoughts of Winston drew her mind back to Rock Harbor. She had forgotten her cell-phone charger. When her phone went dead, she put it back in her bag. It was an intentional isolation, as she, at that time, wanted no connection to her life on Orcas Island. She didn't want to quarrel with Sandra. But then she purchased a universal charger at the hardware store and never used it until now. She plugged her phone into the charger and waited for a few minutes until the battery had enough power for it to turn on. She was afraid to look at the screen. *Was Sandra looking for her to reopen the coffee shop? Were people mad at her?*

She picked up the phone and looked at messages. Eight voicemails from Sandra, one each morning for the past eight days. Halem was not sure if she would ever return to Rock Harbor. Too painful to think about.

She stared at the phone for several minutes before pushing the voice-mail button. There was a pause and then Sandra's voice, shrouded in emotion, "Oh, Halem, please call me! Halem, hon, as I said in my other messages, the woman in Port Angeles... well... it turns out was a swindler herself. She had never met Winston. She was, like you warned me, trying to con *me* out of money. Halem, I'm so sorry, but I think Winston was legit. Please call me!"

The phone fell out of Halem's hand onto the linoleum floor. She burst into tears. Shaking so hard she didn't know what to do. Then she grabbed a paper towel and wrote a note on it to her dad, "Pop, I had to go back to Rock Harbor to find somebody. I'll be back soon. Don't regress! Buy flowers. Don't eat out of a box! Keep going out! I WILL BE BACK!"

She quickly stuffed her backpack with her essentials; grabbed her phone and her coat and ran out the door. She flagged a taxi, trying to think of the fastest way to get to Anacortes. She caught the 8 p.m. Amtrak back to Mount Vernon and then the local bus to Anacortes, arriving at ten-thirty. Now, she didn't know what to do. Her phone rang. It was Sandra.

Halem told her, "I just got your message and I'm on my way home... uh, home to Rock Harbor."

"Where are you sweetie?"

"I'm stuck at the Anacortes Safeway."

Sandra gave Halem the number of a taxi company and told her to meet her at the Skyline Harbor. Sandra was on her way in her boat.

The taxi dropped Halem off in the graveled and weedy parking lot, next to Sandra's BMW. From there, she stepped over the horizonal telephone pole, which acted as a barrier between the parking lot and the beach. Sat on a drift log and looked across the water. Dots of moving lights here and there, looking south across Burrows Bay. She thought Sandra would be coming in from the northwest, but she wouldn't see her until she was around Burrows Island.

It was a lovely night where the stars completely covered the expanse of the velvet sky, flowing down to meet the silhouetted mountains of the San Juan Islands. It dawned on her, looking at those wading mountains, that the San Juan Islands were just where the North Cascade mountain range danced with the sea. The mountains were up to their knees in water, which made them islands. On the island mountains themselves, the stars seemed to continue into the terrain, but more sparsely, representing the isolated homes that enjoy grand easterly vistas from their high roosts.

It wasn't long before a point of moving light came around the corner and through Burrows Pass. She could hear the familiar sound of the twin Honda outboards pushing Sandra's boat across the dark crystal waters of the nocturnal Salish Sea.

Halem stood, dusted the sand off the seat of her pants, and walked toward Sandra's slip. She arrived just as Sandra was coasting up. Motors in idle. Sandra standing outside the cab with a rope. Before Halem could react, the rope, with a loop in the end, was heading directly toward her. She jerked her hands out of her pockets and caught it, just before it hit her in the face. Halem pulled the bow toward the forward dock cleat. Sandra jumped to the dock as soon as the boat was a foot away and tied the stern rope, with just a twirl and flip of her wrist onto the rear cleat. The two women embraced. Tears were in Sandra's eyes as she repeated over and over how sorry she was.

With the big Honda's still idling, Sandra helped Halem step into the boat's cockpit. Then Sandra untied Halem's twisted knot and threw her the bow rope. Then she yanked, in a reverse of her wrist twirl, and the stern rope came off the cleat. Sandra jumped back into the boat and entered the cab, with Halem following right behind.

The winds chilled Halem's face, as she ventured outside the cabin to inhale the familiar smells of the sea. The moving lights of boats and ships, ranging from small day-sailers to cargo ships and oil tankers, dotted the night.

The Washington State ferries make the most visible appearance on the waters with their well-lit triple floors, two for riders and a crew floor on top. They navigated just behind one such ferry, and Halem held on as they rode over the crests of its wake. Sandra asked about her time with her father, and Halem gave her the whole story.

Halem asked Sandra about Winston and the Port Angeles lady to which Sandra explained, "Like I said, she was a complete fraud. This bleached-blonde lady with a tube top and a face that was at least in her forties trying to appear in her twenties, wanted money from me, and it was obvious, after I went over to meet her, that she probably never laid eyes on Winston. I described him as five-foot seven and a long, gray beard, and she answered, 'yes, that was him.' It was all a big fat lie… every stinking word was a lie."

Sandra focused on navigating them back through the dark waters. "Oh, Ms. Van Dijk has been looking for you. She said she needed to talk to you as soon as you returned. Do you have any clue what that's about?"

"None… Oh, maybe. I think it is related to something I overheard Winston say to her. Speaking of which, where's Winston now? Does anyone have a clue?"

"No. No one knows. I tried to find him up north, and one person responded from Bellingham that he was there a few weeks ago, but then it dawned on me, this was the same way I found that Blossom woman in Port Angeles. Maybe I'm cynical now, but I put the odds of her telling me the truth as quite low."

"Do you have her address?"

"Yeah, I have her e-mail contact information. You can pursue this, but I would warn you to use caution. Make sure this lady can describe Winston clearly on her own before you give her any tips. I've told her nothing about Winston, except that he's a man."

"Yeah, and I hope I can find that man."

Chapter Nineteen

Return

Sailing through the rift was like a reunification of the lost pieces of her soul. Halem had never thought of Rock Harbor as home before that moment. Resolve had now replaced her previous uncertainty about the merits of the move there. It had certainly been the right thing to do. Before coming to Rock Harbor, it seemed to be too exotic to be more than an iconic post card. The village perched on the mountainside was beyond the weight of what the word *beautiful* could carry. But now it was home, and the entire village was her family.

As Halem stepped outside the cabin door again, the mist falling back from the bow's spray felt refreshing to her, except for the sting from the salt in her eyes. She was tempted to capture the moment on her cell-phone's camera, but she quickly realized that it would be as hopeless as trying to capture the essence of someone's life… within the brim of an espresso cup.

In a moment they were coasting, silently down between docks C and D. There was no kayak in the way this time and moving into the designated slip was undemanding. It was just the two of them and no cargo, save Halem's simple, over-stuffed JanSport backpack, well-worn from years of use and habitual—and hastily—overstuffing. They didn't have to use the trolley and immediately started the climb up to the fourth shelve. Halem noticed, for the first time, how winded Sandra got by the time they were just above the second level. They paused at the third landing while she caught her breath. Halem turned to look down on the harbor while she was waiting to resume their climb. She saw the vacant slip that Winston's boat had occupied for seven weeks. Behind her, she heard the wheeze coming from Sandra's labored breath… slowing between each draw. Finally,

Sandra spoke, still puffing. "Sorry, it's that time of year when my asthma acts up... and I left in such a hurry that I forgot my inhaler."

"Are you okay?"

"I'll be fine, let's just take it slowly." Sandra started to climb again. "So, what's your plan?"

"I don't know. Winston's long gone, and I'm afraid I'll never be able to find him. This would be so much easier if he had a cell-phone number, e-mail address, or even a friggin marine radio. I just don't know what to do."

They reached the fourth level, and Sandra bent over to catch her breath once more; then, she stood back up, putting her hand on Halem's shoulder. "Well, let's sleep on it and tomorrow I'll work with you to figure out a plan."

They walked down to Sandra's door. Once inside, just as Halem was entering her bedroom and poised to close the door behind her, Sandra said, "I do take responsibility for this. I still say that Winston seems too good to be true, but then, what do I know?"

Halem said nothing.

Sandra added, "Don't worry about the coffee shop, I'm managing okay, but everyone's anxious for your return, especially Ms. Van Dijk." Then Sandra gave a silly little wave, as to say goodnight, and Halem waved back and closed her door in search for sleep.

Tinkling ceramic chimes, which hung from the neighbor's eave, moved by the rhythmic morning drafts coming down the mountain, pulled Halem awake in the otherwise silent house. Unlike the past two weeks of trying to do so much to help her dad, this morning she had no reason to get up early.

Halem took advantage of the linger of languor and just laid in her bed, reflecting on her plan. She couldn't let Winston go... not like this. She had to find him, but how? She could go back to the mainland and continue with the northbound Amtrak to Vancouver, BC, but then what? What if Winston wasn't there. How could she move on up the coast? It had been over two weeks since his departure; he could be loitering at the next port in the same way he did in Rock

Harbor, or he could have moved on after one night. Who knows? He told Halem several times that his long stay in Rock Harbor was unusual.

No. Halem knew that she needed to be mobile on the water if she was going to do a thorough search for Winston. Could she ask to borrow Sandra's boat? Sandra was in such a state of remorse for what she had done to Winston, she might be willing to loan it to the cause of finding him. She didn't seem to be possessive of her material wealth, as she didn't hesitate to share things with others, such as her house with Halem or an apartment building with Bret. Halem had overheard her offer her boat to others, but the others were experience captains. Halem quickly realized the impossibility of the thought. She didn't know much about piloting a boat, especially in the narrow, turbulent, and busy waters between Rock Harbor and Alaska. She thought about borrowing a kayak, but that was even more ridiculous than the power boat idea, as she would never catch up to Winston, who no doubt was under sail.

She could also hitch a ride with the next tourist heading north. But water hitch-hiking seemed less predictable than the same on the asphalt highways.

Then, Halem realized that taking Jamie with her as her captain and borrowing Sandra's or Jamie's family's boat would be the best solution. He would know how to navigate the channels and would love to have the opportunity to be so valuable to Halem. She overheard him telling Winston he had a certificate for being a power boat captain. It could work out great with them as a pair, if only he could keep his hands to himself.

Sandra came by the house at a quarter past ten. Halem was still in her pajamas sitting at the kitchen table looking at maps of the Inland Passage, which she had purchased at a map store outside of Pike's Place Market on the way to the train station. Sandra asked, "So, what're you thinking?"

Halem shared with Sandra her idea of borrowing her boat and taking Jamie with her to find Winston. Sandra was silent at first, but then agreed it was the best idea. The only other idea was that she, herself, would captain her own boat and take Halem. But the coffee shop would have to close in their absences, plus Sandra had an important business meeting in Seattle the following week that she would hate to miss. Waiting until after the meeting may not be the best idea either, if they really wanted to catch Winston.

They concluded that it was going to be Jamie as captain, if he agreed. Sandra told Halem that she would bring it up with the boy, who was sitting in the coffee shop at that moment, as her contribution to the mission of finding Winston. She would have to talk to Dale and Molly as well, to persuade them to let Jamie take on this mission. Sandra also voiced that she felt obligated to speak to Winston herself. While she would not have the time to go chasing him now, which could take weeks, that once found she would like to fly up and talk to him face to face, apologizing for her belying his character. She had a friend with a floatplane in Seattle, who could take her to almost any harbor within a few hours.

Over the next five days, the plan fell into place. Jamie agreed to be the boat captain and seemed nervous but thrilled about it. Sandra took him out in Puget Sound in her boat, so that he could learn the controls and navigation system. She reassured Halem that he was familiar with all the components and took only minutes to gain an expertise. Sandra admitted to Halem that Winston was right about Jamie being smarter than she, or most other people, had given him credit for.

Halem and Jamie worked together for the next couple of days, packing supplies, looking over navigational charts (which Halem was only beginning to understand) and planning their course. Jamie's dad was a big help; fortunately, he was in town... and on board with the mission. But were they too late?

Chapter Twenty

The Search

The silver KingFisher Coastal Express sat peacefully afloat in San-dra's slip, all prepared for a multiple-week excursion north. Near where the boat's bottom pierced the brackish water was one long, brown arm of a kelp tentacle, held to the surface by its gaseous ball. Between the sea plant and the hull were the remains of a Starbucks coffee cup, having made its way from Anacortes… or perhaps Seat-tle, probably tossed by a thoughtless ferry passenger. The stern held three large gray plastic boxes filled with carefully selected supplies for the journey. Jamie had deposited his drab olive canvas duffle of personal belongings in the cabin earlier that morning before he made his way up the bluff to the coffee shop.

As Jamie was leaving the boat, he raised his three-by-five-foot, black Jolly Roger flag on the main antenna above the front of the metallic cabin. It fluttered and rolled in the wind. Halem didn't care about the flag and considered it just one of Jamie's quirky idiosyn-crasies.

Sandra met Halem at her house and helped her with her old backpack and large-capacity yellow waterproof duffle with "REI" stamped on the side in bold black letters. Sandra had loaned her the bag so that she wouldn't have to resort to using trash bags for lug-gage. It was so big and heavy that the two of them carried it together. They threw it up on the trolley's tub. "I don't like the idea of that flag flying over my boat," said Sandra.

They started down the cold-stone steps of the escalator. "Who cares? I think it's part of Jamie's fantasy of adventure."

"Well, I'm taking it down."

"I don't know why you always have to pick fights for such trivial things. Who cares if Jamie wants to fly a pirate flag? I've seen the same on other boats during the summer. Even the big sailboats. The yacht that was so big that it barely fit through the rift, was flying a Jolly Roger."

"Well, you'll be sailing in international waters, speaking of which, make sure Jamie has his passport. I wouldn't do anything that draws attention, such as flying that silly flag."

Halem mumbled, "I doubt if a Columbian drug boat or a boat full of Chinese refugees would sail under a Jolly Roger."

Sandra continued down the staircase, as the tub was already at the bottom. Sandra carried her breath much better this morning than the night she went to pick up Halem. It was the combination of using her inhaler faithfully and descending rather than climbing. The two women grabbed the yellow duffle and carried it toward the KingFisher. Sandra asked Halem, "Are you still mad at me... you know, for making a scene about Winston in the coffee shop?"

Halem nodded. "Honestly... yeah, I'm still a little pissed. Even if those rumors from Port Angeles were true, that was a harsh way to confront him, in front of everyone. I'm grateful for your help in finding him, but this whole thing wouldn't have happened if you had not stuck you nose where it didn't belong, just like with Jamie's silly flag."

Halem had never spoken with this much self-assurance to Sandra. But it felt like the process of going into her father's life and taking control to save him had given her a new confidence that she had not had since losing her mother. She saw Sandra as a strong and sometimes intimidating woman but now, for the first time, felt that she could hold her own with her.

"Well, Winston was leaving sooner or later anyway," said Sandra.

They arrived at the slip. They put the duffle in the open cockpit area of the boat. Carried her backpack through the open door and into the enclosed cabin, laying it on the table. "Don't you want to put this in the cabin too?" asked Sandra, still standing outside and pointing to the duffle.

"No. It's waterproof and with Jamie's huge bag already in there, it would be too crowded. I want to create enough space between me and the boy to feel comfortable without stumbling over things. I trust him, but not fully. He's always asking to kiss me… or more."

Sandra stepped over the duffle and plastic boxes, reaching the cabin door, and came inside. Sandra sat in the captain's chair. Halem stood behind her left shoulder. Sandra reviewed the radar, GPS, marine radio, and distress signaling process.

"I'm showing you all of this again," said Sandra, "because, you need to be watching Jamie and making sure he's doing things right. Also, what would happen, may God forbid, if Jamie became incapacitated?"

Once they were done reviewing the instruments, Sandra asked again, "Halem, what's your plan? I mean specifically."

"As I said, I'll go to Bellingham and ask questions around the harbor and see if I can find any trace of the man. Then, I'll move on to Vancouver, the city, or Vancouver Island for my next stop, depending what I find out in Bellingham."

Sandra redirected the question: "I know your trip's 'flight plan' but I mean, what're you gonna say to Winston if you find him, and what do you expect from him? You're not going to tell him you love him, are you?" Before Halem had the chance to answer, Sandra added, "I just don't want to see you get hurt again. What I'm worried about is that you're in love with the man, and he will hurt you by not reciprocating the affections. Not that he's a bad guy, but simply he loves the sea more."

"Sandra, that's not my expectation," said Halem with her eyes rolling. "Winston made it clear that he wasn't interested in romance… and if he were, it certainly wouldn't be with me. I accept that. So, no, I would never tell him that I'm in love with him."

"But you are, aren't you?"

Halem let the cool wind tickle her face. "What time is it?"

"Don't you have a watch? It's a quarter to ten."

"Yeah, I have a cellphone and that's how I keep time, but I stuffed it into my backpack. I told Jamie to meet me here before ten, hoping to cast off at ten o'clock on the dot."

"He'll be late… he's always late."

The two women stepped off the boat, back onto the dock, and walked from the floating dock to the fixed one, where a metal bench was firmly fastened. They sat down and looked over their shoulders and back up the bluff for some sign of Jamie. Three seagulls landed near them and walked in their direction, as if they had hopes of breadcrumbs. They ignored the birds, Halem feeling like it was a fair retribution for the gulls snubbing her the morning her heart was in such anguish from Winston's departure.

Then Sandra glimpsed the coffee shop, about eighty feet above them. "Halem, I've got to run back up to the shop. I had a customer come in, just as I was leaving, and I need to go up and fix his order." Sandra looked up the bluff. "Yeah, that guy was a bit odd… he was wearing a stove pipe hat. I'd thought I'd seen everything, but I have never seen anything like an Abraham Lincoln impersonator in Rock Harbor before."

Halem's heart began to race; her palms became sweaty. The thought that came to her mind was the fact that Finn owned such a hat and wore it out occasionally. He is the only person she had ever seen with such a strange hat. But how would he have found her? How would he have gotten here? Surely, it couldn't be… or could it? Maybe he had visited her father and her dad told Finn where she was living. *Wish she had never divulged Rock Harbor as her new home.*

Sandra made her way up the escalator. As she studied the woman, she noticed Jamie walking down the fourth level, toward the stairs, his father walking with him. The comforting thought came to Halem's mind that there was no better time to be leaving town than now, if that was indeed Finn. But she wished that she could talk to Sandra before she re-encountered the stranger. *Her cellphone!*

Halem ran to the boat. She opened the cabin door, grabbed her backpack, and pulled her cellphone out of a side pocket. She looked up again: Sandra was between the third and fourth levels, pausing to talk to Jamie and his father, who were in the same spot heading down. Then she started up the stairs again. texted: "The man in the stovepipe hat could be Finn, my old boyfriend. Please don't mention that I live here. He's bad news!"

Halem watched Sandra come to a dead stop and look down the bluff. She smiled, nodded, and waved. Halem smiled in the feeling of the assurance that she had read the message. Sandra put her phone back in her pocket and continued walking toward the shop.

About that time, Jamie and his dad were approaching the boat. They engaged Halem in casual conversation about the trip and preparation. Dale wanted to board the boat and re-check the electronics once more, even after Sandra just did. He seemed to be confident in Jamie's ability to navigate the waters up to Alaska (if they needed to go that far). His confidence, being the experienced sea captain that he was, was reassuring to Halem.

Soon they had packed everything in its place, the fuel tank was topped off, and they were on their way. They missed Halem's desired departure time of 10 a.m. by over an hour. But, as they started through the rift, Halem looked back at the beautiful harbor. No artist could improve on the scene. Standing on the fourth level were a group of people outside the coffee shop waving. She couldn't make out all the people but certainly didn't see anyone wearing a stovepipe hat.

She watched Jamie sitting at the wheel in great confidence and his face open with gleam. He was wearing his dad's Greek navy-wool seaman's hat. The hat was well-worn, had one yellow and green fishing fly embedded in the brim, and carried a faint salt stain around the edges, possibly from the sea, but more likely from the sweat of the previous wearers. He was looking to his right and left, as they navigated between the basalt cliffs, out to the Samish Sea. Seagulls, resting on the edge of the bluffs above them, took to flight, escorting them out into the deeper waters but soon turned back after seeing no opportunity for bait. The hills to their starboard were lush in their wet early autumn's green, and Mount Baker stood a head taller behind them with his head all covered in new snow, which looked like melted paraffin. The volcano just needed a giant wick sticking out of it to appear as a gigantic pillar candle.

After a while, they had to turn south to navigate around Lummi Island and then continued northeast toward Bellingham Bay. Halem expected that their visit there would be brief as surely Winston had moved on by now.

Halem stepped into the cockpit of the shiny metallic boat. Outside the cabin, the wind was brisk and carried the chill of cold water from the inside passage. New Bellingham-based seagulls were coming out to escort them into the harbor. Halem caught glimpse of a solitaire bald eagle soaring a hundred feet above the gulls. Maybe he was looking for a salmon for lunch... or maybe a seagull? *Do eagles eat gulls?*

To the far west, she saw a big green and white Washington state ferry crawling carefully across the shimmering water, heading from Anacortes to the San Juans. Between the ferry and her boat, Halem saw three other boats, one in full sail. It was a spectacular day on the water, but her heart felt anxious.

Halem was uncertain about finding Winston, actually locating him and how to react if she did. There was no longer a point in denying the truth of the magnitude of her affection. It was the magic that she had always dreamt of, a natural and deep attraction that required no thought. It pulled her into his atmosphere the night of the coffee roasting. It was uncontainable. She felt their hearts becoming interwoven in the mood of that moment, exalted into the celestial firmaments themselves. She never felt this with Finn, a relationship of convenience, helping her to escape the drabness of her father's self-inflicted catacomb. A liaison built simply on the attractiveness of each one's face to the other. No further depth.

Sandra had warned her, she had to expect nothing in return from Winston. There was even a good chance he would be angry, even though he didn't show her anger on his departure.

But Winston was a unique man, a man who would normally only live between the pages of a trade novel, with a glossy cover of Fabio without a shirt. A man created by the perfect imagination of a romantic woman but not assembled from a man living anywhere in reality. Yet, there he was. When you tally up his incredible handsomeness, his great kindness, his wisdom, his incredible story of ruggedness and adventure, you arrive at a man that could walk into Hollywood, and the most glamorous starlets would have pursued him. That's if the directors didn't grab him first with the hopes of making him the hero of their next movie project, replacing their aspirations for the aging Brad Pitt. But his looks no longer mattered to Halem. She didn't care if he looked like a rotted dock post covered in seagull crap. She still loved him.

Halem looked inside the cabin to see Jamie still in control, looking at the electronic GPS map, which he'd turned into an orange radiance per his adjustments of the color scheme; the orange glow mirrored off his glasses. Then she caught a glimpse of her own reflection in the cabin's tinted window.

She felt embarrassed and inadequate. She looked down at her feet still in her dirty tennis shoes. Her now, straight hair, thin face, and ordinary looks disappointed her. Her naturally auburn roots had grown out leaving the lightly bleached ends, but the corkscrew curls long gone. She was a quiet woman, introspective, with minimal ambitions and no personality. With her personal tally, she didn't arrive at much... certainly not enough to find a place in Winston's memory, and that was just the way it was. But, following his advice, she was trying to steer away from those negative thoughts about herself.

She felt special to Winston when he was in Rock Harbor, but that was just the way *he* was. She was sure all the regulars in her coffee shop—Jamie, Kane, Hank, and maybe even old Ms. Van Dijk—all felt special in Winston's eyes. It was his character, to embrace and shroud all his conversationalists with the feeling that they were his friends, and in that moment, his best of friends. *Ms. Van Dijk wanted to talk to her, didn't she? Maybe the woman held a secret about Winston.* But she remembers overhearing him say, "You need to reach out to Halem." Maybe she would look her up when she got back.

She wished that Sandra had been partially right. That Winston had a dark side... not as dark as Finn's, mind you... but dark enough to make him obtainable to an ordinary woman. Maybe sleeping with a couple of shady women and stealing a few hundred dollars would suffice.

Halem shook her head to clear her thoughts. She had to prepare her heart for the certainty of Winston being kind, maybe hugging her, and then casting off to his life of adventure, and her never seeing or hearing from him again. This is the way this story will end. This is the written destiny of her life as if by the Moirai, the three goddesses of fate, themselves. The perfect man and a simple, imperfect woman saying goodbye forever.

But Halem knew that it would not be forever because Winston would inhabit her soul, the very cells of it, for the rest of her life, no matter who came along later. *Was she ruined?* No other man could displace the Winston-shaped space occupying that heart. If this had been two hundred years earlier, at this juncture she would be entering a convent to take a vow of life-long celibacy, because of her ruin as a woman and lover. Halem, at that moment, felt sorry for any man that she would meet in the future... that is if there were any men to meet.

Then Halem thought about Finn. Was that him in Rock Harbor? The thought frightened her. When he was intoxicated, he was scary. But when he was sober, he was funny. Maybe that was the most that she deserved, a man like Finn... or Finn himself. Maybe he would be the only man ever interested in her. It could be that the choice would be between Finn and a life of solitude. Solitude isn't so bad, which Sandra seemed to wear with glory, although she did seem to have friends in Seattle—of whom Halem knew almost nothing, like they were ghost writers to Sandra's love life.

Maybe it was all those formative years, when Halem had lived alone with her muted father that she became so lonely. That lonesomeness had seeped so deeply that it filled all the porous places. While Sandra thrived, the thoughts of being alone to Halem seemed, itself, dark.

Maybe it was worth reuniting with Finn... if that was him searching for her. She never doubted him loving her, or at least being infatuated with her. Bruises do heal with time, as do broken bones. She could become skilled in handling Finn, hiding his booze, and dodging his swings. Maybe they could find a place of equilibrium. Maybe Winston was wrong, and she *was* the one to venture into Finn's nautilus' spirals and to take him by the hand, saving him like she did her father. He was very funny… when he was sober.

Her thoughts carried her all the way to the harbor in Bellingham Bay. She noticed the green slopes of the shoreline mountains closing in on both sides, the mainland on the starboard and Lummi Island on the portside. The visit there was brief as the harbormaster looked in his log and found Winston's registration from three weeks earlier, the day he left Rock Harbor. The records showed that he had stayed for just one night, the harbormaster recollecting, that he had slept on his boat and sailed out on the sunrise the next morning. Halem asked him if he knew where he was going, and he looked again at his log. "Uh… Vancouver, Vancouver the city."

With that, they took off heading north, crossing the international boundary in the early evening, and Jamie trying to avoid the turbulent waters at the mouth of the Fraser River. Fortunately, the early September sun was still tardy in its descent into the sea, giving them the light they needed to make it to Vancouver Bay. Halem had overheard Dale telling Jamie that False Creek Harbor would be the easiest to navigate, although their slips were usually taken, especially by the end of the day.

Jamie watched carefully as he steered their way into the harbor, being mindful of the constant flow of boats going out and coming in. Billowing clouds were forming in the east, high in the troposphere, all along the craggy ridges of the North Shore Mountains.

Jamie called on his radio: "False Creek Harbor, Harbor Master, Harbor Master, Harbor Master."

There was no answer except for the occasional chatter of other boats, which they had been hearing since leaving Rock Harbor. He called again: "Harbor Master, False Creek Harbor Master, Harbor

Master, this is the…" He looked at Halem and said with haste, "What's the name of this boat?"

They heard a loud voice emitting from the radio speaker: "Harbor Master here, please identify yourself, over."

"I don't know," Halem said. "Uh, is it written anywhere?"

Jamie looked around the cabin and shook his head.

Halem thought for a second. "Call it the *Silver Sandra*… that'll work. You know, the boat is silver as is her hair."

Jamie pressed the button on the mic. "False Creek Harbor Master, this is the *Silver Sandra*."

A loud booming voice came over the speaker: "This is the False Creek Fisherman's Warf Harbormaster. Please switch to channel 60, over."

Jamie mumbled to Halem, "I keep forgetting to say 'over.'" He switched the channel.

"Harbormaster, Harbormaster, Harbormaster, this is the *Silver Sandra*. Do you have available slips for the night? … uh… over."

The harbormaster explained that it was to their good fortunate that a flotilla of five boats, circumnavigating Vancouver Island, had just left that afternoon, vacating their slips. Three, however, were quickly filled. There were also four more marinas in False Creek alone, but he knew that they were full for the night because the three new boats had checked them first. He knew of some available buoy moorings for a lower price, but Jamie and Halem wanted to avoid those, which would have added complexity to their ability to get to shore.

Once they arrived at the False Creek Harbor, the harbormaster was not as nice as he had seemed on the radio. He was also younger than they had imagined. He was, at the most, in his upper twenties and appeared to be taking his job very seriously, as if it were above his head… but he was trying to grow into it. He made it clear that he could not give out information on other boats. "It's against Canadian maritime law!" he announced several times.

Jamie listened to the harbormaster's rant and then blurred out, "I don't like you!"

The man started to yell back at Jamie; then Halem asked Jamie to check on the boat. He walked away like an obedient child. "He has a learning disability and speaks his mind," she said to the man. "He meant no harm."

"And he's your captain?"

"Yes—and a very good one."

"Does he have a Washington state boater license?"

"Hey, Jamie!" Halem cried. "Come back and show the man your boater license."

Jamie did an abrupt about-face, showed the man his card, and then they were at peace.

As they made their way back to the boat, Halem noticed that Jamie had pulled out of his pack a Ziplocked bag of bologna and crackers. "Hey," she said. "Let's go into downtown Vancouver and let me buy you a good dinner at a nice restaurant. You can save your food for when we're on the water."

"But aren't we going to look for Winston?"

"Did you see his boat anywhere in the harbor?"

"No. But I didn't look closely. The man also said on the radio that there were four more marinas to check out. My dad and I had stayed at this one before. We were running out of fuel due to a strong headwind coming out of the south and it was late at night. We had to stay until morning to refuel."

"Well, Mr. Jamie, why don't we split up and go up and down each floating dock looking for it, and if we pass anyone along the way, we will ask them if they've seen Winston?"

Jamie frowned; cracker crumbs stuck to his lip. "I don't want to do that. I don't like talking to strangers."

Halem sighed. "Okay, follow me then."

"Jamie, you seem to have no qualms about speaking to strangers in the coffee shop."

"Only if I have to."

Then Halem had an epiphany. "Jamie, speaking of strangers, did you notice someone new in the coffee shop this morning? A guy wearing a stovepipe hat... you know, like Abe Lincoln?"

"No... I don't think so. But I wasn't looking around much. I was with my dad and we were talking. Why are you asking me this? Who would be wearing such a dumb hat? I mean besides Abe Lincoln. He wasn't dumb."

"Never mind."

They walked down all the floating docks speaking with several people, each of whom seemed like they had been there for a while. There was an older couple, the man sporting a Fort Belvedere silk neck scarf and his partner in white Capri pants sipping something from long-stemmed crystal glasses from the bow of their sailboat. In the next couple of slips were two pairs of well-tanned, muscular seniors, docked side by side in their intimidating Nordic Tugs. Most were boats tied to the cleats with no one on board. None of the boaters had seen Winston, but again, the longest visitor was a younger man in a sailboat attempting to do the figure of 8 of the earth, which means circling both Antarctica and the Artic. He said he had moored in Vancouver for two weeks. He was about to set out for Anchorage, where he would moor for the winter. He had heard nothing about Winston.

That night, the two of them, Jamie and Halem, walked into downtown Vancouver where they entered a high-end Italian Restaurant called The Medici's Kitchen. They had a wonderful meal, which Halem paid for. She was shocked when it cost the two of them well over one hundred and fifty Canadian dollars. Halem knew that she couldn't keep spending like this. The facelift she'd given her father's Belltown apartment had almost depleted her savings. Fortunately, she had saved a lot because there was no place in Rock Harbor to spend money, except for the coffee shop, and everything there was free for her. After eleven months, Sandra had yet asked to collect one dollar of rent.

That night, they slept on the boat, Jamie inside the cabin on the floor in the aisle between the captain and the passenger seats. Halem unrolled her mummy bag in the cockpit and slept in it, twisted between and around the duffels and boxes like a python. She never knew how noisy downtown Vancouver could be at night. Both Capitol Hill, where she was living with Finn, and her father's side-street apartment were much quieter, although they were in a city almost as large.

Halem must have nodded off just before sunrise. The first thing she remembered was reaching up to scratch her nose and feeling that it was cold and wet. Had it rained? She sat up and looked at her nylon sleeping bag to see that the morning dew had soaked it completely through. The sea's mist had poured in, engulfing the entire city and its inhabitants within its white shroud. You couldn't even see the tops of the aqua green-glassed buildings and certainly not the lofty North Shore Range. She was chilled. She reached for her phone and drops of water had covered it too... fortunately, it still worked. 7:47 a.m. She heard a strange noise coming from somewhere in the boat. Crescendoing and de crescendoing came the sound. She stood up, allowing her sleeping bag to slump around her ankles, like her python was shedding its skin. She sat upon a box. Got her bearings. Stood again and walked to the cabin to find the rhythmic sound was Jamie's snore.

They had a quick snack of smoked salmon and mixed nuts, sitting at the little booth and table on the portside of the boat's cabin, soaking up what morning sun was now penetrating through the lifting fog and the smoked-glass windows. They sat in silence as neither were habitual morning people. As Jamie was finishing up his "breakfast dessert," as he called it, which was a big oatmeal and raisin cookie, he cleared his throat, breaking the morning's tranquility. "Do you love Winston?"

Halem wanted to ignore him. But she knew from experience that Jamie never takes the hint that a conversational snub meant to drop the topic. He always repeated his questions... until he had a reasonable answer.

Just as he was starting to speak again, Halem quickly interrupted him. "Jamie, I've told you before that Winston's not my boyfriend, but just a good friend. Why's everyone asking me this? You like him too, don't you?"

Halem stared at him, as he reached down to open another break-fast cookie, this one chocolate chip. He wrestled with the cellophane wrapper until he got it off. Took a bite and then tried to speak, as crumbs fell to his lap. Stood up to make the crumbs and the wrapper fall further down, into the cabin's floor. "Uh, I like Winston a lot. But you seem to love him."

Halem shook her head. "Jamie… you know, it really doesn't matter what I feel. Winston would never have interest in someone like me… especially when we, the citizens of Rock Harbor, treated him so badly."

"I would have interest in you, Halem, if you would only like me. I think you're beautiful." Jamie smiled.

She crossed her arms. "I do like you! Jamie, I love you… in the same way Molly and Dale love you… as do all the residents of Rock Harbor. You're adorable, and we would do anything for you."

"Would you sleep with me?"

"What do you mean?"

"Sex."

"Jamie Baker! I told you to never say things like that again. This isn't funny! I overheard what Winston told you that having sex doesn't make you a man. So, for the rest of the trip don't bring anything up like that again or (and she regretted saying this later), I will stop even liking you. I'll turn this damn boat around and take you home."

"Sorry."

Halem then sat in the cabin's front chair on the portside and watched downtown Vancouver slowly coming alive. The crazy thought came to her mind that maybe if she did sleep with Jamie, just once, like a friend with benefits, that just maybe he would shut up. But then the thoughts of sex with him gave her a chill. Not that she saw Jamie as repulsive… but as a little brother.

That morning, they searched up and down each floating dock of every marina along False Creek, completely encircling the canal. They were coming back around toward their boat with no new information. They were trying to decide what to do, with their options being to cross over to Vancouver Island or continue up the coast of British Columbia's mainland. As they passed the Heather Civic Marina, Halem wanted to use their public bathroom while Jamie stood outside waiting.

It was a large, multi-stall, bathroom, including two private showers at the left end and on the right, a row of four ceramic sinks, above which were four large mirrors. After Halem finished her business, she walked up to the sink to wash her hands and then paused to look in the mirror. Her hair was a mess, and she didn't know what to do with it. She was in the process of growing it out, but she felt like long hair made her uglier, so maybe a pixie would work better. With the shape of that morning hair, she could even tell which side she had slept on. She felt embarrassed that she had been walking around all morning looking like that. She wet her hand to fix her hair. She reflected on that one morning, what then seemed like a long time ago, when she was wetting her hair with her dishtowel and looked above her expresso machine to get her very first glimpse of Winston... a black dot bobbing on the distant sea.

A woman with long red hair came up to the sink beside her. She had obviously been taking a shower. Her hair was wet, and she started combing it out. Halem looked at the woman's reflection in the mirror and said, "Good morning."

The stranger smiled. The two of them soon engaged in a conversation as the woman continued combing her hair and putting on her makeup. She explained that rents were so high in Vancouver that her boyfriend and her decided to buy a sailboat, moor it in the harbor, and live on it. She mentioned that, while her boat has a head with a shower, it is so cramped that she lets her boyfriend use it, and she comes ashore to use the marina's shower. Halem then questioned her about Winston.

The woman smiled big. "Yeah, I met Winston. I remember him well. Wow, what a nice guy. He was here about four weeks ago in his little sailboat. He moored just down from us and we shared a meal.

He was only here for a few days, maybe three or four, and took off."

"Where, uh, where did he go?"

"Oh, he was going to try and sail that little boat all the way to Campbell River, on Vancouver Island, in one day... and that was about two weeks ago when he left... or maybe ten days... I'm not sure as I can't remember the details."

"Thanks!" Screamed Halem, running out the bathroom door.

Chapter Twenty-one

Assignation

Halem and Jamie immediately left the protected waters of Burrard Inlet, watching the green-glassed city of Vancouver delicately fade into the mountainous backdrop behind it. They cruised out into the main channel and started their five-hour taxing crossing of the Strait of Georgia to the village of Campbell River. The journey was uneventful, as Jamie remained attentive to navigating the shifting currents. Halem stood on the deck, the cool wind against her face, her heart filled with the anticipation of seeing Winston again. The traffic was heavy at times. Jamie was constantly passing by and cutting between pleasure boats, ferries, container ships, barges, and two large cruise ships loaded with passengers out on their decks under British Columbia's late summer's sun, bound for or returning from Alaska.

As they approached the more peaceful waters that encompass Vancouver Island, they found a beautiful and serene setting, where, like Rock Harbor, the velvety-avocado hills softly slip down to embrace the blue waters of the Salish Sea. At the Campbell River Marina, they found the harbormaster, a wiry man with an Australian accent. He seemed impatient until Halem started to describe Winston. He nodded his head in confirmation that he knew him.

"In fact, this Winston guy just left the marina this morning."

Halem's heart started to beat fast. She felt as short of breath as Sandra was on the escalator a few days before.

The harbormaster further explained, "Unless he had a running wind at his back, he would have to wait for slack tide before entering the Seymour Narrows five miles to the north. I told him that the perfect slack tide today would be occurring about 6:50 in the evening. I remembered that Winston said that he wanted to wait to ride an outgoing tide through the narrows. That will come a little later."

Jamie looked at his watch. "We can make it!"

Halem thanked the harbormaster; then, they ran down the floating dock so fast that it rocked back and forth, almost causing Jamie to fall off the side. They jumped into the *Silver Sandra* and took off, quickly coming to a dead halt. Halem noticed that a stern rope was still on the cleat. She hastily removed it and shouted up to the cabin, "Okay, Jamie, you're free!"

Jamie guided the boat through the marina exit channel then between the rows of giant speckled granite boulders on each side, forming the breakwater. While most of the rocks were gray, a few carried a hint of pink or amethyst hue as the low sun tripped across them.

There was an old man in a red baseball hat and wife-beater fishing at the very end of the breakwater, on their starboard side. Halem couldn't imagine how difficult it would be to climb over all those boulders to get there. But then she noticed a small royal blue rowboat turned up on the rocks, just below the man, realizing that he had not made the precarious journey by land. The man did the odd thing of putting his cigarette in his mouth, standing at a full attention, and then giving them a big salute as they passed by. Jamie stood erect and saluted in return.

Once back out in the deeper water of the Discovery Passage and past the last "no wake" sign, Jamie jammed the throttle and headed northwest toward the narrows. Halem lost her balance in the sudden acceleration. She grabbed the door and held on as the momentum of her body caught up with that of the boat beneath her feet. She entered the small space. When she closed the door, suddenly it was much quieter, hearing only the rushing water against the bow, with the wind and sound of the Hondas now muted.

Jamie turned to Halem. "That man... the man who saluted us?"

"Yeah?"

"Well, I think he's a pirate too. That's what pirates do; we salute the Jolly Roger when we see it." He smiled like a little an excited boy at a birthday party. Was he the same boy who keeps asking her for sex?

On both sides of the dark indigo sea were hills leading to mountains, all carpeted in Douglas Firs and Western Red Cedar trees, with rectangle patches of clear cutting visible higher up. Beautiful wooden and glass homes in sparse locations interrupted the seashore. Wide decks wrapped the homes, giving them the appearance of wearing brown ballet tutus but adorned with outdoor furniture, grills, and hot tubs. Between the houses were rocky shorelines where Pacific Madrone trees, dressed in the peeling skins of cognac-colored leather, leaned over the water like they were looking for something on the bottom.

The slopes gradually closed in on them as if to squeeze them into submission, especially as they approached the narrows proper. From a distance, the tight channel did not look as intimidating as Halem feared. It was at least a half-mile wide at that point and with no observable obstructions, except for an occasional weathered floating log. Halem knew, as Jamie's father had told her, that beneath the waters are some rocky shoals that they must navigate carefully.

Jamie seemed a bit nervous as his eyes bounced between the window in front of him, the navigation map on the screen, and the dashboard indicators telling him about his speed, direction, and fuel. He told Halem during their voyage from Rock Harbor that his father let him pilot his big fishing boat; however, whenever they approached treacherous places such as the Seymour Narrows, his father would take the helm, Jamie observing over his broad shoulders. This was his first solo navigation of the narrows.

Halem saw no movement in the flow of water beside them because they were traveling with the current, although slightly faster. However, when she saw a large drift-log sticking out of the water, whose other end was obviously impaled in the bottom, she could see how fast the water was moving around it. Only then did *she* start to feel nervous.

Her heart was also full of anticipation, as they were drawing near to Winston, who was somewhere within the thrashing narrows ahead of them. Halem used Sandra's field glasses, which hung from a small chrome cleat inside the cabin, to scan the horizon, looking for any signs of Winston's little boat. She wasn't sure if his sail would be up, as they did have a favorable wind behind them, but only a narrow navigable course ahead, maybe too narrow for a sailboat drifting on the wind.

She spotted a large object directly in front of them but at some distance. It turned out, as they drew closer, to be a tugboat pushing a barge full of machinery, also going north. It surprised her that such a large boat would be going through the narrows at anything but a slack tide.

Halem pointed the barge out to Jamie who wasn't surprised. He remarked, "Those people are on a strict time schedule and keep a steady pace no matter what the weather or currents put against them. Also, riding with the current, the way we are, saves them some fuel."

It wasn't long before they were catching up with and passing the barge, which was traveling around eight knots while they were moving at thirty-five. The narrows continued closing in on them, especially up ahead, where a cluster of large islands, on their starboard side, reduced the channel by half. After passing the barge and tugboat, Halem could see whitecaps in the water ahead, like a river's rapids. She was getting more uneasy... as was Jamie at the helm.

With the barge out of the way, she could also see several boats farther ahead, including what looked like a Nordic Tug going north and a cluster of sailboats in a line, surprisingly heading in the opposite direction, southeast and against the current. Beyond the Nordic Tug, and not quite as far away as the southeast bound sailboats, was a white northbound object, entering part of the canal that doglegged to the northeast. *Winston?* It did appear to have a single sail sticking up from it. She quickly lost sight of the object as it disappeared completely in front of the Nordic Tug.

With the water pushing them along, the current, as rough as it was, wasn't perceivable to the *Silver Sandra*, unless Jamie tried to change its course to the starboard or portside. He had to do precisely that, as the depth finder was showing the starboard shore shallowing out beneath them. Just ahead were the infamous remains of Ripple Rock.

The original Ripple Rock formation was a submarine mountain, which stuck up just a few feet shy of the surface in the most fearsome stretch of sea rapids. That rock had caused the demise of many great sailors, starting in the eighteenth century. The original rock used to cause so much disturbance on the surface that the British explorer George Vancouver described it as, "One of the vilest stretches of water in the world." The Canadians destroyed it, all but these still-present remnants, in 1958, when the largest explosion in the history of the world—outside of a nuclear bomb—blew out over a half million tons of rock from the infamous mountain. But still it creates problems, and boat captains must navigate it with respect. The Nordic Tug and, what Halem presumed to be Winston's boat, had cleared the hazard. Now it was their turn.

To the starboard side, between them and the steep bank of Gowlland Island, Halem caught the rotation of a piece of driftwood around a large circular path. Right behind the old gray tree branch was a chunk of Styrofoam, dirty and green-stained from algae. She then noticed the objects were forming the outer boundaries of a large whirlpool, whose center was now dipping below the ocean's surface like an aqueous black hole. This sent a chill of terror up her spine as the power of the sea seemed incredible. She was hoping that Jamie would steer them clear of the depression's "event horizon." Jamie was dead quiet, and his eyes focused carefully on the path ahead. She saw fear in his eyes too, but she knew it was up to her to offer him some comfort, to circumnavigate a full panic.

Halem mustered up a façade of courage and said to Jamie, "It must be easy going with the tidal flow than going against it, like those sailboats up ahead."

Jamie nodded.

She had not looked at the sailboats for several minutes, then she noticed they seemed to struggle, especially the very last one. Oddly, it had its main sail up and fully trimmed, although the winds in the narrow pass between the mountains were shifting and often heading directly across the bow of the oncoming boats. The first two sailboats seemed to be clearing the rapids intact and under motor power, but the third boat was falling farther behind and swinging wildly from starboard to portside, back and forth in the gushing head current as it tried to push southeast.

"Why does that boat have its sails up?"

Jamie, focused on his own navigation, said, "I don't know. It isn't helping them. Maybe their on-board engine isn't enough power to go against the current, and they thought having the sail up would help to get them through. Maybe they had favorable winds when they entered the narrows. But the wind is so unpredictable here that I think the sail is more of a problem."

"Why didn't they wait to slack tide?"

After a few minutes of silence, to either gather his anxious thoughts or to focus on his own steering, he answered, "My dad always says that that's the number-one reason sailors here get in trouble is impatience and over-confidence. I bet they were planning on going south through a slack tide but got to the entrance of the narrows late. Rather than just waiting six hours to the next slack tide, they decided to take their chances against the current. But it can get nasty here."

Halem smiled. "That's two. You know, two reasons. Your dad said the 'number one reason.'"

Jamie looked perplexed. "What?"

"Oh, forget it."

Soon the two leading sailboats passed to their portside, and they waved at them. It was only then that Halem recognized them as the San Diego flotilla that had stopped off in Rock Harbor earlier in the summer, on their way to Anchorage. She stepped back outside into the cockpit with her field glasses so that she could see them better. She could tell that they, looking over their shoulders and behind them, were equally concerned by their last boat, which continued its scuffle against the outgoing tide.

Jamie guided the *Silver Sandra* into the most difficult part of the passage. The current was so powerful that, within spasmodic surges, it would rise and pour over the transom and into the cockpit. Some of the lighter plastic boxes were starting to float, and Halem's feet were getting wet. She felt the boat slow down as they navigated up and across a five-foot standing wave, crowned with a tumultuous whitecap, whose spray coated the front tinted window and filled her nose and mouth with the taste of saltwater. The sea looked angry, overpowering, as if there were no rhythm or geometric plan directing it but an oceanic world of chaos.

The head current pushed the struggling sailboat to its starboard, despite the woman at the helm pulling the wheel with the opposite intent. The woman looked desperate, trying to navigate back toward the center of the lane, into deeper, safer water. However, the winds, now coming briskly out of the east in bursts, along with the rushing river of seawater, pounding their bow, made such navigation impossible.

Halem looked through the binoculars. It was only then that she realized that the woman hanging on to the wheel was the same obnoxious blonde, Diane, the woman who made fun of Jamie in the coffee shop. She looked terrified.

Halem swung the field of view to her right to visualize the small white boat just ahead of them. There was also no question that the man in the small boat was Winston. This realization caused her heart to flutter once more. Winston was seated, managing the lines of his main sail, and easily taming the muddled winds, which was causing havoc with the larger sailboat, but he was going in the direction that favored the wind. His oars were extended as he rowed intermittently to correct his course. He was in no state of distress, watching with a disquieted expression the sailboat, still ahead of him and off to his portside.

Then he stood up, alarmed. Halem looked back to the left, at the sailboat. Now on its side, sail in the water. Apparently, the strong current had pushed it backward; it had bottomed out on a shallow rock shelf, the current pushing the boat over. The weighted keel was not enough to upright the boat in the shallow sea, as the river of saltwater was forcing it up on the bottom rock behind it, now pinning the boat to its side.

The woman was still holding to the wheel but swinging over the side of the boat, with her tiptoes feeling for the gunwale. Her partner, donning a bright red raincoat beneath what appeared to be a yellow inflatable flotation device, wrestled with their small Zodiac boat, which was firmly strapped on top of the cabin but now perpendicular to the water. He stood precariously on the bow's railing, reaching up, trying to untie the raft.

Jamie, who was apparently now watching the same drama play out, said, "My dad always said, when you enter stormy waters, make sure your life raft is free and easy to launch in a hurry."

The sailboat suddenly rotated farther into the water, snapping off the aluminum mast against the rocks like a toothpick, leaving the big white sail flapping flaccidly on the surface of the fast-moving stream like a film forming on boiling milk. The woman fell into the crazy waters and began to go with the current, until she reached the terminus of the white line she had grabbed during her fall.

The man on the sailboat, intentionally, dropped into the water right behind her and swam, more like thrashed, in her direction until he too, had a grasp of the same line. The man's automatically inflating life jacket suddenly inflated. It was not clear if it was the shock of the sudden inflation on the man, emotionally, or the actual physical pressure that it caused between him and the woman, but suddenly the rope slipped out of his hand. He grabbed at the woman's arm. Hung on to her jacket's sleeve and the forceful flow of the water pulled them both off the end of the rope. They floated quickly downstream until they came up against a large, fixed log, just protruding above the surface and not noticed by Halem until that moment.

Halem scanned her binoculars back toward Winston. He was turning his small boat sharply in the direction of the capsized sailors who were being force against and almost under the log. He rowed his boat up against the log, pinning it between its weathered trunk and the pressure of the current. When the boat seemed to be locked into position, he dove into the raging water and swam up behind the two sailors, fighting to keep his body on top of the log rather than being swept under it and probably to his death. Unfortunately, a surge in tidal flow dislodged his boat, and it began to rotate counter-clockwise and out from the grips of the forces that had held it in place. Halem panicked. She watched Winston pull himself up, throw his leg over the log, then ride the water-logged tree like a horse in full stride. He inched along, scooting toward the sailors as water flowed over his back.

Halem dropped the binoculars and looked at Jamie. He seemed to have the *Silver Sandra* under control. "Jamie, head over to Winston's boat... it's about to float away."

He looked perplexed. "Winston's boat?"

"Don't you recognize it, that white boat is Winston's. The man on the log is Winston!"

"I don't know. I should just try and get to the other end of the narrows."

"Jamie! Winston and those sailors are in trouble. We must help them! Besides, Sandra said this boat is virtually unsinkable."

Jamie then turned the boat and pushed the throttle, moving diagonally across the river of sea pushing behind them.

"Pull up next to Winston's boat!" she screamed as she hung the binoculars back on their cleat and went out the cabin door into the noise of rushing water. She focused on the task in front of her so she would not feel the danger of the situation. She threw her raincoat's hood over her head, as she was getting drenched by the spray from the sea and drops now falling from the sky.

Winston's boat was moving with the current until it hung up on the far end of the same tree. The boat continued to rotate counter-clockwise and was about to be tossed back into the free current. As the *Silver Sandra* bumped up against the smaller white boat, Halem banged on the cockpit window and brought her hands together like a slow-motion clap, as a signal for Jamie to keep the boats together. She closed her eyes and leaped into the smaller craft. The wooden boat rocked wildly. She grabbed the limp mainsail to avoid getting tossed over the gunwales. Then she took a seat, grabbing the handles of the oars, planted her heels against the wooden footrest in front of her, and then steered the boat back toward the log. The edge of Winston's big canvas sail flapped meaninglessly above Halem's head as nothing more than a nuisance; its line was unsecured, edge untrimmed.

Halem watched Winston pull Diane up and onto her belly over the log. He then helped the man into the same position.

Halem pushed the oar out and against the water, trying to reverse the small rowboat's direction, turning it clockwise and back into the grips of the full log, next to the victims in the water. In her first two attempts, the oar blade popped completely out of the water and the shaft out of the oarlock. She had never rowed a boat before, not since a one-day rowing class in high school on the calm waters of Seattle's Lake Union. Getting the feel for what had seemed like an easy task was not so straightforward, after all.

As the bow of the white boat contacted the log, closer to where the victims were hanging on, only then did Winston look up and seem to understand that his empty boat was now back under human control. The starboard gunwales came sliding in his direction. Then he helped the man and woman roll off the log and into the open craft. Then he climbed in after them. Halem, exhausted, allowed the boat to drift and rotate back in a counterclockwise direction, under complete command of the tide and into the main course of the current.

Winston stood, arms outstretched, as to keep his balance in the rocking boat. He slowly rose until his eyes were fixed on the person sitting at the oars. He didn't recognize the mysterious rower in the yellow raincoat, hood over her head, wet bangs covering her eyes. *Puzzled*. This woman suddenly appeared in his boat out of nowhere. *An apparition?*

He also didn't notice the *Silver Sandra* now slipping past them in the background and farther out in the main channel and downstream. He stooped back down, stepping over the two water-logged rescuees, now resting inside the bow's hull. He sat down beside Halem and reached for the oars.

Halem surrendered the oars and moved to the stern seat, between Winston's packs of supplies. She turned and faced Winston, who was sitting in the center seat with his back to the bow in typical rowing position. Winston worked the oars, struggling to cross the current and back into the main channel. Halem's eyes were fixed on his face as it swung from side to side with each powerful stroke. Water dripped from his chin. The overwhelming presence of the man sucked the breath out of her lungs once again, leaving her winded and muted.

When Winston finished the most difficult part of the transition, surrendering to the current's northern tow at the center of the canal, he sighed and relaxed. He extended his neck and look straight up, relieved. What had started as a beautiful blue-sky morning now was framed in by billowing pewter clouds releasing large random drops of crystalline sprinkles. Halem looked up too, feeling water splatter on her nose. Winston was staring at her. He pointed at the tiller, which was linked to a wooden rod so that it would reach the center seat. She pushed it in his direction and had to lean to the portside to make way for the rod reaching back to the rudder. Winston just kept staring at her, his back to the bow, looking over his shoulder now and then to confirm the boat's position in the channel.

She lifted the yellow hood and tossed it backward as an accommodating gesture to his probing eyes.

"Halem?" *It can't be.*

"Yes! It's me."

Winston pulled the tiller to move the boat more to its starboard side. "What are *you* doing here?"

"Looking for you."

"Why?"

Halem leaned forward, as if to make the conversation private.

Winston looked around and seemed satisfied that the boat was now tracking in the center of the current, where he wanted it. He spoke to his passengers in the bow of the boat, who were then sitting up on the bottom of the hull, facing forward, and holding on to the gunwales. They nodded to show understanding. She assumed it was something about where they were heading and his plan for getting them back to their sailboat. Winston did not carry a marine radio. Help would not be on its way anytime soon.

Winston then dropped the tiller's rod so that Halem didn't have to contort herself around it. The rudder centered itself. She could smell peanuts on his warm, moist breath and see droplets of water, like dew, clinging to his stubby beard growth. He looked more handsome to her than she remembered. "Winston, I wanted you to know that you've been vindicated in Rock Harbor. The woman who reported you as a fraud... well, she turned out to be one herself. Sandra's so sorry and wanted to tell you once I located you... and now I have. Winston, the whole village's sorry for how they treated you."

He smiled and shook his head. "That's okay Halem. I wasn't mad at anyone but felt like it was my time to leave, as the tide there had turned against me. That's what good sailors do you know; they follow the tides." He looked over his shoulder again, checking his passengers and location in the current, the flow of which was clearly slowing down, as the hills on both side of the passage were moving further apart, and the waters stretching out and relaxing between them. They had survived the narrows.

Winston guided the boat into still calmer waters, and the boat came to a crawl. He grabbed the loose end of the line to the main-sail, handed it to Halem, and pointed beneath her seat to the small wooden pully mounted to the frame. She passed the line through the wooden pully and handed the end back to him. He gave her a thumbs up. He then tightened the rope until the sail billowed in an appropriate trim and locked the line in a cleat beside the center seat. He pulled in his oars and laid them in the boat. Both the winds and the moving water quieter now, and his hands now free so that he could lean closer to her, he spoke, "I was shocked to see *you* here in my boat. I still just can't believe it's you! Halem... I was afraid that I would never see you again."

"Really? You were worried about not seeing *me* again?" asked Halem, although she assumed that he meant that he missed everyone in Rock Harbor... or did he?

In the awkward silence, she added, "I found my dad. I followed your advice. I think you're right... I can save him."

"Of course, you can!"

He stared into her soul with the dark eyes of the pharaohs, passed in his bloodline. Eyes that were like an ancient and mysterious forest. She wanted to get completely lost in them. *She loved this man!*

"Yes, Halem. I was very worried about never seeing *you* again."

With that, the blush was impulsive as was a big smile that came across her face. Trying to hide her feelings, she looked down between her wet tennis shoes and inside the hull, which now held several inches of water. She rubbed her finger along the nylon line that was taught as it passed through the pully beneath her seat. She looked back up. "I don't think so, Winston. You must have a thousand people who you consider your friends... scattered between here and Singapore's bays."

He nodded. "I'm sure I do. I've met a lot of wonderful people over the past few years." He then looked up and to his right as if he were trolling for memories of those people.

He pulled in the mainsail line a bit more taught. The canvas sheet responded by drawing drum-like and solid as if it were a hardened plaster cast material, holding the fractured wind in its proper place. "But Halem... you're the first of those persons that I..." he seemed, uncharacteristically for him, to stumble for words, "that I've ever fallen in love with."

She wasn't sure if she heard him right, so she did the awkward thing of shaking her head and nervously asking, "What?"

He softly touched the back of her left hand. His finger was long, each crease, lined with dirt and the nail quite grubby, but the touch was with great tenderness. "Halem, I've honestly fallen in love with you… uh… and I'm not sure what to do about that." He looked down into the boat and back up at her. "I had to leave town when I did because of the rumors, but I wasn't sure what to do or say to you. I pulled away from you before I left, and I'm sorry about that, but the goodbye seemed unbearable to me. But I knew I had to leave soon, after the things that Sandra had said about me, and I was feeling an angst about losing you. I pulled away because it was too painful to deal with. It was during my journey here that I realized that I've been hopelessly smitten, and that it was too late, that my love was irreversible, even with an ever-expanding sea between us. I realized then that no amount of brine could dilute this love enough so that I could live again."

He paused like he was gathering his thoughts.

"I only knew I was in love with you when I rowed away from Rock Harbor on that terrible morning and couldn't see anything because of the tears in my eyes. I almost hit the wall of the rift. I knew I was leaving my heart that day. I was less of a man rowing out than I had been rowing in."

His words completely befuddled Halem, as if the world around her had faded into a dim black and white postcard of some forgotten place. But Winston's face stood out above the dreary of the card, as if it had been hand-painted with living colors of tanned skin, a stubby beard, and dark taupe eyes. The muscles over his sharply angled jaw, repetitively flexed and relaxed like he was ruminating on his thoughts. Why was he saying this? Was he mocking her? Was he trying to be funny? She felt bewildered. Nothing made sense. She didn't notice, but she was shaking her head, and her state of shock projected onto her face through her emblematic crooked smile. Was her own heart about to burst? Was it more than her soul could carry?

"Halem!" snapped Winston. "Did you hear me? I'm totally in love with you! You are the ristretto, the very best extraction of what's good in my life."

She noticed Diane looking back at them over Winston's shoulder.

She must have been listening to them, as her face was beaming with a huge grin. Was it joy about the evolving love story playing out in the back of the boat... or maybe it was just her personal elation about not drowning with her own ship?

"Why are you saying this, Winston? Why are you saying these things to me?"

"Because it's true! If you don't love me in the same way, I'll understand, but I knew I had to take my chances and tell you how I felt, if I ever saw you again. But then, if there's a small chance that you do love me back, then I want you to come with me... barista girl."

Tears were starting to run down her cheeks. Wiped them off with the back of her hand. Leaned forward again for more privacy. Her heart was starting to accept what her head could not, Winston, the greatest man she had ever met, honestly loved *her*. "Why?" she whispered to him, once again. "If you're not sincere, then you're the cruelest of men, and I'll hate you for this."

"Why would I want to take you with me? Of course, I'm sincere."

She was now crying so hard, it was almost impossible to speak, "No! Why would you love *me*?"

"Why wouldn't I? There's only one Halem, and I got to discover her myself, hidden away behind a shiny red expresso machine, in a big hole on the side of a mountain, on the edge of an island, in the middle of nowhere."

"But Winston, I'm not loveable... I'm just a coffee minion!"

He pulled her close, until their noses were almost touching, and whispered, "Halem... you're truly the most lovable person I've ever met. You just don't realize it. Your self-deprecation is a delusion."

Winston looked back over his shoulder once again to see where they were in the water, as a boat dock and resort were coming into view on their portside. He recognized Sandra's boat tied up there already. *Was that Jamie standing in the cockpit waving? Wasn't that his Jolly Roger also waving in the air above him?* He reached for the tiller and steered toward the dock.

"I knew I loved you that first night in the shop when I saw the confidence you had around the roasting machine but denied that same confidence about yourself." He smiled. "I knew I had found a jewel, a real gem in the rough. I knew it wouldn't take much for you to shine, and making me the luckiest man on the planet, having found you. But if I can't have you, I will sail on, over dark waves, through the mountain gaps, and beyond the horizon, and like a note in a bottle, a treasured message forever lost in the sea. I will then be less of a man and you... barista girl; you will be chiseled in my heart like a timeless, lichen-covered stone escalator... but leading no-where."

He moved closer and tilted his head. His eyes meticulously moved down her face to her lips. They were wet with tears and rain. Trembling, those lips conformed to his. They gently kissed. It wasn't the overpowering kiss of passion like she remembered with Finn. With each one of Finn's kisses, she felt a piece of her soul was being drawn away from her, pulled into him, and devoured by his own unquenchable thirst. Winston's kiss was simple. Lips lightly touching lips. But it was so virtuous, like her first kiss as a sixth grader, backstage with her Little Mermaid costar. The only thing that existed in the entire universe was the boy...

She pushed Winston's damp hair out of his eyes. It felt courser than she had expected. She sank into his overwhelming presence and sobbed. It reminded her of the night in the roasting room with Winston when the grief of her mother first caught up with her. That night he held her as she collapsed within the bottomless sorrow. But now, an implausible joy enshrouded her tears, and an overwhelming delight was raining down on her. It was a refreshing deluge of happiness, a happiness too great to feel deserved. It couldn't be real... or could it? Will she awaken from this fantastical moment, back in her bed, alone? Had the purging of the stockpiled sorrow now made room for an unimaginable contentment?

Finally, she was able to speak and repeated the question in a different way, "Winston, you're Winston, and I'm nothing. How can you love me?"

"Halem, my dear, stop with the nonsense! I'm just a man, a man named after a nasty cigarette, who meddles too much into people's private lives, alone in a tiny wooden boat—by the way, which leaks—lost in a 140-million-square-mile ocean. Nothing more. But my love for you makes me greater than I could otherwise possibly have been without you. Please… please come with me, and we'll chase the setting sun over the horizon together and see what's there… but only if you love me back and can come without remorse."

Halem trembled—not just the cold, being drenched by the sky and sea, it was from love. "Oh Winston, I do love you, of course I love you and have from the moment you walked in my door. I feel my heart is about to burst with joy, and if I'm not careful, my copious tears from such a happiness may swamp your boat. My love for you, it's… it's insatiable."

Insatiable? "I dare to prove you wrong."

They docked at the Brown's Bay Resort. They unloaded their sailboat rescuees, giving them to the care of Captain Jamie Baker at the helm of the Silver Sandra. He would take them back to their boat at the next slack tide. They, Winston and Halem cast off again in pursuit of the setting sun, a giant disk slipping beneath the pewter clouds.

Like a rag doll, she slid off her wooden bench and into the wet boat. He turned and sat in the bottom of the boat beside her. The oars stowed away, and the sail in full billow. With that, Winston held Halem, his left arm around her and his right reaching to the tiller's rod. He looked back over his shoulder at Jamie standing on the dock's end, not much more than a dot, a mustard seed cast against the lavender mountains behind him. Winston stood and saluted. Jamie saluted in return. He sat back down beside Halem, looked at the sea in front of them… and led her out of her nautilus shell that evening… evaporating into a red sky… truly to these sailors' delight.

Thanks so much for reading Ristretto Rain. I hope you found it enjoyable and thought-provoking. I wanted to share with you the story of the novel and how it came into being.

In 2017, after a long career in headache medicine, I shortened my work week from five to four days. With great anticipation, I devoted my Fridays to my passion of writing. I had written countless articles for national and international journals and four nonfiction books but finally had the time to express my unbridled creativity in writing my first work of fiction, Waters of Bimini.

On those glorious mornings I would go to the—now defunct—Acme Coffee Shop in Anacortes, Washington, arriving at the small shop (which was in the storefront of an art gallery) when it opened at 9 a.m. and get a wonderful, hand-crafted cappuccino from one of the two baristas, Adam, or Abby. I sat at my tall, red stool, facing away from the bar and out into the street where our sleepy little harbor village was just waking up. There, I typed my book. I say "typed" because the narrative itself had been flooding into my mind for the whole week, and I only needed the time to transcribe it into text. While I watched the words appear on the white tablet screen in front of me, I kept hearing the most fascinating conversations between other customers and Abby or Adam, whoever was working that morning.

Many of these customers were locals who confided with the barista, like liquor connoisseurs do with their bartenders, the most personal things happening in their lives. It was loves, losses, jobs, and illnesses. But some of the most interesting stories were from transients who were on the road to nowhere... but having the time of their lives getting there.

There was the couple who sold their house and bought a sailboat, loaded it up with their five sons and one Irish Setter and started sailing around the world. They had already spent two years going down America's Atlantic coast, and foundering in the beautiful warm, cerulean seas of the Caribbean archipelago. From there, they went through the Panama Canal and were then coasting around our own archipelago of the San Juan Islands.

Another guy came into the shop for a while. He in the spitting image of a young and blond Brad Pitt, but poor. He had just bought an old wooden sailing yacht that was a ruin and scheduled for demolition in Seattle. He bought it for a few bucks and had to haul it with a small aluminum fishing boat all the way to our waters, where he moored it on a buoy in the harbor. Thanks to his good looks, he had—what I called a harem—of five young women working on the boat for him. I think one (or possible more) was his girlfriend. He shared some his restoration skills with my efforts of restoring an old Land Rover Defender, my other passion at the time.

However, the most interesting person I heard during that time was a young woman (I think in her twenties as she was at my back during the whole verbal narrative of her life) who had a great banking job in Boston, her dream career after finishing with an MBA from Harvard. One day, she realized how empty that career really was. She walked out of her office then down the street to Boston's REI store and loaded up on the best camping equipment her money could buy. She bought a pickup truck, got her little black dog named Micky, and took off. She had been driving across the country for two years, with an eventual tentative destination of Alaska.

While I was doing the dirty work of editing and rewrites of my Waters of Bimini manuscript, my subconscious had already become engaged in creating my next novel, about coffee, boats, lost harbors, fascinating people, and romantic love. This was the genesis of Ristretto Rain.

I began working on the manuscript in earnest as soon as Waters of Bimini was launched in 2018. I was about three quarters of the way through the story in December of that year when I suddenly became quite ill, near death, with what eventually turned out to be cancer, multiple myeloma with associated renal failure. I went from doing mountain hikes with my Saint Bernard, Greta, sailing my own small wooden boat (which makes a cameo in Ristretto Rain) around our lake, to being in an ICU with tubes in my chest and my doctor telling me that I need to prepare for death.

Ristretto Rain had to take a backseat to my full-time devotion of trying to survive and to get better. My treatment forced me to end my career in medicine and spend the summer at the Seattle Cancer Care Alliance, where I eventually had a stem cell transplant. In summary, after what I call "summer camp at Auschwitz" (not reflecting on the great care I got but the suffering I had to endure), that at his juncture, one year post-transplant, my cancer is in remission and my kidneys came back just enough to get off of dialysis. I still must continue chemo and endure the side effects afforded to me by those nasty drugs.

While I did not give up writing, I wrote a new novel, Christina Athena, while in the hospital at the University of Washington getting my transplant, I could not return to Ristretto Rain until October 2019. For one thing, in the chaos of my illness, the manuscript was lost. But I eventually found it on an old thumb drive and when I was starting to feel well enough to get out of bed, I returned to my passion of finishing this work, which I was able to do in early 2020. Then, the COVID-19 pandemic hit. It really didn't make any difference on my lifestyle, as I was already having to do social distancing due to my transplant but was able to focus during this tragedy enough to finish the book.

While it is not my illusion to "make a living" from my writing, I do hope that I can write well enough to have critical mass of readers. I am working hard to improve my word smithery. Putting imaginative thoughts into words is my greatest passion, only second to my family... and Greta. If you have found this book to be enjoyable, please review it on Amazon and places like Good Reads and encourage your reading friends to purchase it. Word of mouth is what we unknown and aspiring authors depend upon. Mike